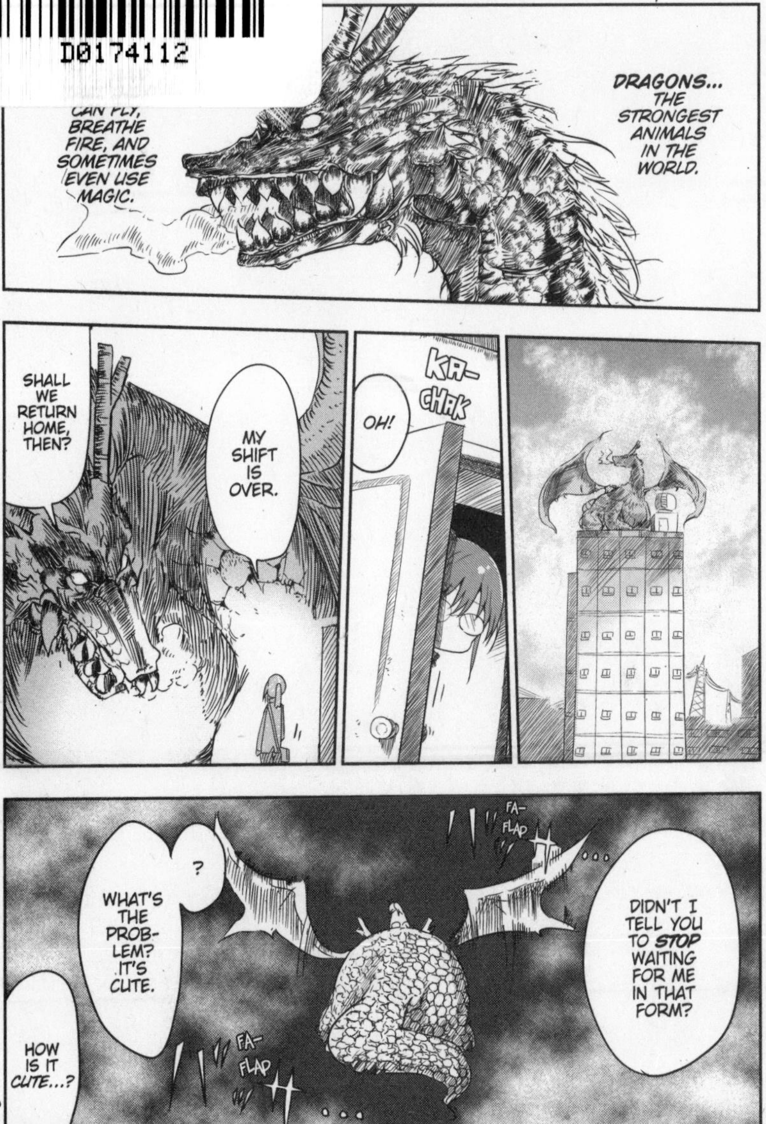
DRAGONS... THE STRONGEST ANIMALS IN THE WORLD.
CAN FLY, BREATHE FIRE, AND SOMETIMES EVEN USE MAGIC.
KA-CHAK
OH!
MY SHIFT IS OVER.
SHALL WE RETURN HOME, THEN?
FA-FLAP
...
DIDN'T I TELL YOU TO STOP WAITING FOR ME IN THAT FORM?
?
WHAT'S THE PROB-LEM? IT'S CUTE.
FA-FLAP
...
HOW IS IT CUTE...?

# CHAPTER 1 : TOHRU & MISS KOBAYASHI

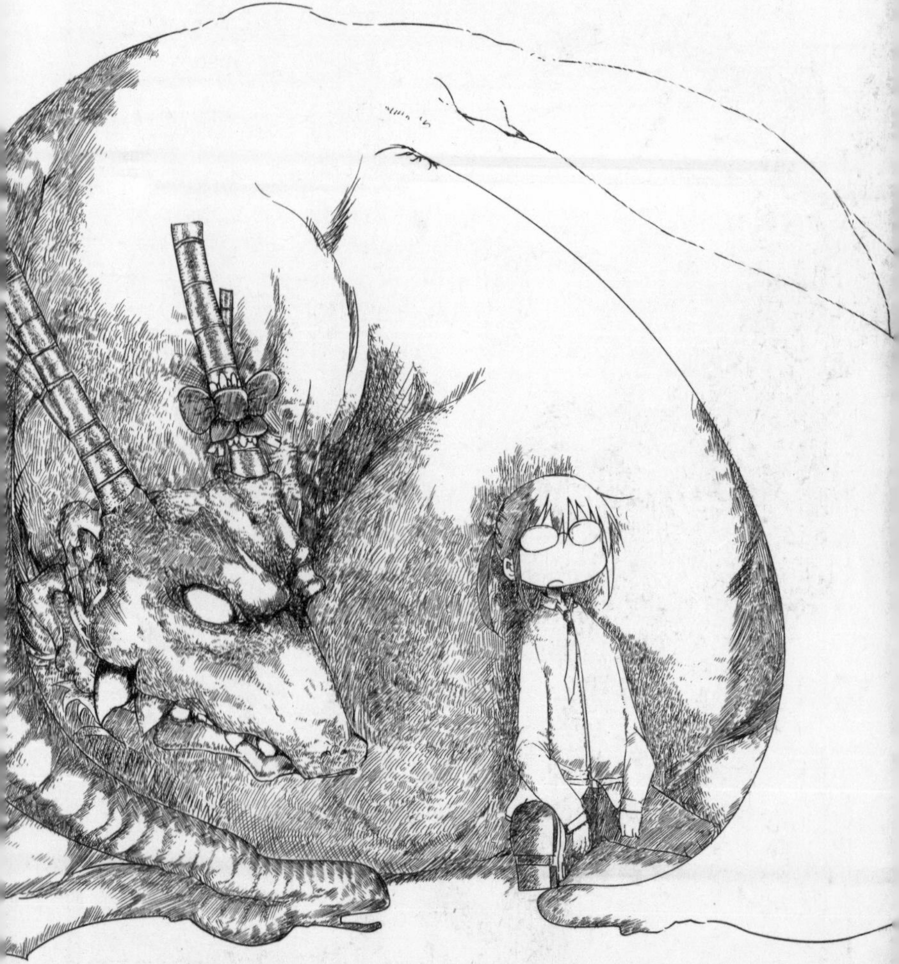

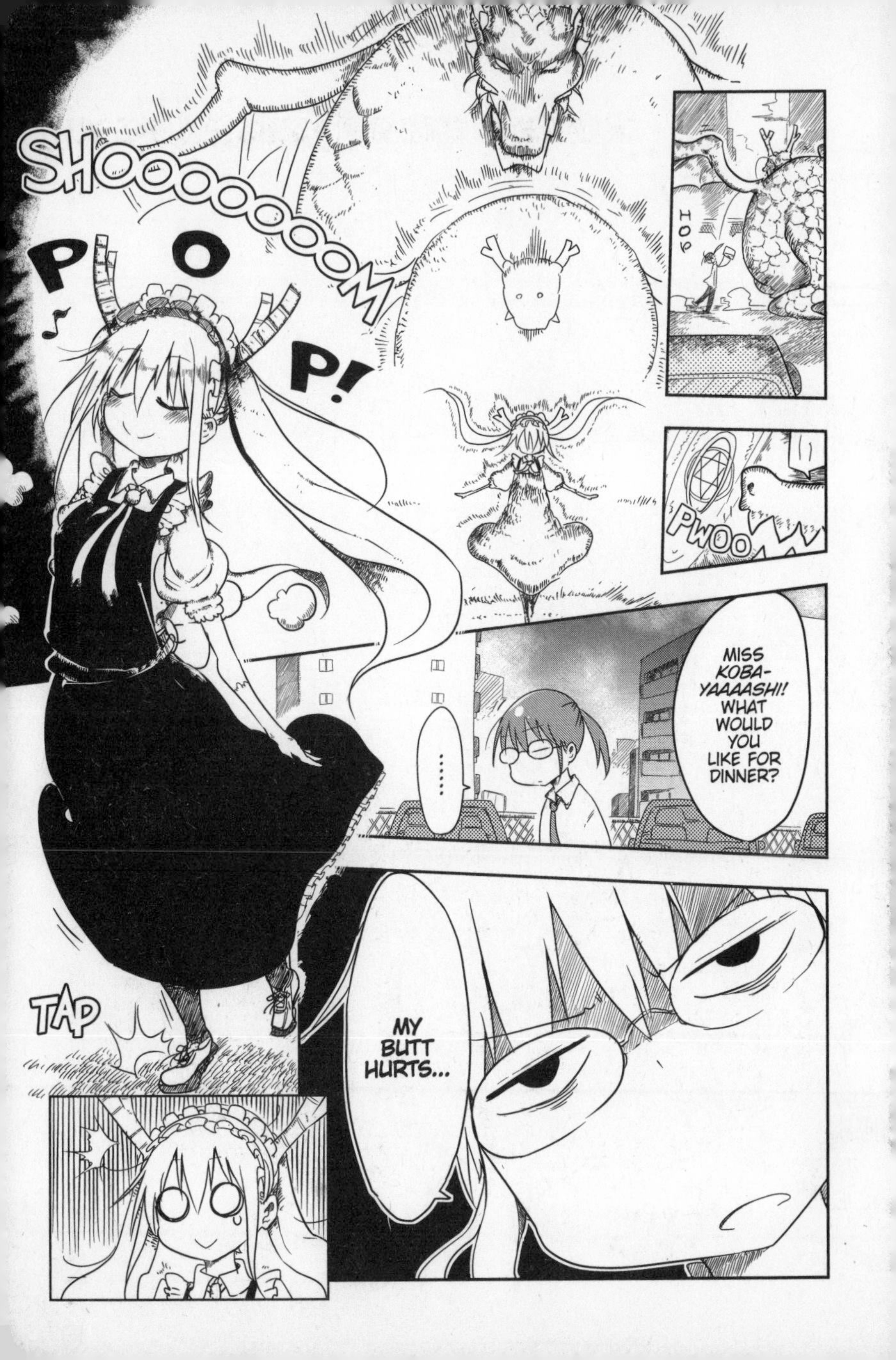
HOP
PWOO
SHOOOOOOOOM
POOF!
♪
TAP
MISS KOBA-YAAAASHI! WHAT WOULD YOU LIKE FOR DINNER?
......
MY BUTT HURTS...

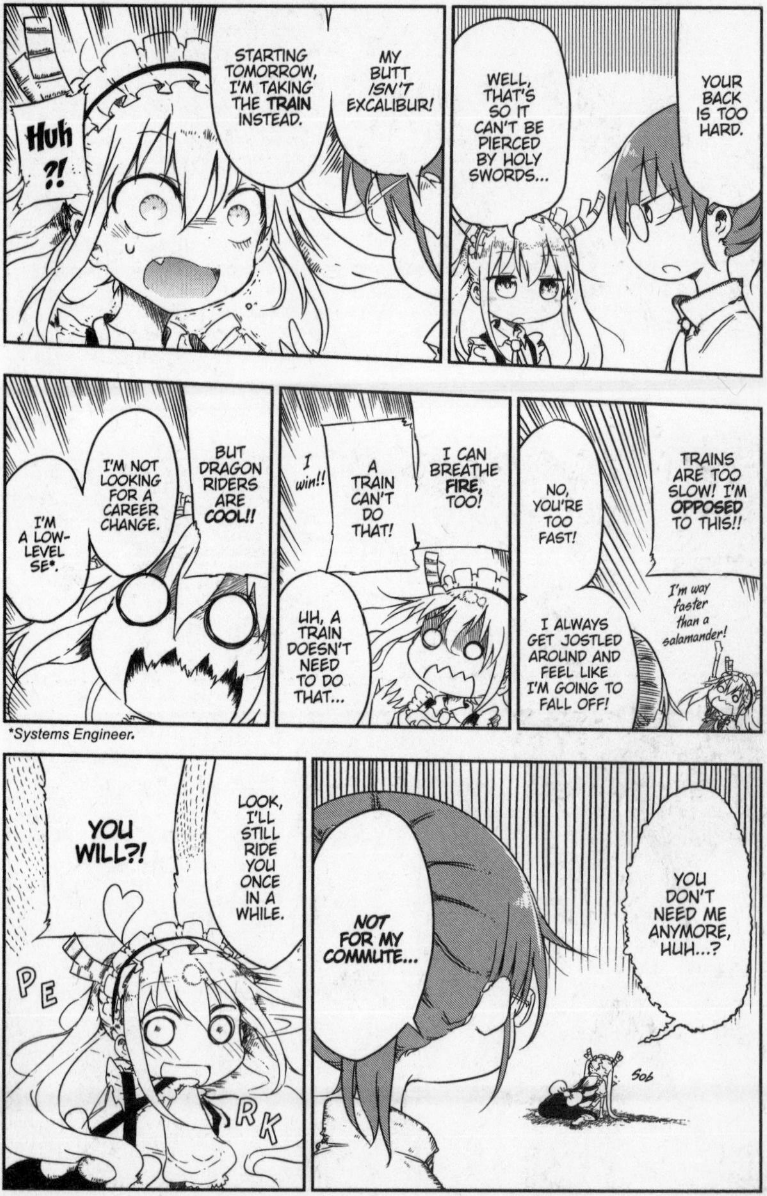
YOUR BACK IS TOO HARD.
WELL, THAT'S SO IT CAN'T BE PIERCED BY HOLY SWORDS...
MY BUTT ISN'T EXCALIBUR!
STARTING TOMORROW, I'M TAKING THE TRAIN INSTEAD.
Huh ?!
TRAINS ARE TOO SLOW! I'M OPPOSED TO THIS!!
NO, YOU'RE TOO FAST!
I'm way faster than a salamander!
I ALWAYS GET JOSTLED AROUND AND FEEL LIKE I'M GOING TO FALL OFF!
I CAN BREATHE FIRE, TOO!
A TRAIN CAN'T DO THAT!
I win!!
UH, A TRAIN DOESN'T NEED TO DO THAT...
BUT DRAGON RIDERS ARE COOL!!
I'M NOT LOOKING FOR A CAREER CHANGE.
I'M A LOW-LEVEL SE*.
YOU DON'T NEED ME ANYMORE, HUH...?
NOT FOR MY COMMUTE...
Sob
LOOK, I'LL STILL RIDE YOU ONCE IN A WHILE.
YOU WILL?!
PE
RK

*Systems Engineer.

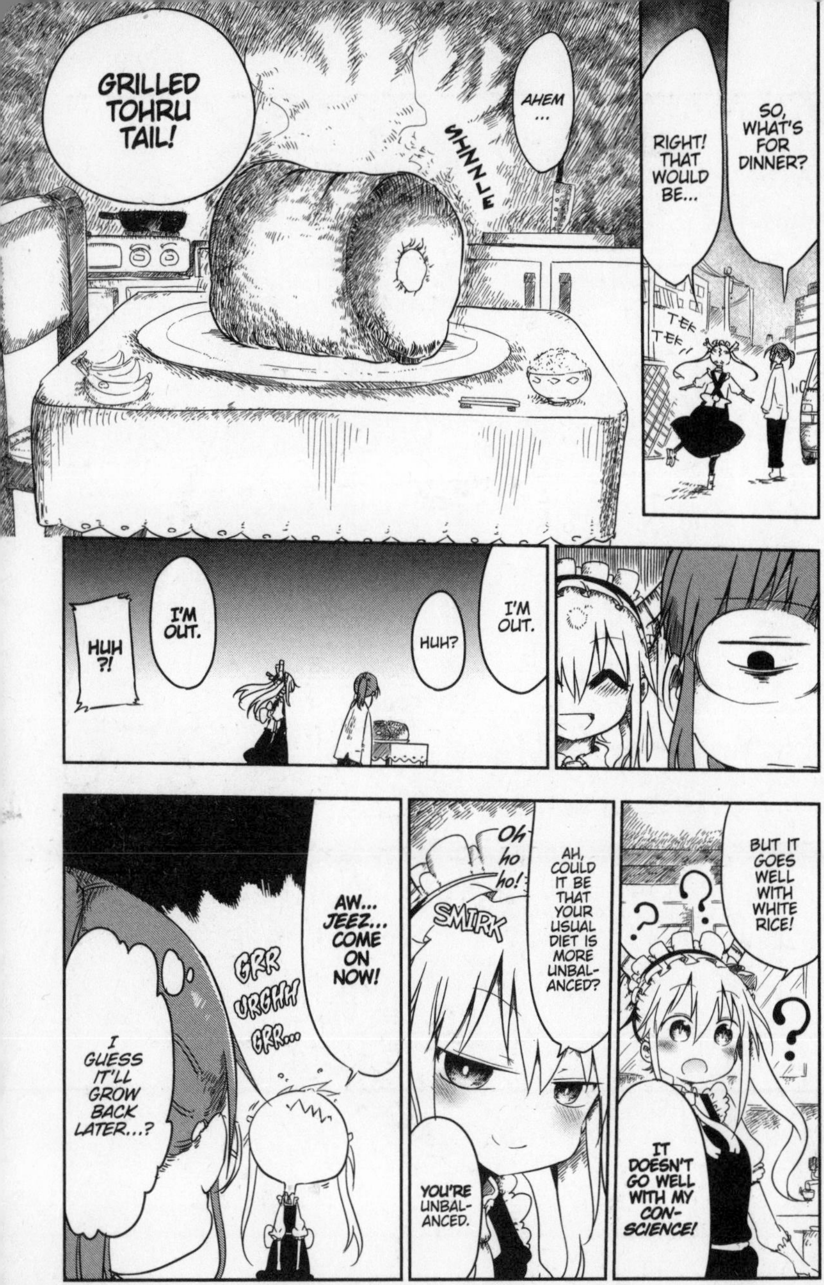
SO, WHAT'S FOR DINNER?
RIGHT! THAT WOULD BE...
TEK TEK
AHEM ...
SIZZLE
GRILLED TOHRU TAIL!
I'M OUT.
HUH?
I'M OUT.
HUH ?!
BUT IT GOES WELL WITH WHITE RICE!
IT DOESN'T GO WELL WITH MY CON-SCIENCE!
AH, COULD IT BE THAT YOUR USUAL DIET IS MORE UNBAL-ANCED?
Oh ho ho!
SMIRK
YOU'RE UNBAL-ANCED.
AW... JEEZ... COME ON NOW!
GRR URGHH GRR...
I GUESS IT'LL GROW BACK LATER...?

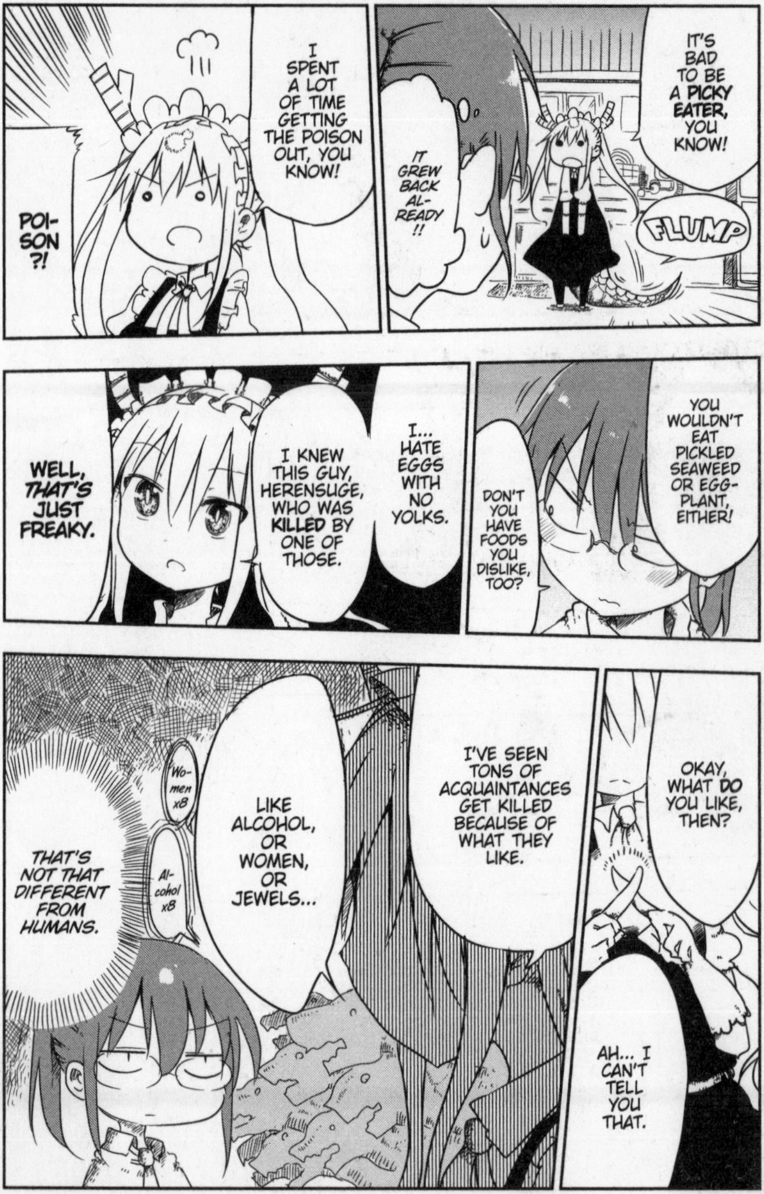
IT'S BAD TO BE A PICKY EATER, YOU KNOW!
FLUMP
IT GREW BACK AL-READY!!
I SPENT A LOT OF TIME GETTING THE POISON OUT, YOU KNOW!
POI-SON?!
YOU WOULDN'T EAT PICKLED SEAWEED OR EGG-PLANT, EITHER!
DON'T YOU HAVE FOODS YOU DISLIKE, TOO?
I... HATE EGGS WITH NO YOLKS.
I KNEW THIS GUY, HERENSUGE, WHO WAS KILLED BY ONE OF THOSE.
WELL, THAT'S JUST FREAKY.
OKAY, WHAT DO YOU LIKE, THEN?
AH... I CAN'T TELL YOU THAT.
I'VE SEEN TONS OF ACQUAINTANCES GET KILLED BECAUSE OF WHAT THEY LIKE.
LIKE ALCOHOL, OR WOMEN, OR JEWELS...
Wo-men x8
Al-cohol x8
THAT'S NOT THAT DIFFERENT FROM HUMANS.

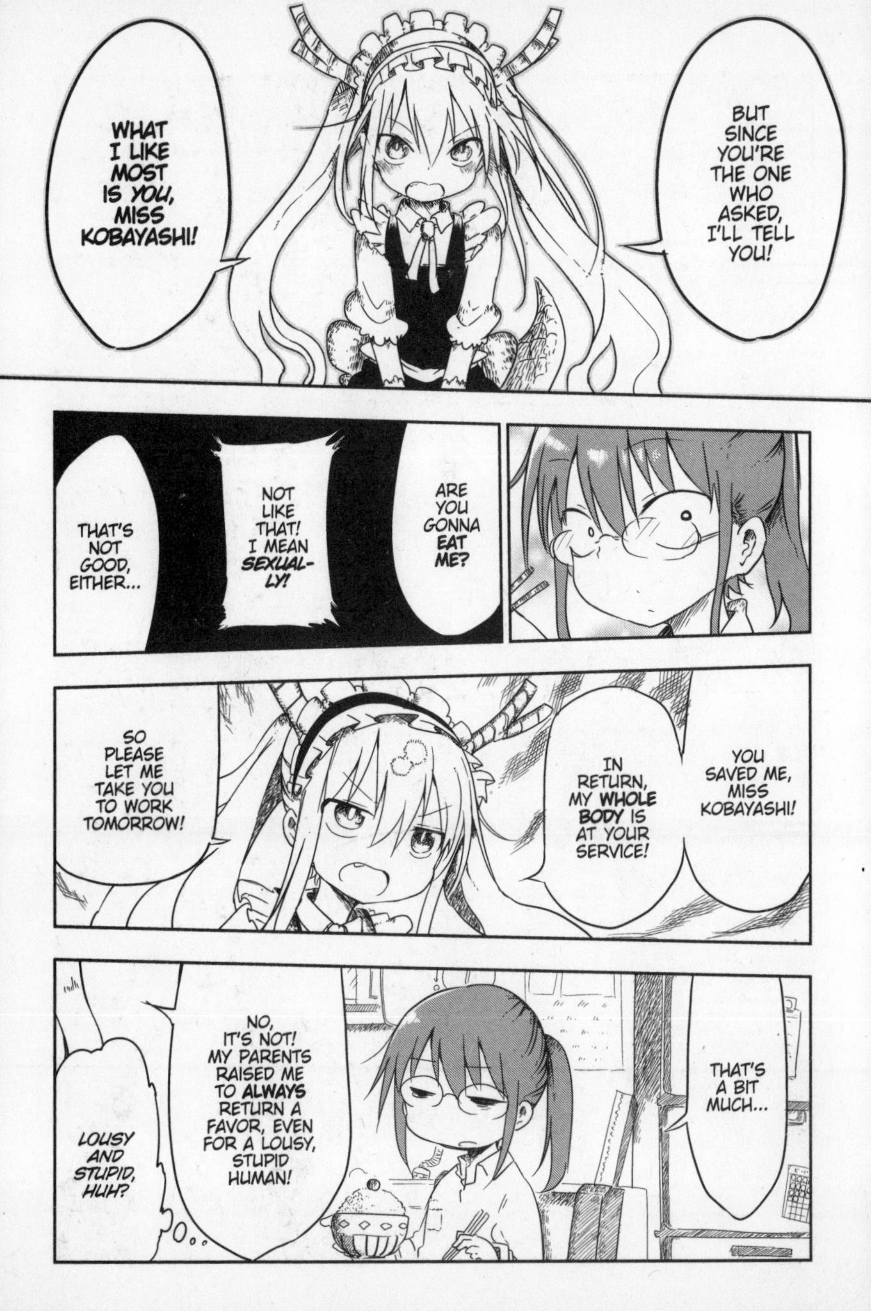
BUT SINCE YOU'RE THE ONE WHO ASKED, I'LL TELL YOU!
WHAT I LIKE MOST IS YOU, MISS KOBAYASHI!
ARE YOU GONNA EAT ME?
NOT LIKE THAT! I MEAN SEXUAL-LY!
THAT'S NOT GOOD, EITHER...
YOU SAVED ME, MISS KOBAYASHI!
IN RETURN, MY WHOLE BODY IS AT YOUR SERVICE!
SO PLEASE LET ME TAKE YOU TO WORK TOMORROW!
THAT'S A BIT MUCH...
NO, IT'S NOT! MY PARENTS RAISED ME TO ALWAYS RETURN A FAVOR, EVEN FOR A LOUSY, STUPID HUMAN!
LOUSY AND STUPID, HUH?

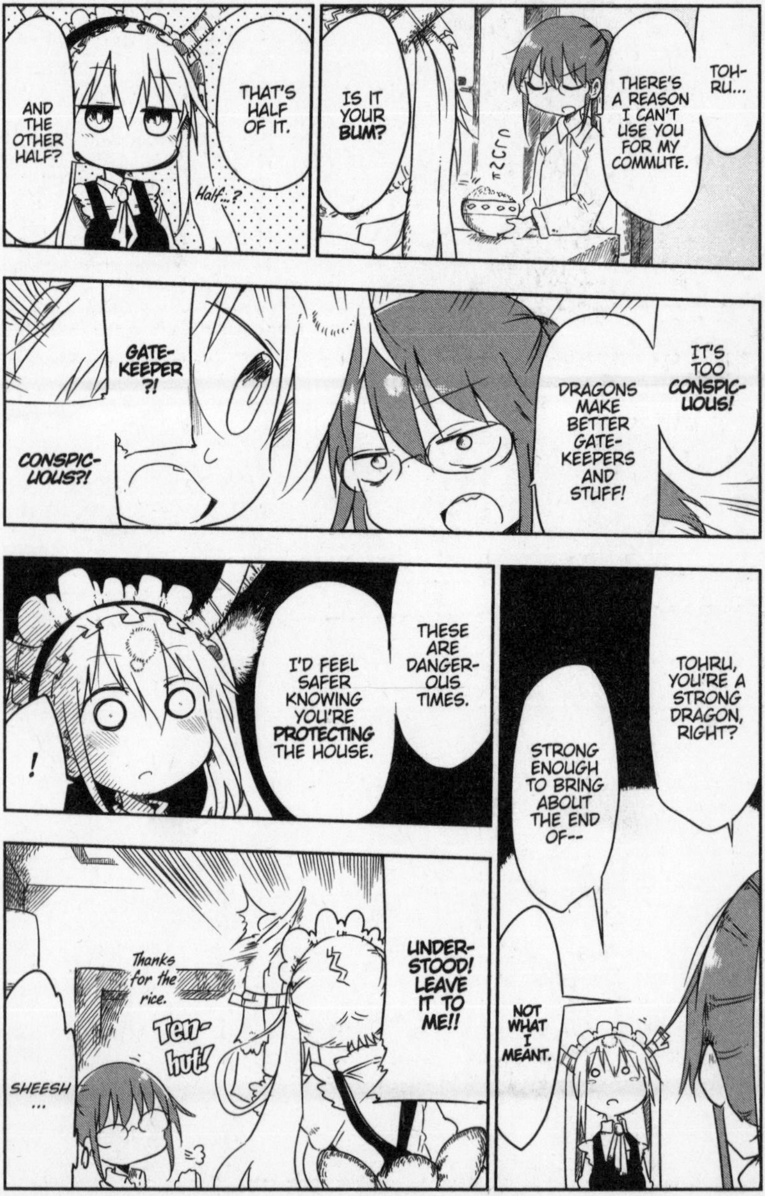
TOH-RU...
THERE'S A REASON I CAN'T USE YOU FOR MY COMMUTE.
IS IT YOUR **BUM?**
THAT'S HALF OF IT.
Half...?
AND THE OTHER HALF?
IT'S TOO **CONSPIC-UOUS!**
DRAGONS MAKE BETTER GATE-KEEPERS AND STUFF!
GATE-KEEPER?!
CONSPIC-UOUS?!
TOHRU, YOU'RE A STRONG DRAGON, RIGHT?
STRONG ENOUGH TO BRING ABOUT THE END OF--
NOT WHAT I MEANT.
THESE ARE DANGER-OUS TIMES.
I'D FEEL SAFER KNOWING YOU'RE **PROTECTING** THE HOUSE.
!
UNDER-STOOD! LEAVE IT TO ME!!
Thanks for the rice.
Ten-hut!
SHEESH...

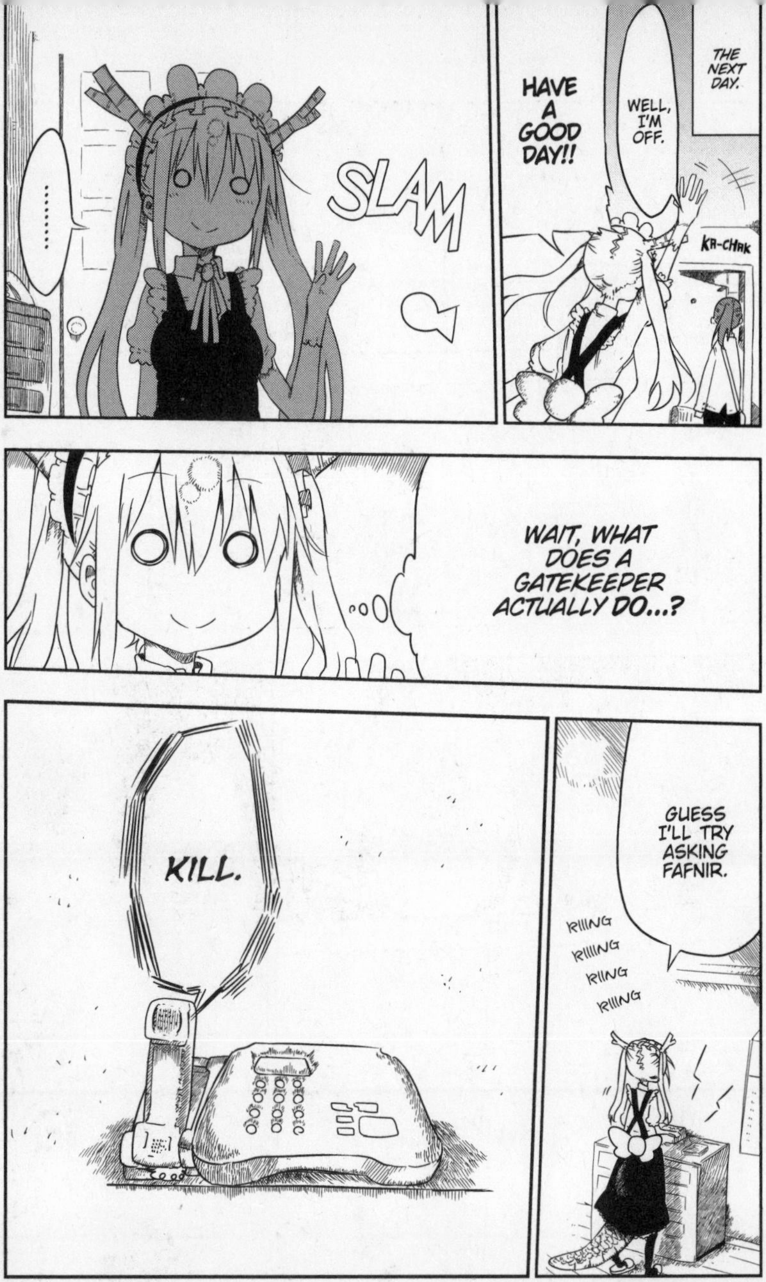
THE NEXT DAY.
WELL, I'M OFF.
HAVE A GOOD DAY!!
KA-CHAK
......
SLAM
WAIT, WHAT DOES A GATEKEEPER ACTUALLY DO...?
GUESS I'LL TRY ASKING FAFNIR.
RIIING
RIIING
RIING
RIIING
KILL.

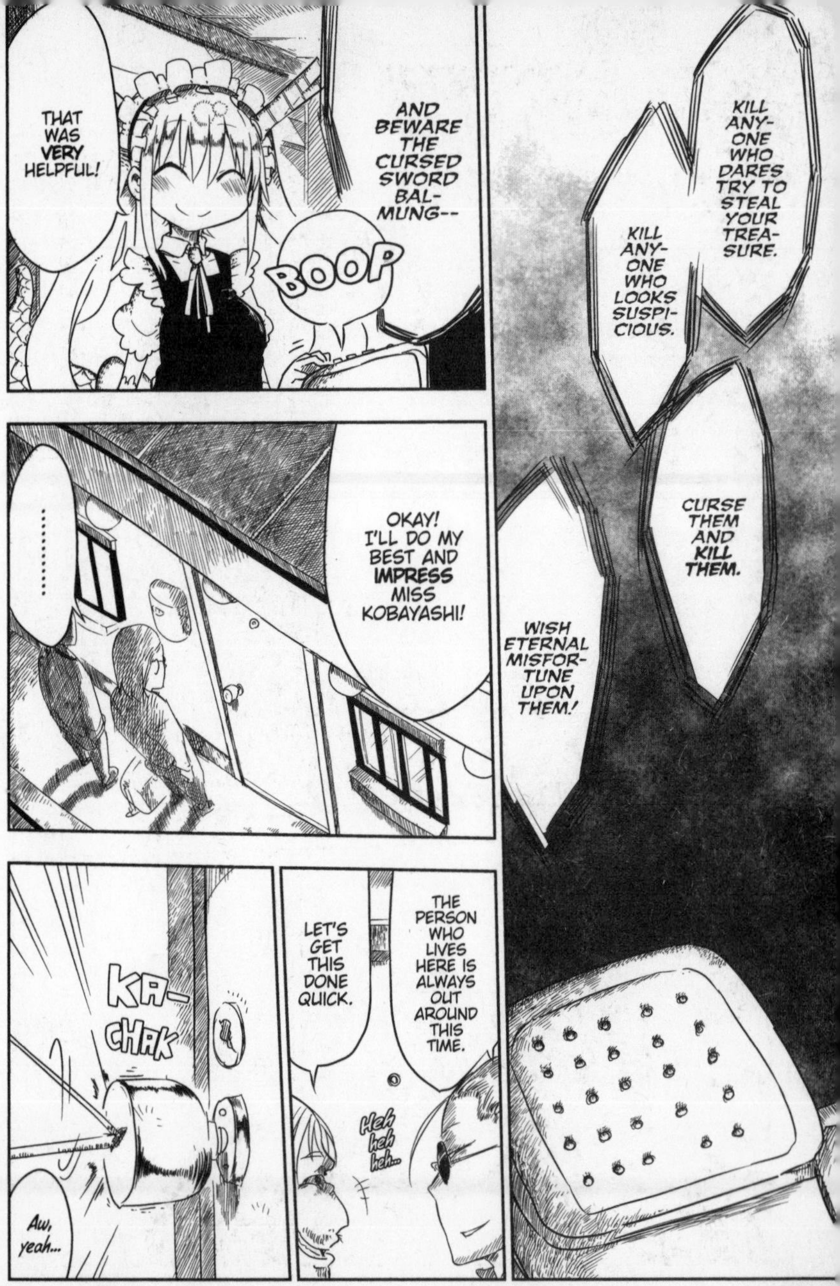
KILL ANYONE WHO DARES TRY TO STEAL YOUR TREASURE.
KILL ANYONE WHO LOOKS SUSPICIOUS.
CURSE THEM AND **KILL THEM.**
WISH ETERNAL MISFORTUNE UPON THEM!
AND BEWARE THE CURSED SWORD BALMUNG--
BOOP
THAT WAS **VERY** HELPFUL!
OKAY! I'LL DO MY BEST AND **IMPRESS** MISS KOBAYASHI!
........
THE PERSON WHO LIVES HERE IS ALWAYS OUT AROUND THIS TIME.
LET'S GET THIS DONE QUICK.
Heh heh heh...
KA-CHAK
Aw, yeah...

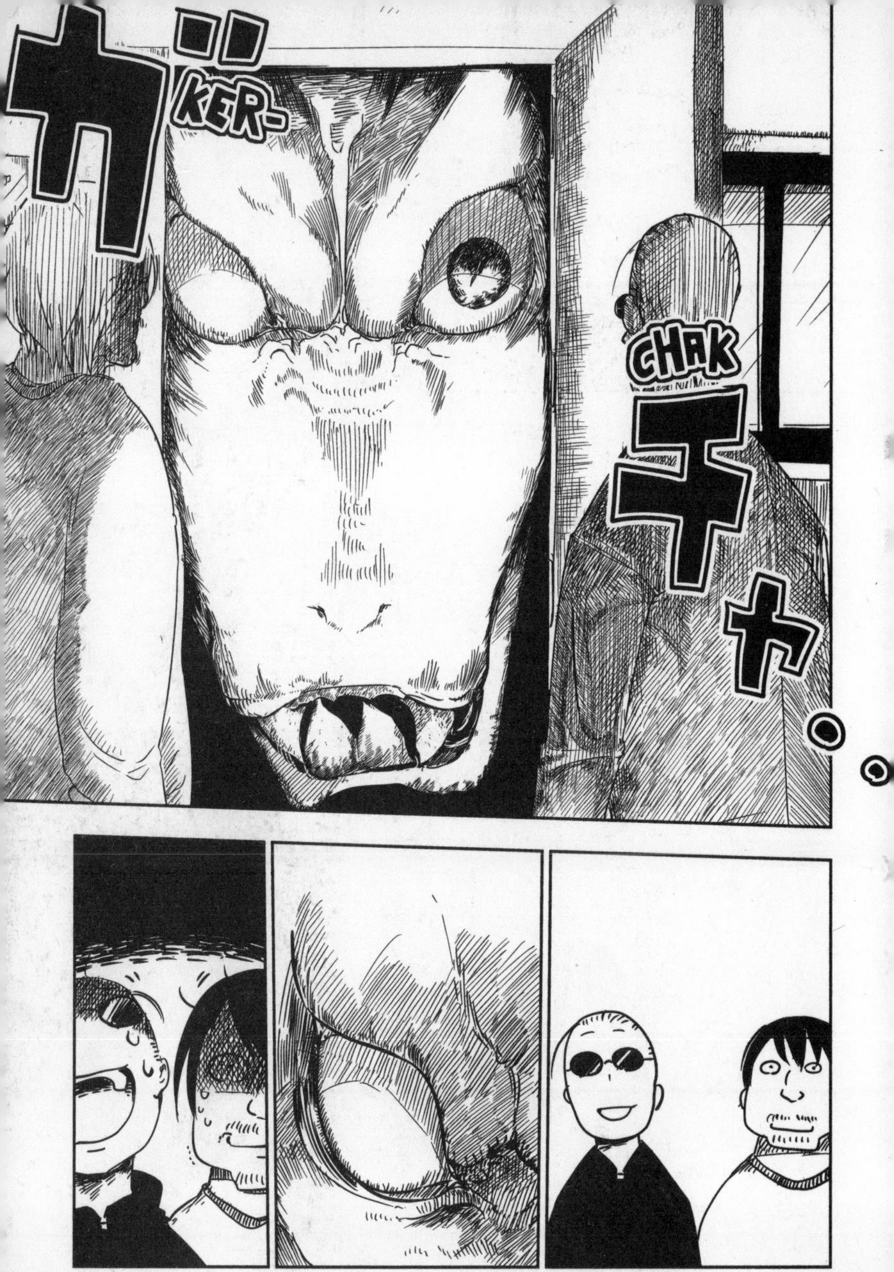
CHAK
チャ。。
KER-
ガ

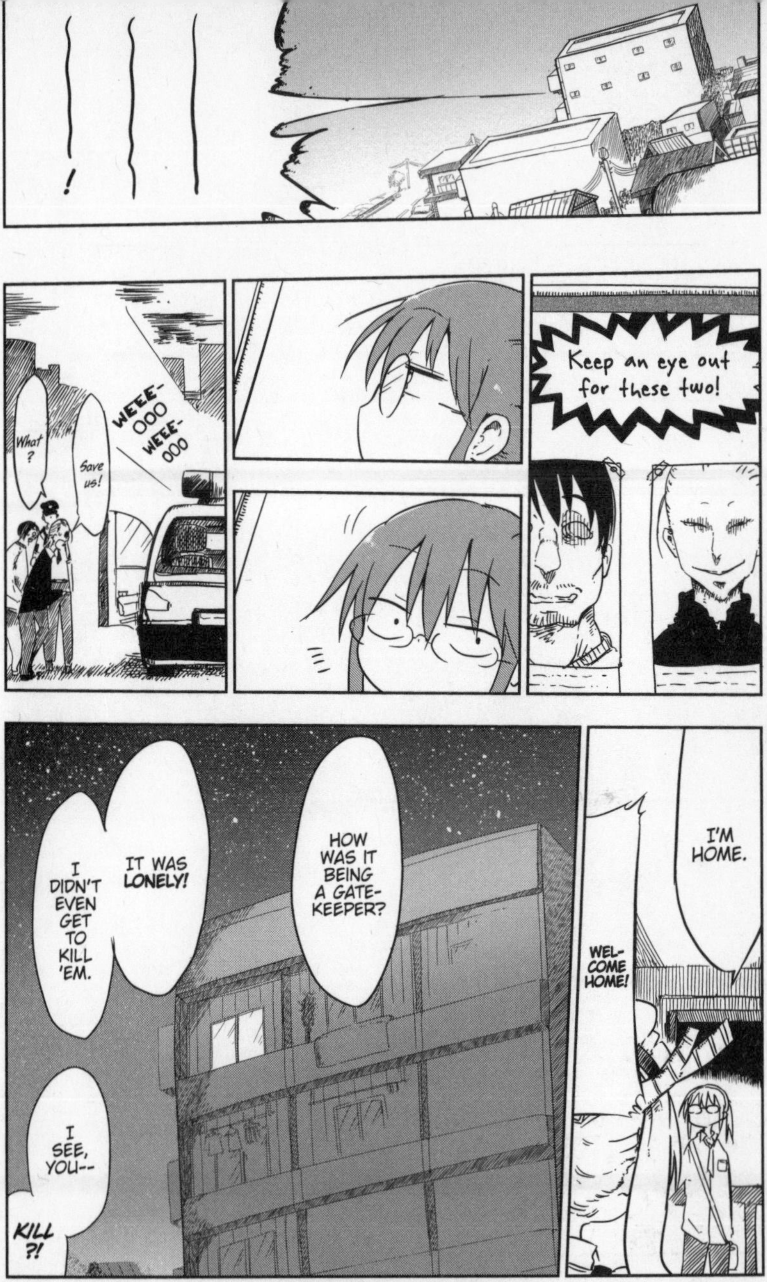
Keep an eye out for these two!
WEEE-OOO WEEE-OOO
Save us!
What?
I'M HOME.
WEL-COME HOME!
HOW WAS IT BEING A GATE-KEEPER?
IT WAS LONELY!
I DIDN'T EVEN GET TO KILL 'EM.
I SEE, YOU--
KILL?!

**CHAPTER 1/END**

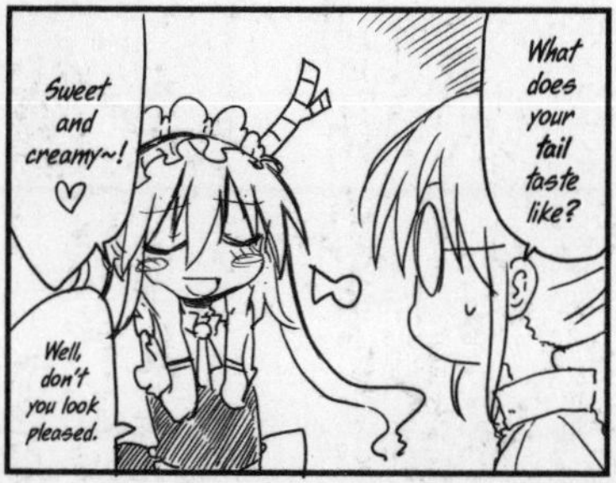
What does your tail taste like?
Sweet and creamy~! ♡
Well, don't you look pleased.

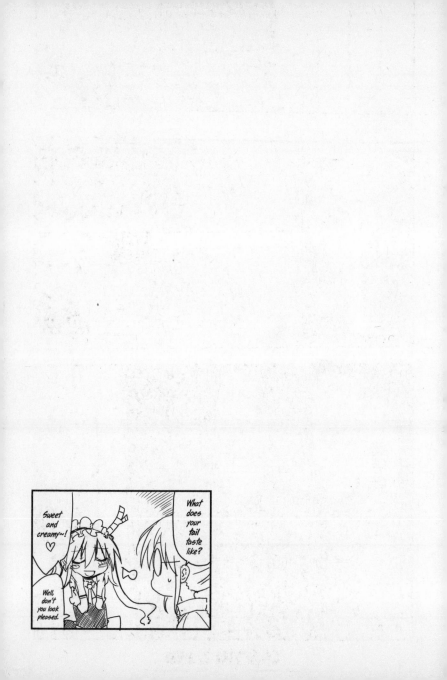

Miss Kobayashi's
DRAGON MAID

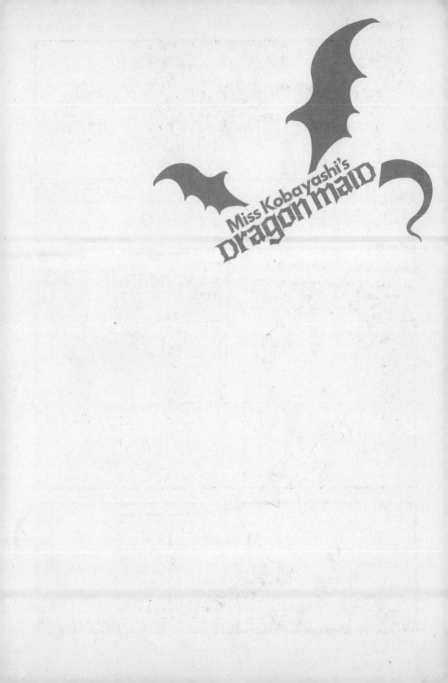

# Chapter 2

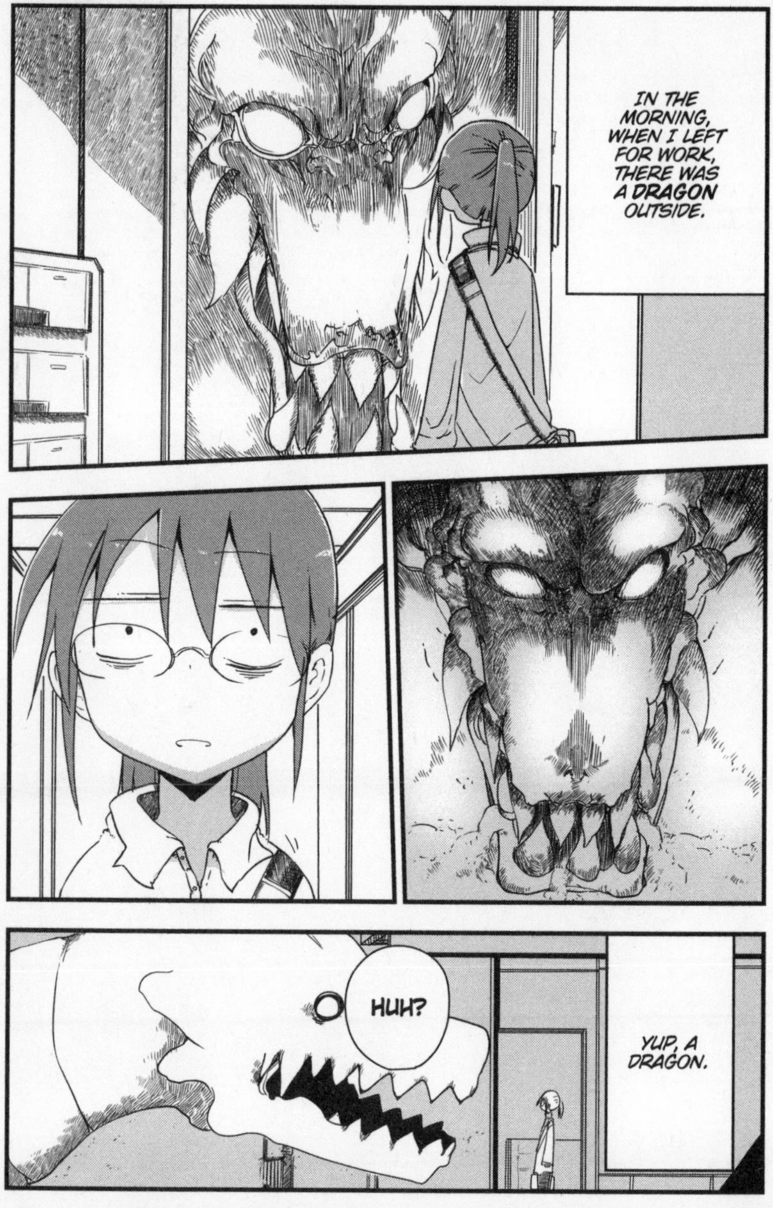
IN THE MORNING, WHEN I LEFT FOR WORK, THERE WAS A DRAGON OUTSIDE.
YUP, A DRAGON.
HUH?

# CHAPTER 2 : TOHRU & THEIR FIRST MEETING

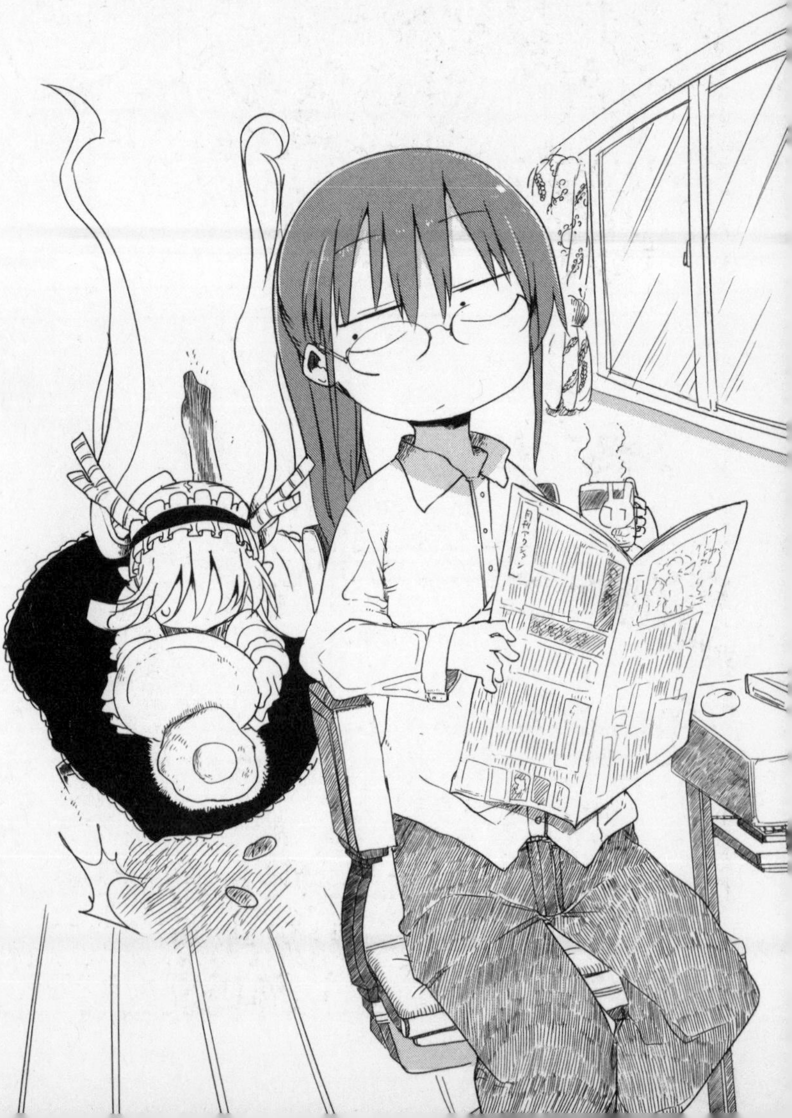

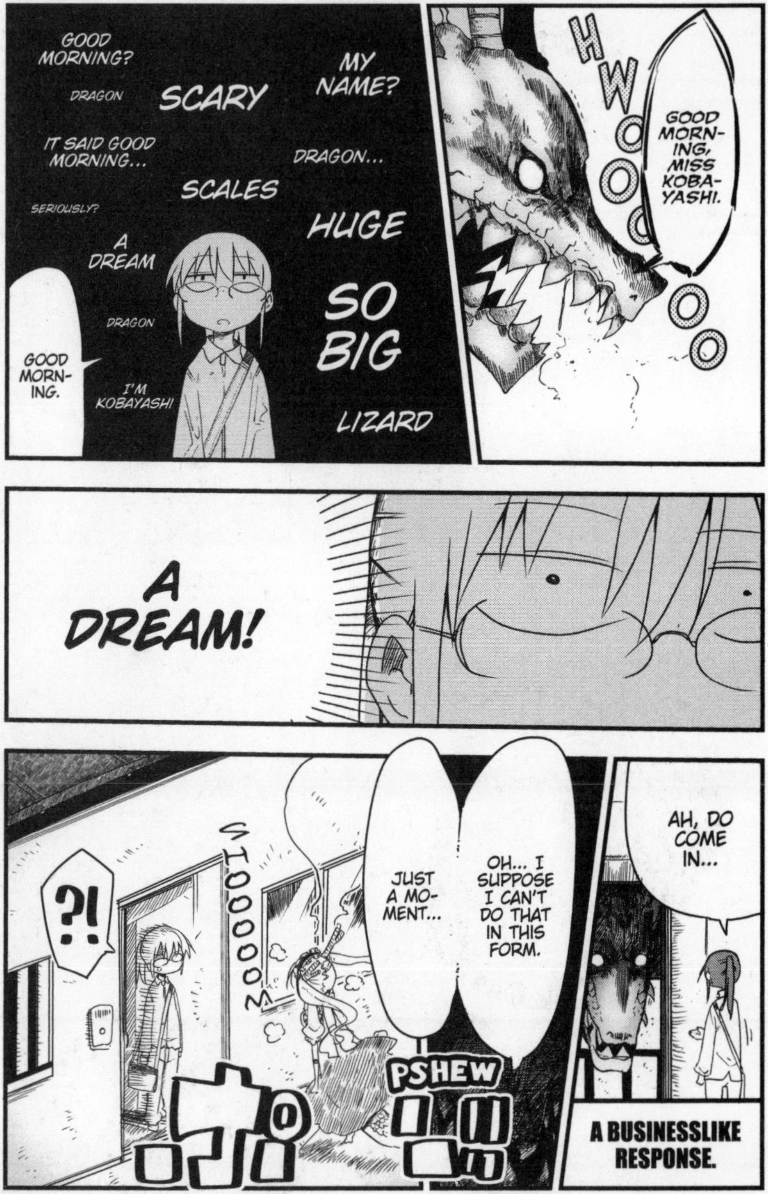
HWOOOOOOOOO
GOOD MORNING, MISS KOBAYASHI.
MY NAME?
GOOD MORNING?
DRAGON
SCARY
DRAGON...
IT SAID GOOD MORNING...
SCALES
HUGE
SERIOUSLY?
A DREAM
SO BIG
DRAGON
GOOD MORNING.
I'M KOBAYASHI
LIZARD
A DREAM!
AH, DO COME IN...
A BUSINESSLIKE RESPONSE.
OH... I SUPPOSE I CAN'T DO THAT IN THIS FORM.
JUST A MOMENT...
PSHEW
SHOOOOOOM
?!

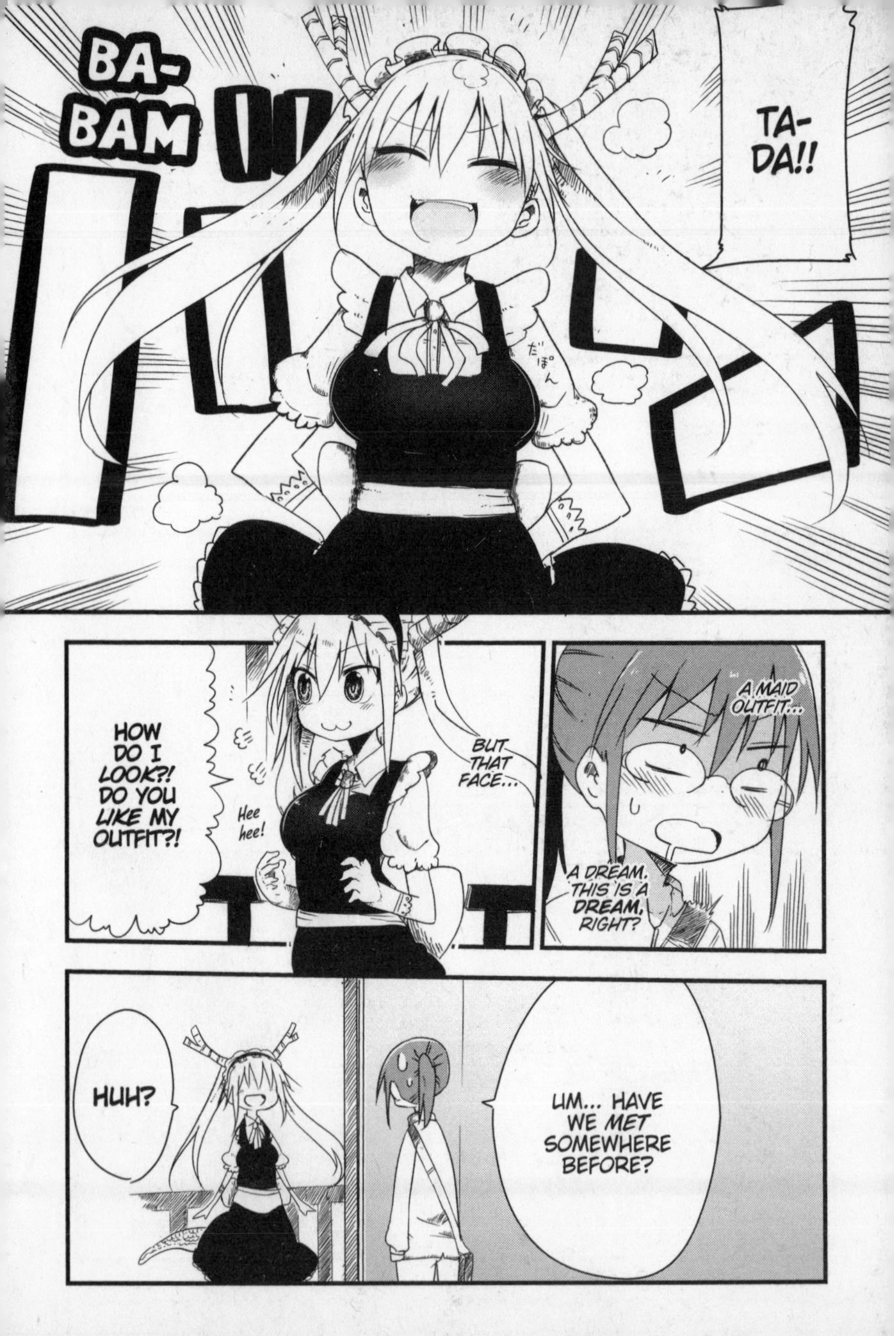
TA-DA!!
BA-BAM!!
だぽん
A MAID OUTFIT...
A DREAM. THIS IS A DREAM, RIGHT?
BUT THAT FACE...
Hee hee!
HOW DO I LOOK?! DO YOU LIKE MY OUTFIT?!
UM... HAVE WE MET SOMEWHERE BEFORE?
HUH?

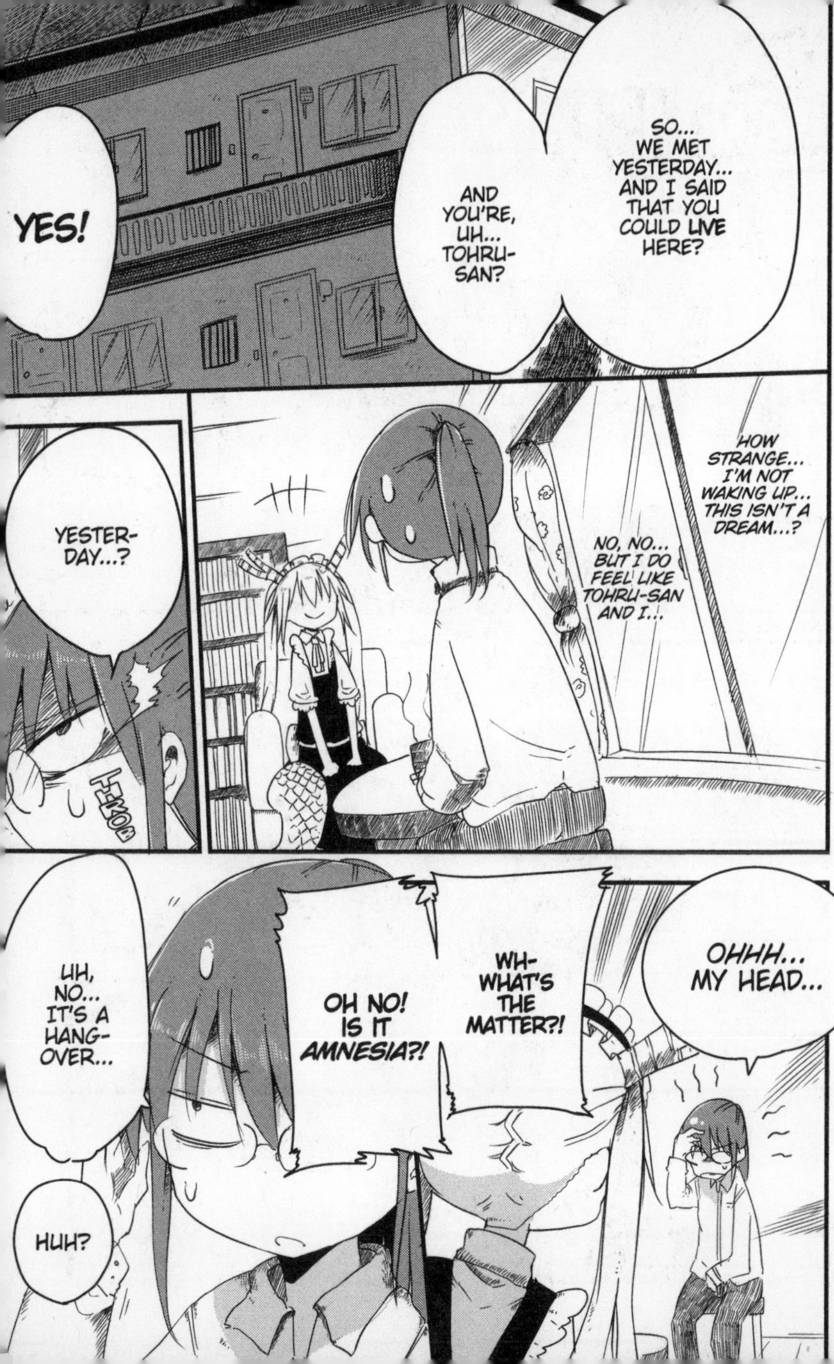
SO... WE MET YESTERDAY... AND I SAID THAT YOU COULD LIVE HERE?
AND YOU'RE, UH... TOHRU-SAN?
YES!
HOW STRANGE... I'M NOT WAKING UP... THIS ISN'T A DREAM...?
NO, NO... BUT I DO FEEL LIKE TOHRU-SAN AND I...
YESTER-DAY...?
OHHH... MY HEAD...
WH-WHAT'S THE MATTER?!
OH NO! IS IT AMNESIA?!
UH, NO... IT'S A HANG-OVER...
HUH?

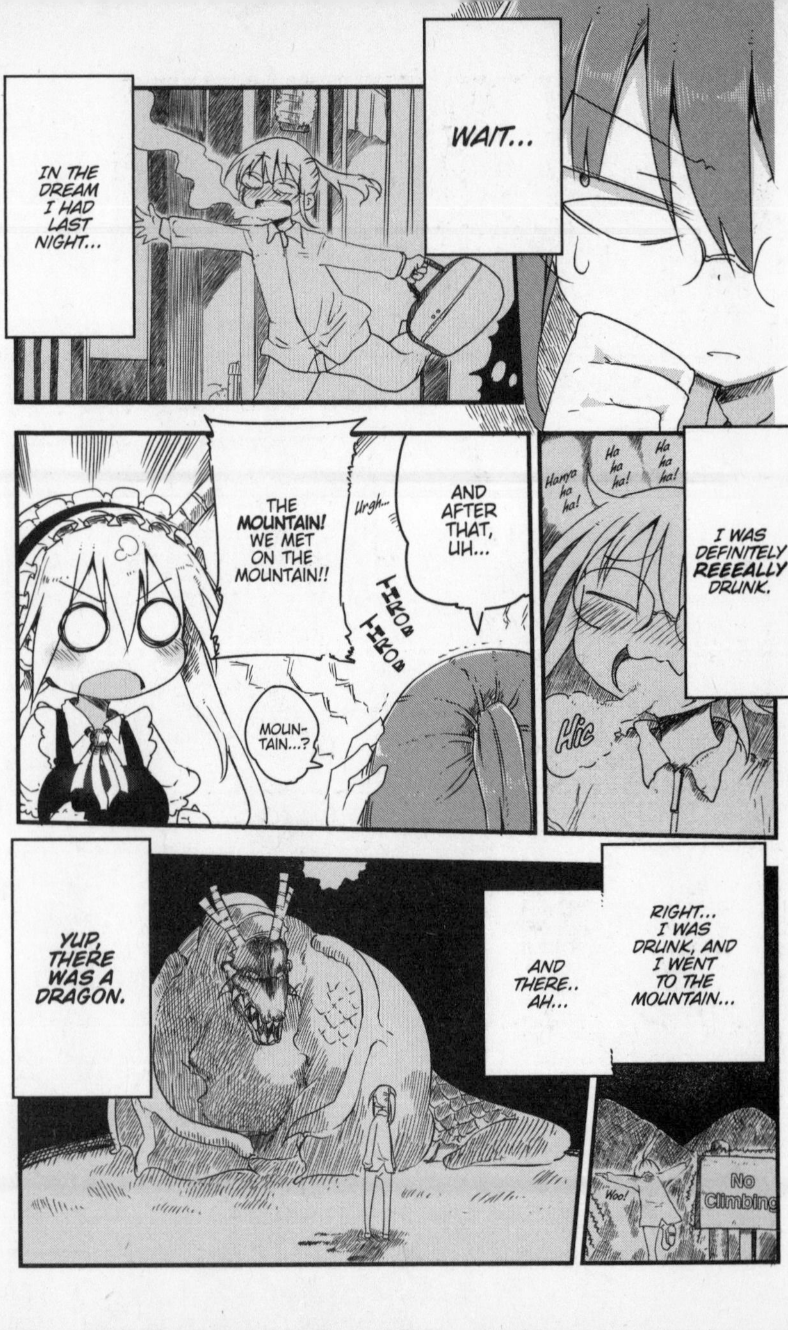
WAIT...
IN THE DREAM I HAD LAST NIGHT...
Ha ha ha!
Ha ha ha!
Hanya ha ha!
I WAS DEFINITELY REEEALLY DRUNK.
Hic
AND AFTER THAT, UH...
Urgh...
THROB THROB
THE MOUNTAIN! WE MET ON THE MOUNTAIN!!
MOUN-TAIN...?
RIGHT... I WAS DRUNK, AND I WENT TO THE MOUNTAIN...
AND THERE.. AH...
Woo!
No Climbing
YUP, THERE WAS A DRAGON.

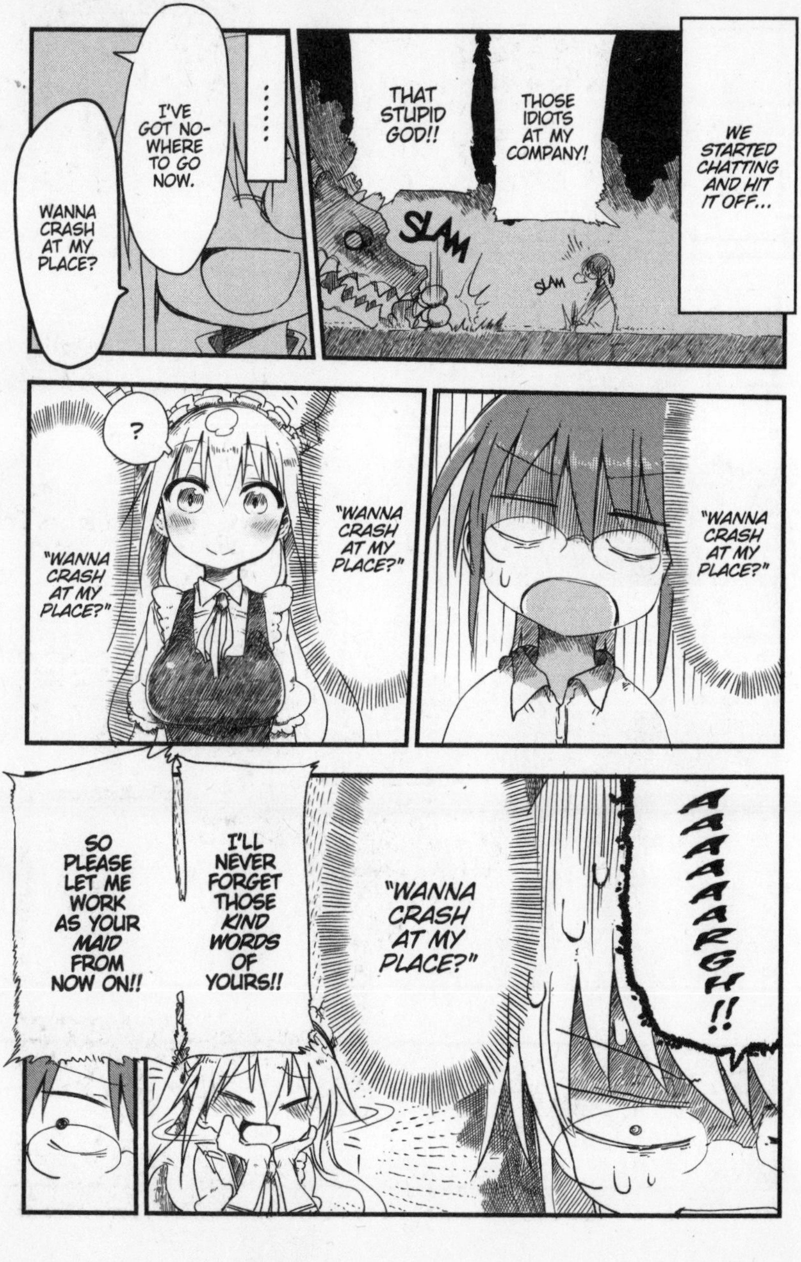

WE STARTED CHATTING AND HIT IT OFF...
THOSE IDIOTS AT MY COMPANY!
THAT STUPID GOD!!
SLAM
SLAM
......
I'VE GOT NO-WHERE TO GO NOW.
WANNA CRASH AT MY PLACE?
"WANNA CRASH AT MY PLACE?"
?
"WANNA CRASH AT MY PLACE?"
"WANNA CRASH AT MY PLACE?"
AAAAAARGH!!
"WANNA CRASH AT MY PLACE?"
I'LL NEVER FORGET THOSE KIND WORDS OF YOURS!!
SO PLEASE LET ME WORK AS YOUR MAID FROM NOW ON!!

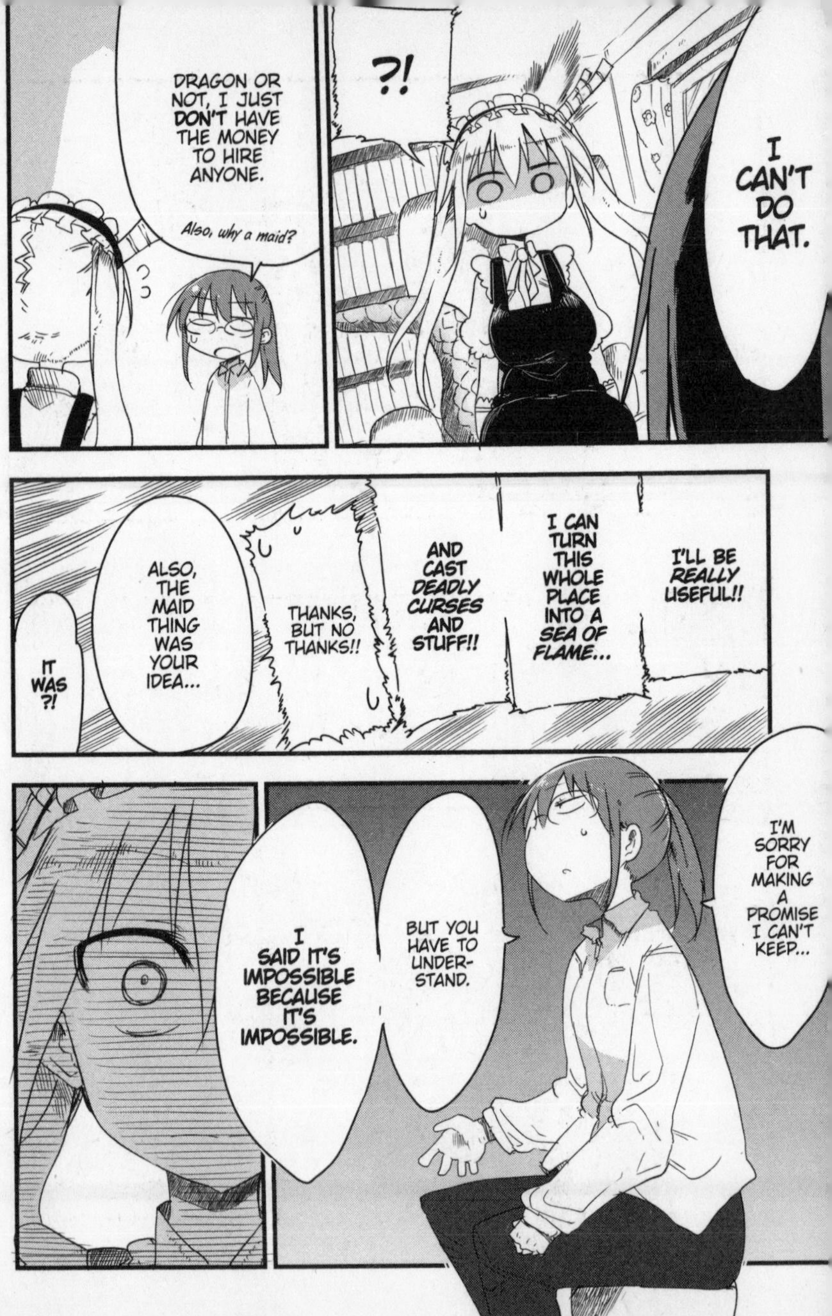
I CAN'T DO THAT.
?!
DRAGON OR NOT, I JUST **DON'T** HAVE THE MONEY TO HIRE ANYONE.
*Also, why a maid?*
I'LL BE *REALLY* USEFUL!!
I CAN TURN THIS WHOLE PLACE INTO A *SEA OF FLAME*...
AND CAST *DEADLY CURSES* AND STUFF!!
THANKS, BUT NO THANKS!!
ALSO, THE MAID THING WAS YOUR IDEA...
IT WAS ?!
I'M SORRY FOR MAKING A PROMISE I CAN'T KEEP...
BUT YOU HAVE TO UNDER-STAND.
I SAID IT'S IMPOSSIBLE BECAUSE IT'S IMPOSSIBLE.

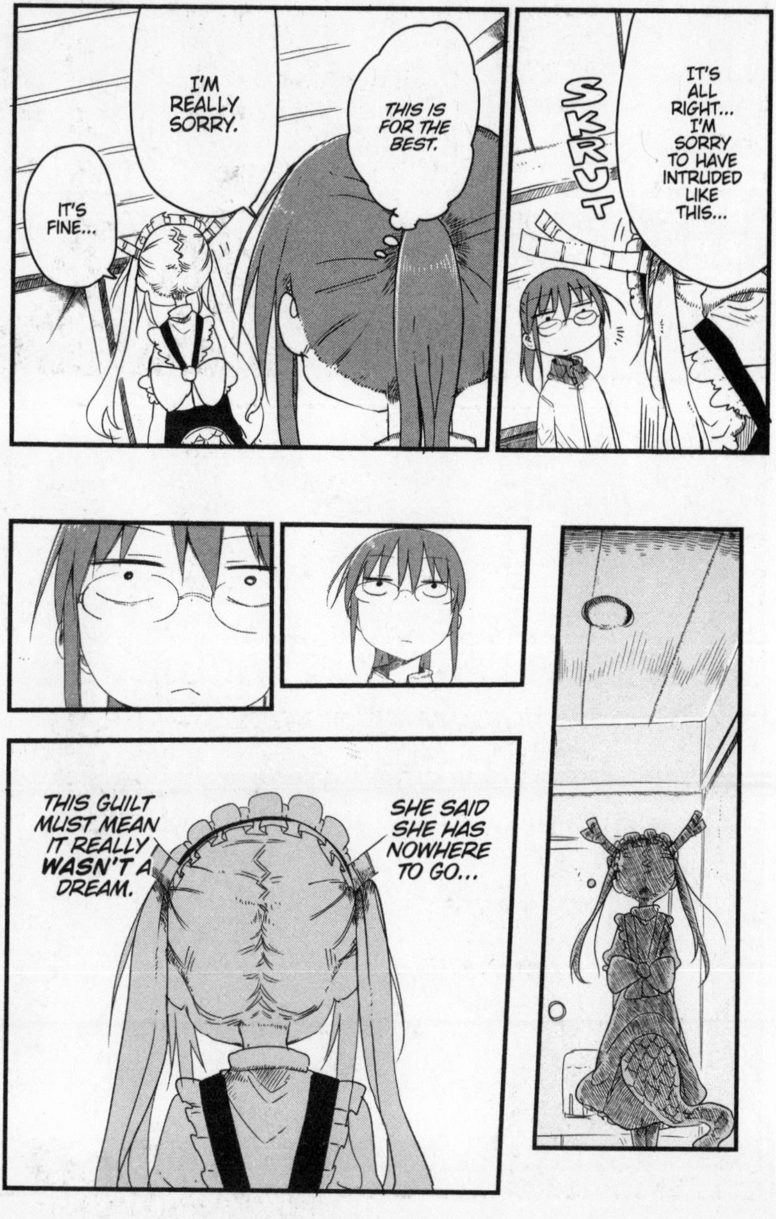
IT'S ALL RIGHT... I'M SORRY TO HAVE INTRUDED LIKE THIS...
SKRUT
THIS IS FOR THE BEST.
I'M REALLY SORRY.
IT'S FINE...
SHE SAID SHE HAS NOWHERE TO GO...
THIS GUILT MUST MEAN IT REALLY WASN'T A DREAM.

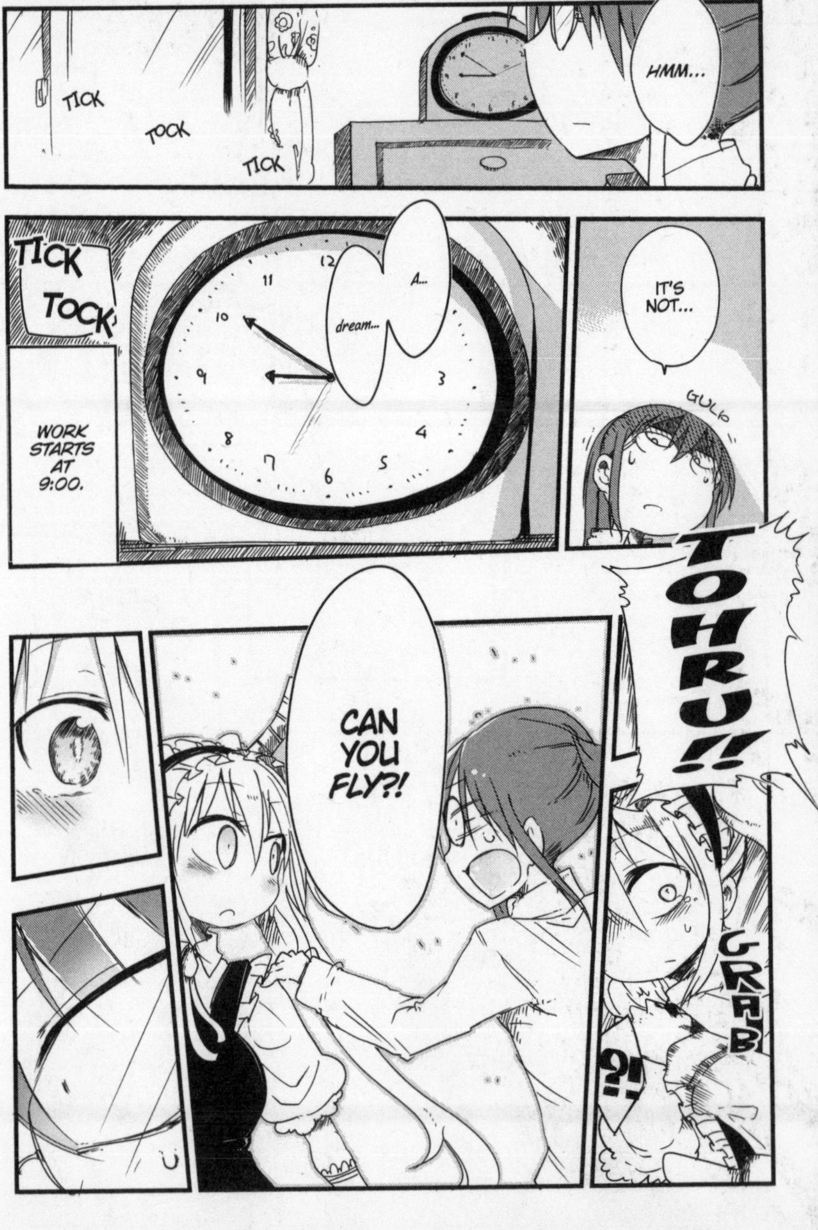
HMM...
TICK
TOCK
TICK
IT'S NOT...
GULP
A... dream...
TICK TOCK
WORK STARTS AT 9:00.
TOHRU!!
GRAB
?!
CAN YOU FLY?!

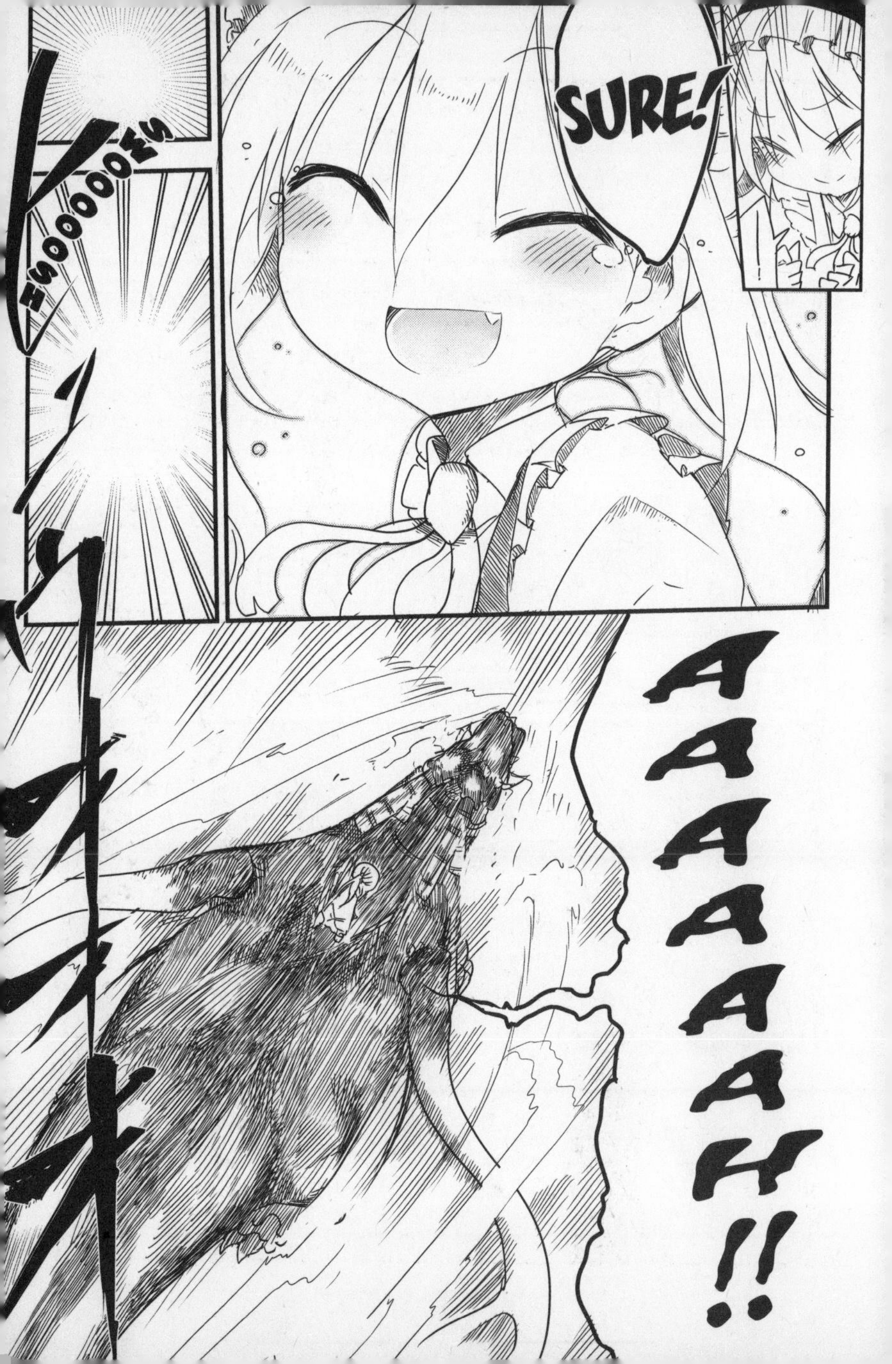
SURE!
SWOOOOOSH
AAAAAAH!!

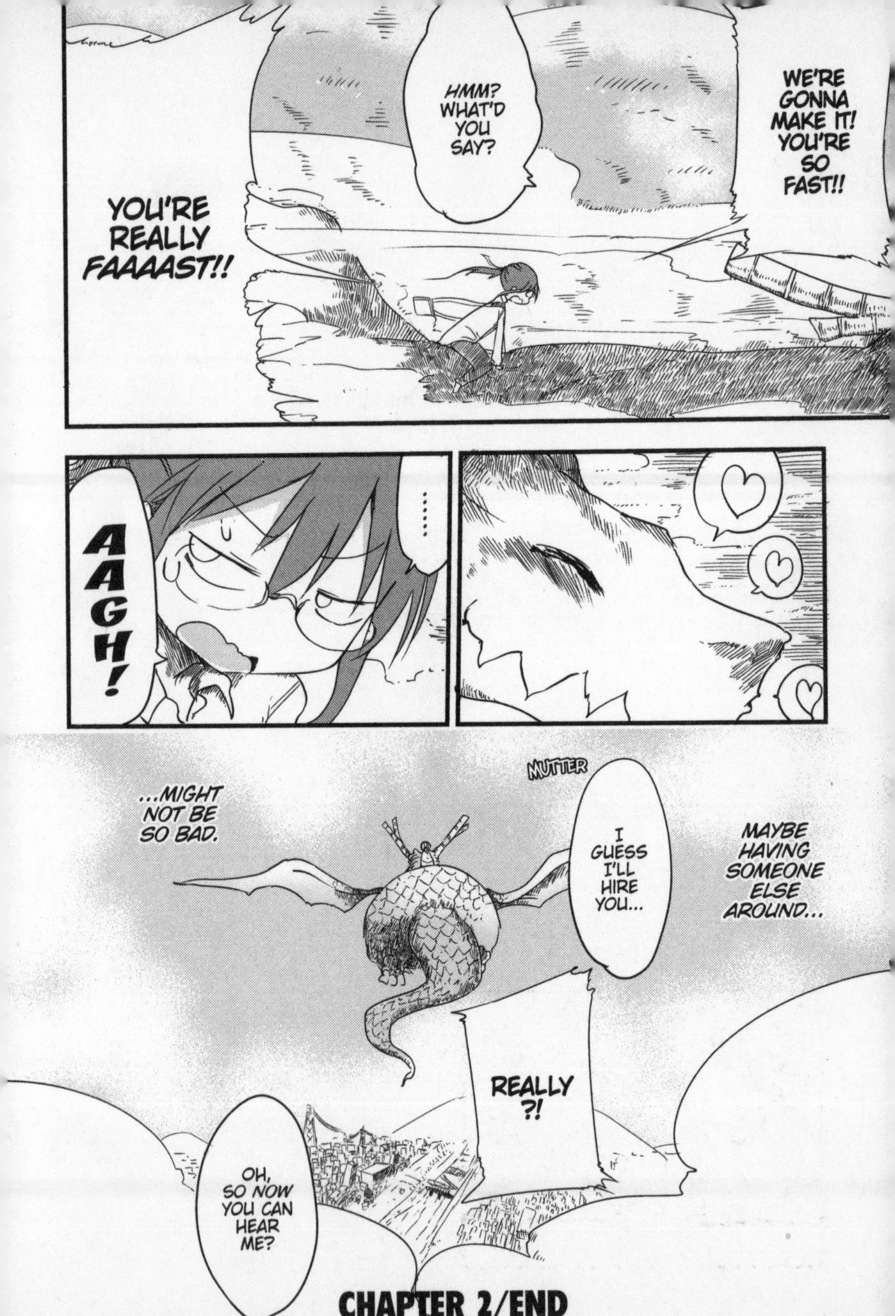
WE'RE GONNA MAKE IT! YOU'RE SO FAST!!
HMM? WHAT'D YOU SAY?
YOU'RE REALLY FAAAAST!!
......
AAGH!
MAYBE HAVING SOMEONE ELSE AROUND...
MUTTER
I GUESS I'LL HIRE YOU...
...MIGHT NOT BE SO BAD.
REALLY?!
OH, SO NOW YOU CAN HEAR ME?

**CHAPTER 2/END**

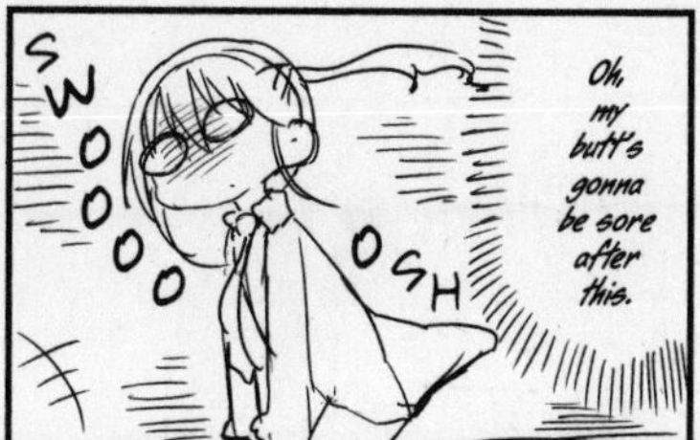
Oh, my butt's gonna be sore after this.
SWOOOOOSH

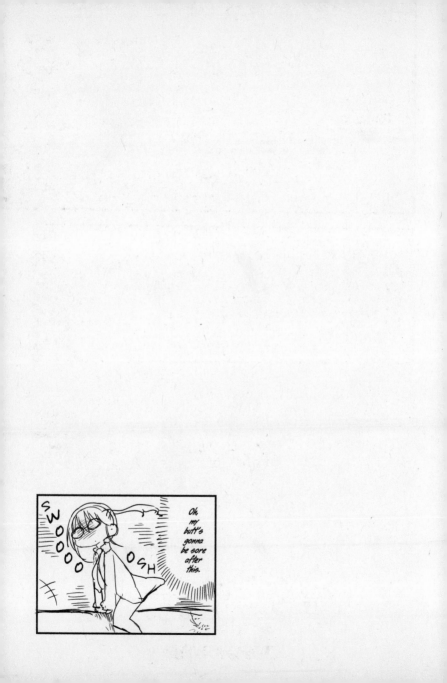

Miss Kobayashi's
DRAGON MAID

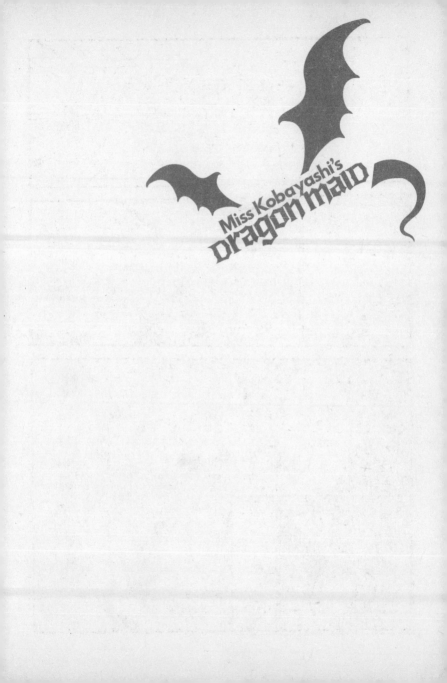

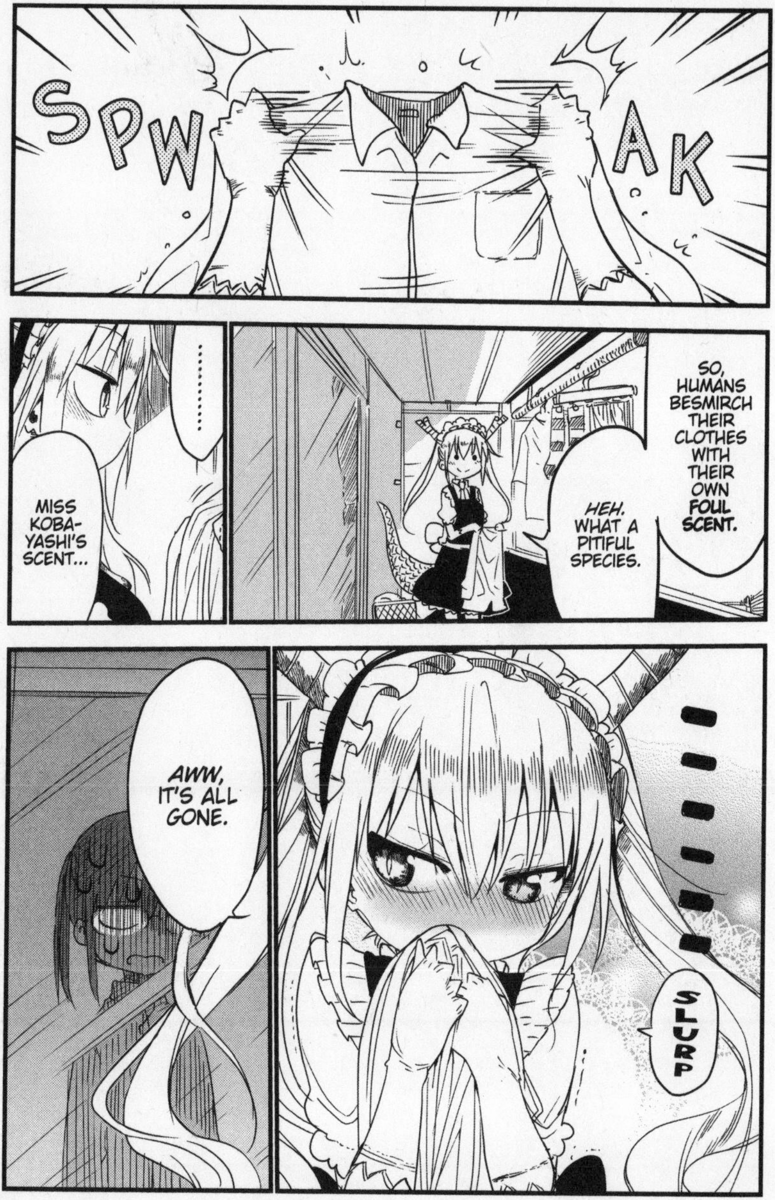

SPWAK
SO, HUMANS BESMIRCH THEIR CLOTHES WITH THEIR OWN **FOUL SCENT.**
*HEH.* WHAT A PITIFUL SPECIES.
......
MISS KOBAYASHI'S SCENT...
SLURP
*AWW,* IT'S ALL GONE.

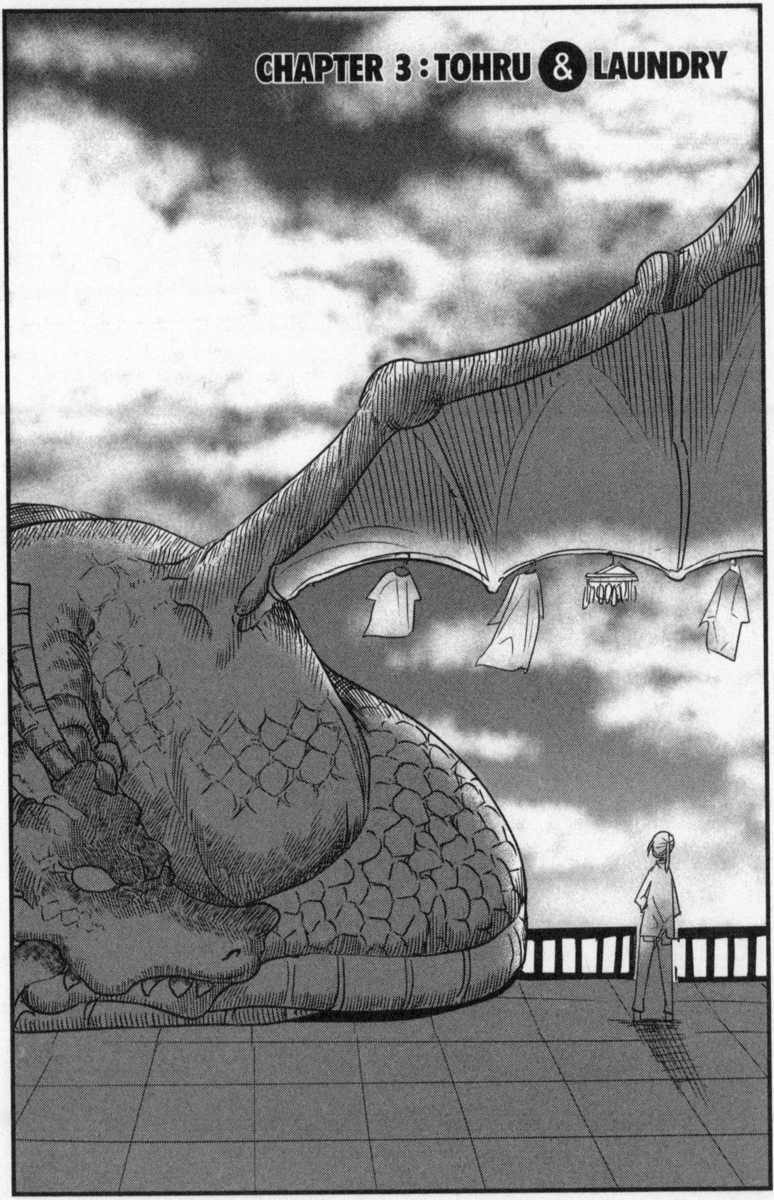
CHAPTER 3 : TOHRU & LAUNDRY

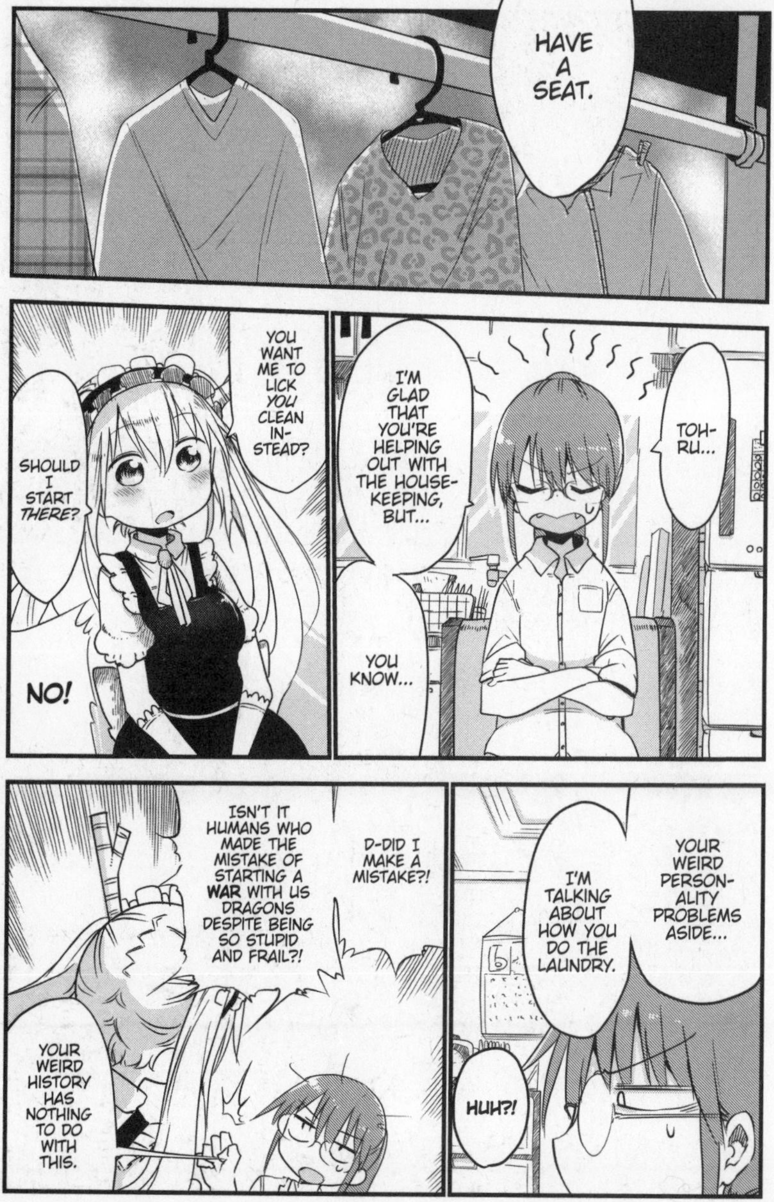
HAVE A SEAT.
TOH-RU...
I'M GLAD THAT YOU'RE HELPING OUT WITH THE HOUSE-KEEPING, BUT...
YOU KNOW...
YOU WANT ME TO LICK *YOU* CLEAN IN-STEAD?
SHOULD I START *THERE?*
NO!
YOUR WEIRD PERSON-ALITY PROBLEMS ASIDE...
I'M TALKING ABOUT HOW YOU DO THE LAUNDRY.
HUH?!
D-DID I MAKE A MISTAKE?!
ISN'T IT HUMANS WHO MADE THE MISTAKE OF STARTING A **WAR** WITH US DRAGONS DESPITE BEING SO STUPID AND FRAIL?!
YOUR WEIRD HISTORY HAS NOTHING TO DO WITH THIS.

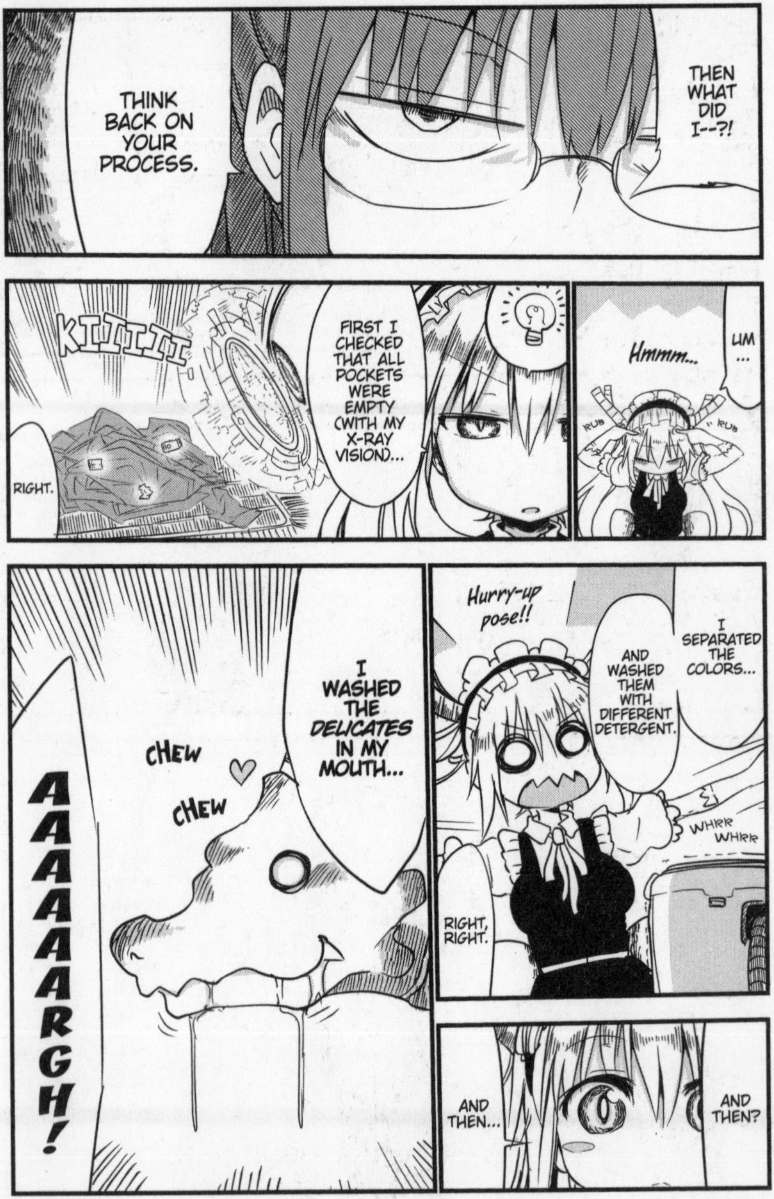
THEN WHAT DID I--?!
THINK BACK ON YOUR PROCESS.
UM ...
Hmmm...
RUB RUB
FIRST I CHECKED THAT ALL POCKETS WERE EMPTY (WITH MY X-RAY VISION)...
KIIIIII
RIGHT.
I SEPARATED THE COLORS...
AND WASHED THEM WITH DIFFERENT DETERGENT.
Hurry-up pose!!
WHRR WHRR
RIGHT, RIGHT.
AND THEN?
AND THEN...
I WASHED THE DELICATES IN MY MOUTH...
CHEW
CHEW
AAAAAAARGH!

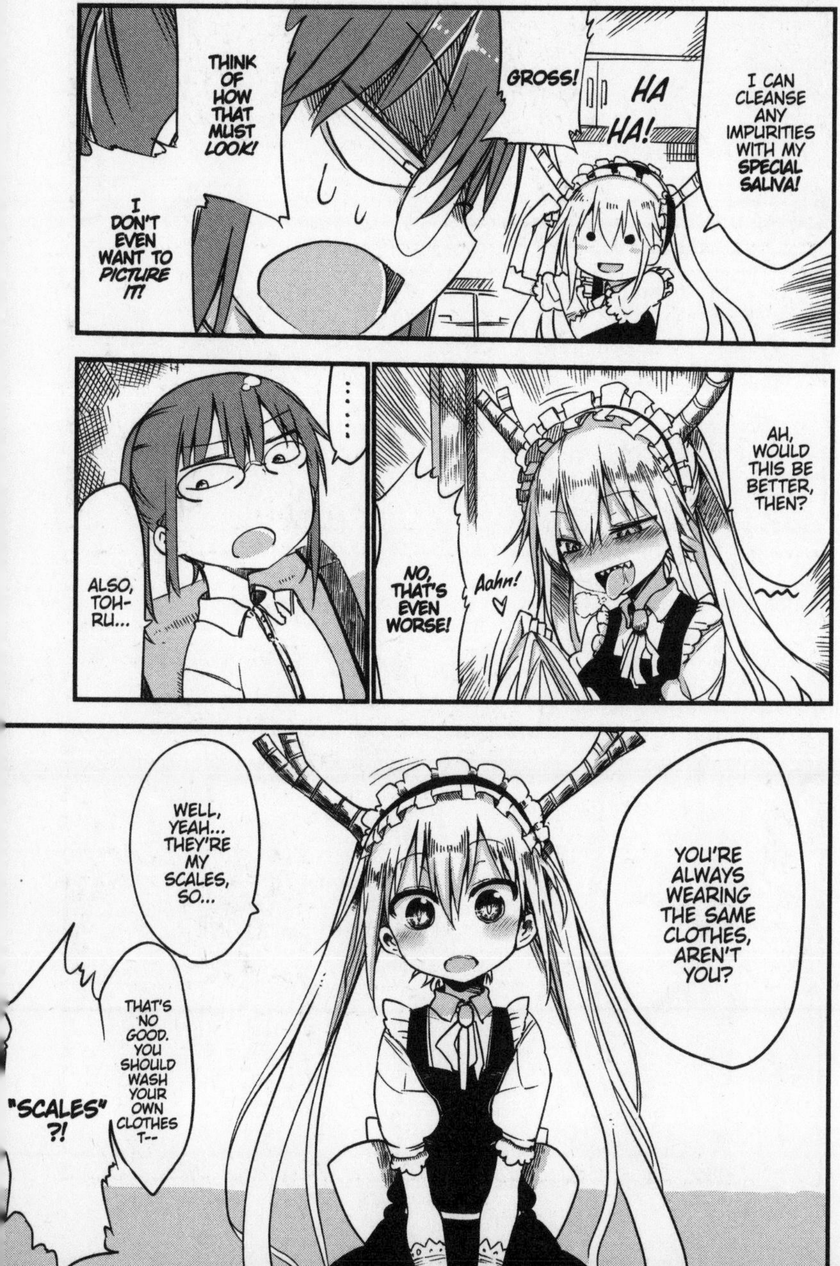
I CAN CLEANSE ANY IMPURITIES WITH MY SPECIAL SALIVA!
HA HA!
GROSS!
THINK OF HOW THAT MUST LOOK!
I DON'T EVEN WANT TO PICTURE IT!
AH, WOULD THIS BE BETTER, THEN?
Aahn! ♡
NO, THAT'S EVEN WORSE!
......
ALSO, TOHRU...
YOU'RE ALWAYS WEARING THE SAME CLOTHES, AREN'T YOU?
WELL, YEAH... THEY'RE MY SCALES, SO...
THAT'S NO GOOD. YOU SHOULD WASH YOUR OWN CLOTHES T--
"SCALES"?!

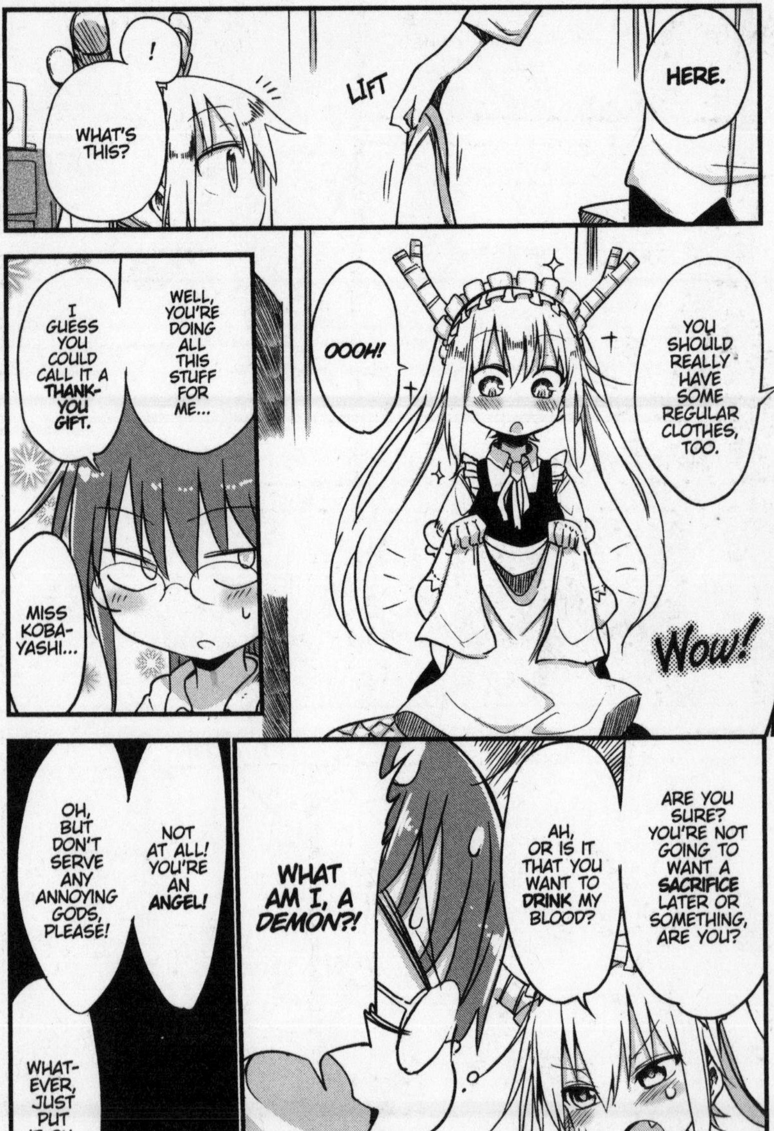
HERE.
LIFT
!
WHAT'S THIS?
YOU SHOULD REALLY HAVE SOME REGULAR CLOTHES, TOO.
OOOH!
WOW!
WELL, YOU'RE DOING ALL THIS STUFF FOR ME...
I GUESS YOU COULD CALL IT A THANK-YOU GIFT.
MISS KOBA-YASHI...
ARE YOU SURE? YOU'RE NOT GOING TO WANT A SACRIFICE LATER OR SOMETHING, ARE YOU?
AH, OR IS IT THAT YOU WANT TO DRINK MY BLOOD?
WHAT AM I, A DEMON?!
NOT AT ALL! YOU'RE AN ANGEL!
OH, BUT DON'T SERVE ANY ANNOYING GODS, PLEASE!
WHAT-EVER, JUST PUT IT ON.

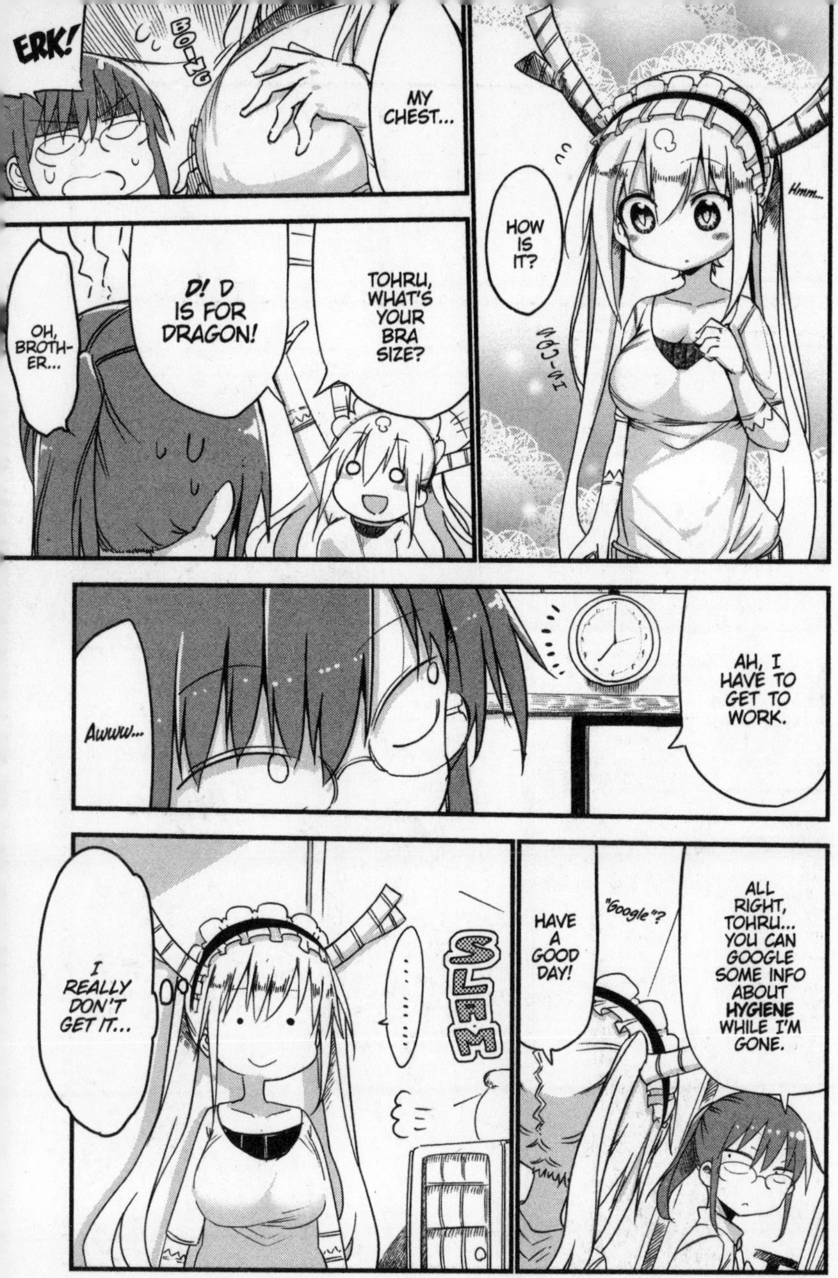
Hmm...
HOW IS IT?
MY CHEST...
BOING
ERK!
TOHRU, WHAT'S YOUR BRA SIZE?
D! D IS FOR DRAGON!
OH, BROTHER...
AH, I HAVE TO GET TO WORK.
Awww...
ALL RIGHT, TOHRU... YOU CAN GOOGLE SOME INFO ABOUT HYGIENE WHILE I'M GONE.
"Google"?
HAVE A GOOD DAY!
SLAM
......
I REALLY DON'T GET IT...

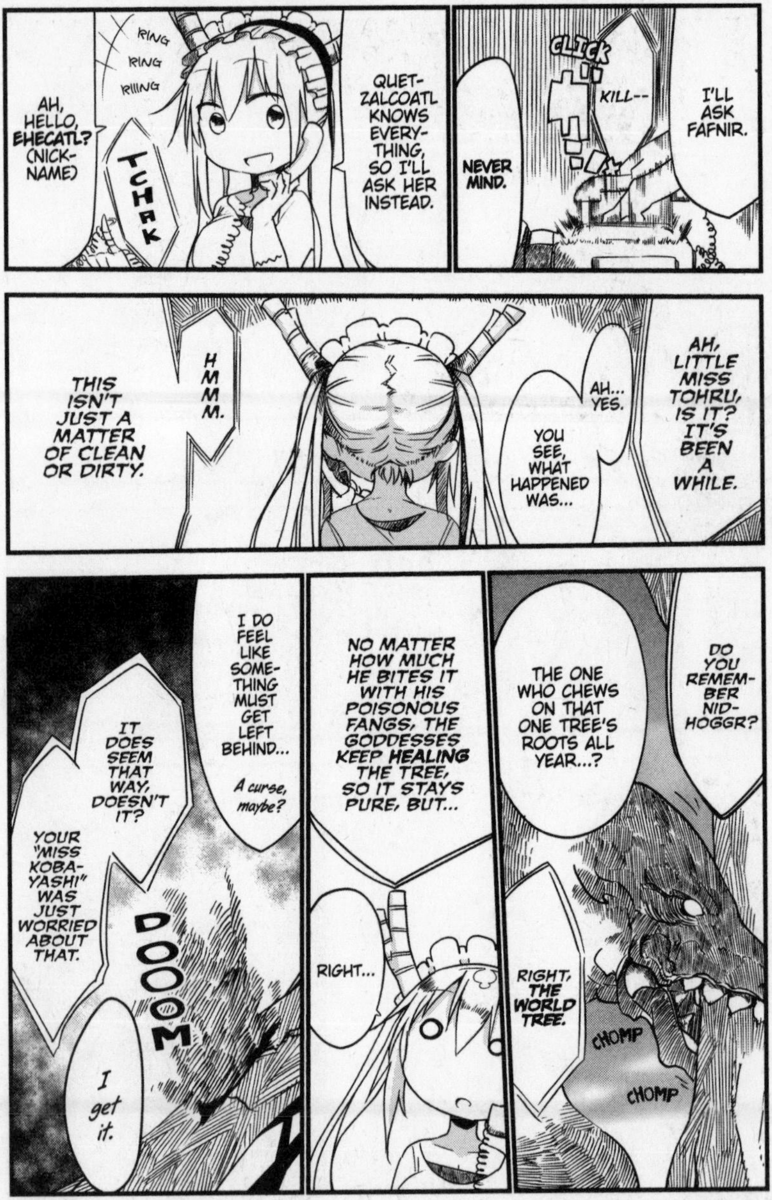
I'LL ASK FAFNIR.
CLICK
KILL--
NEVER MIND.
QUETZALCOATL KNOWS EVERYTHING, SO I'LL ASK HER INSTEAD.
RING RING RIIING
AH, HELLO, EHECATL? (NICKNAME)
TCHAK
AH, LITTLE MISS TOHRU, IS IT? IT'S BEEN A WHILE.
AH... YES.
YOU SEE, WHAT HAPPENED WAS...
HMMM.
THIS ISN'T JUST A MATTER OF CLEAN OR DIRTY.
DO YOU REMEMBER NIDHOGGR?
THE ONE WHO CHEWS ON THAT ONE TREE'S ROOTS ALL YEAR...?
RIGHT, THE WORLD TREE.
CHOMP
CHOMP
NO MATTER HOW MUCH HE BITES IT WITH HIS POISONOUS FANGS, THE GODDESSES KEEP HEALING THE TREE, SO IT STAYS PURE, BUT...
RIGHT...
I DO FEEL LIKE SOMETHING MUST GET LEFT BEHIND...
A curse, maybe?
IT DOES SEEM THAT WAY, DOESN'T IT?
YOUR "MISS KOBAYASHI" WAS JUST WORRIED ABOUT THAT.
DOOOOM
I get it.

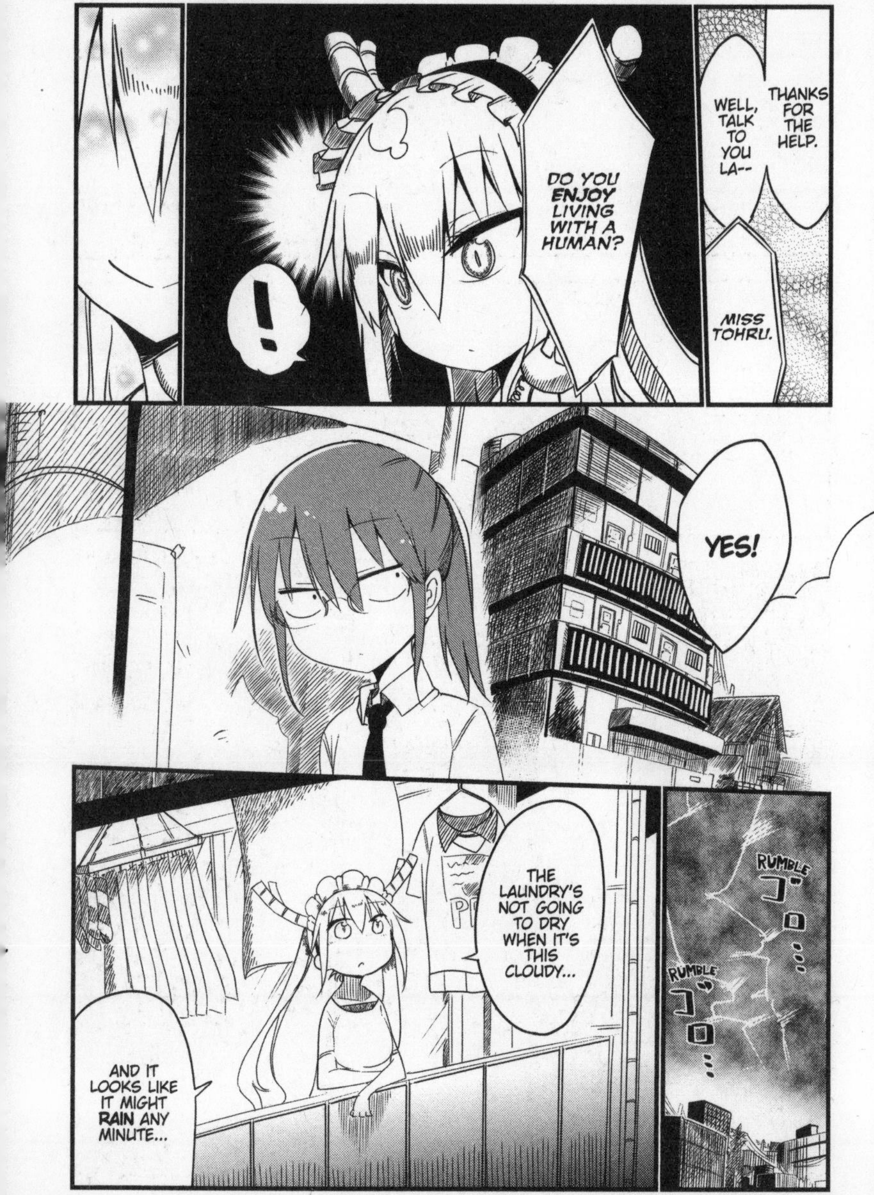
THANKS FOR THE HELP.
WELL, TALK TO YOU LA--
MISS TOHRU.
DO YOU ENJOY LIVING WITH A HUMAN?
!
YES!
RUMBLE
ゴロ…
RUMBLE
ゴロ…
THE LAUNDRY'S NOT GOING TO DRY WHEN IT'S THIS CLOUDY...
AND IT LOOKS LIKE IT MIGHT RAIN ANY MINUTE...

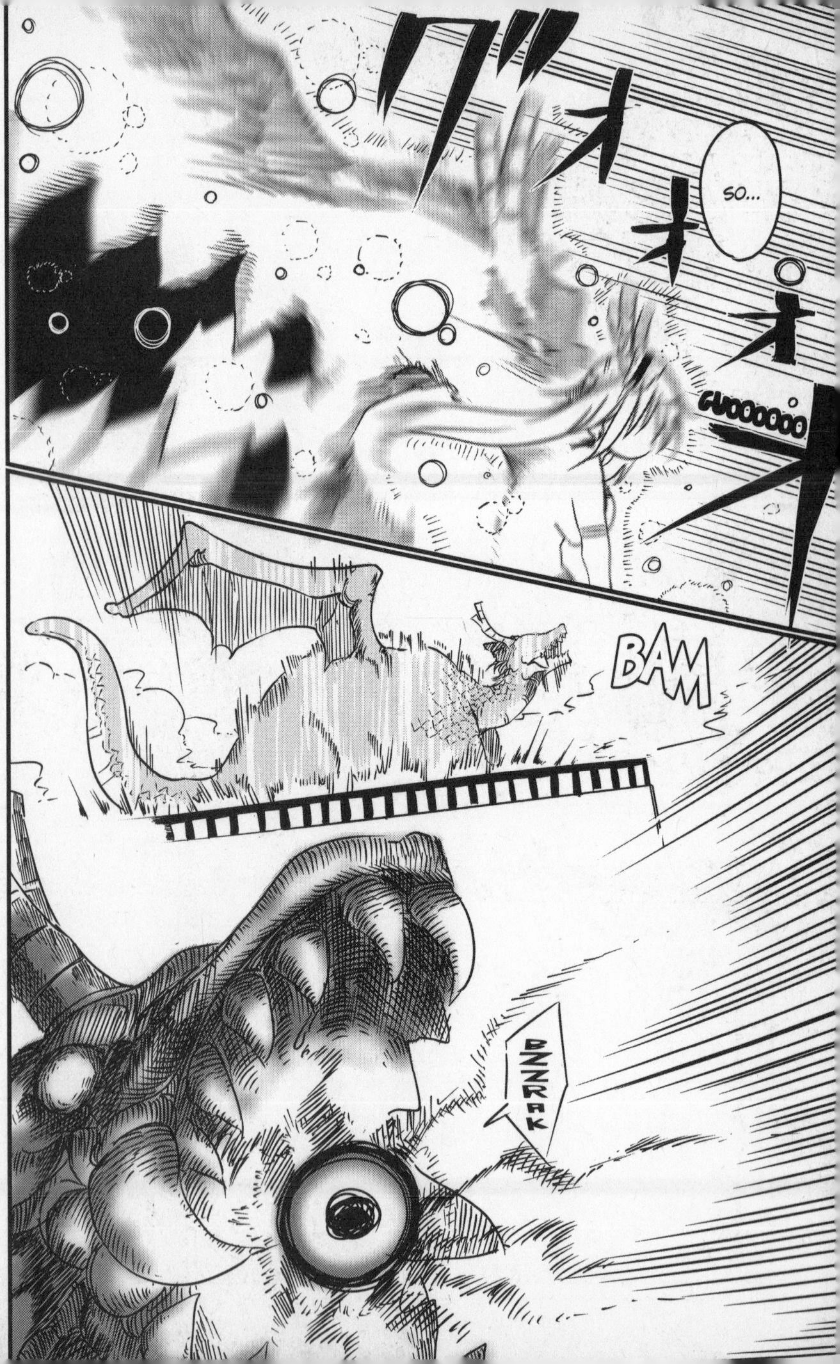
SO...
GUOOOOOO
BAM
BZZRAK

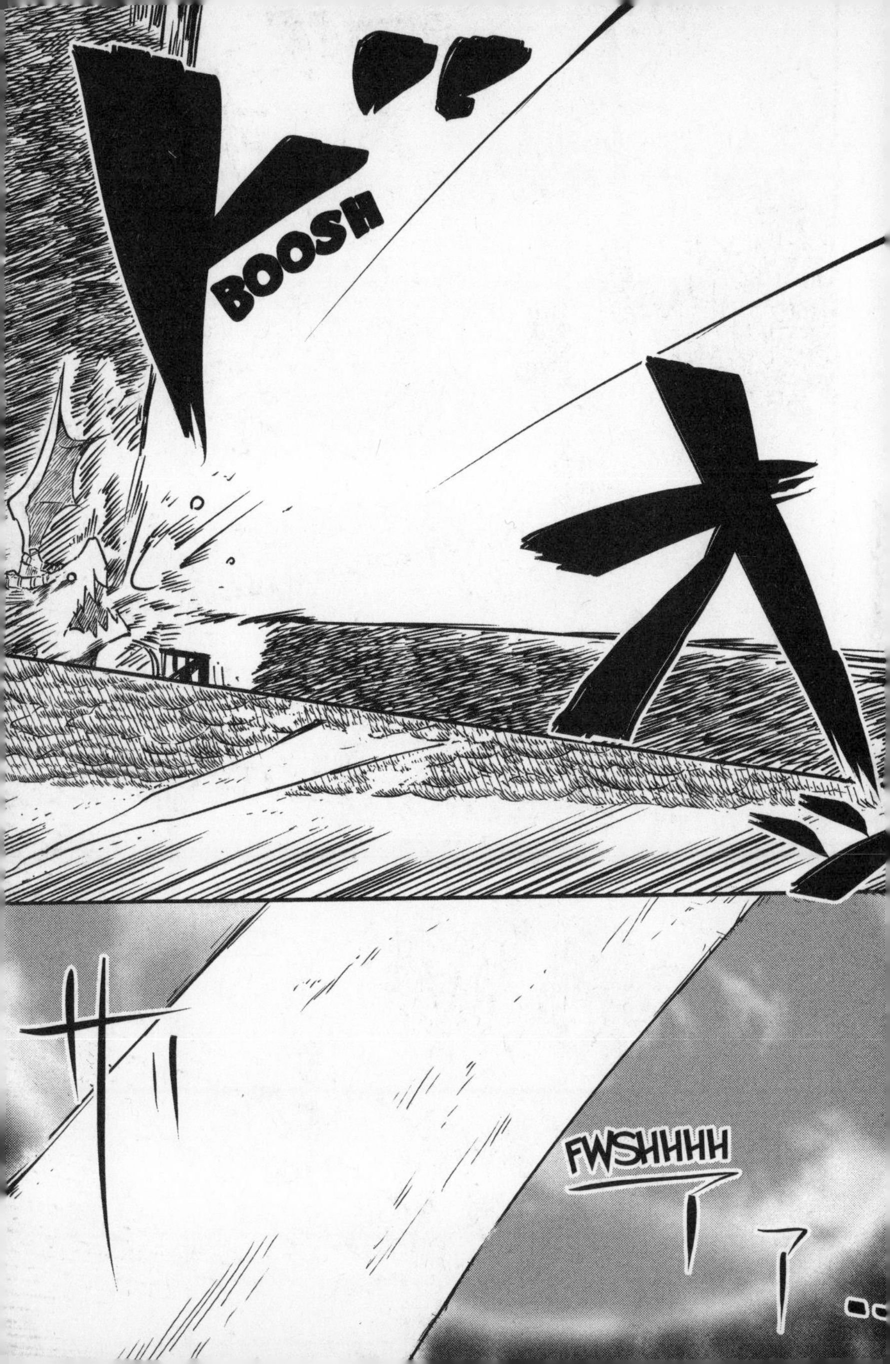
BOOSH
FWSHHHH

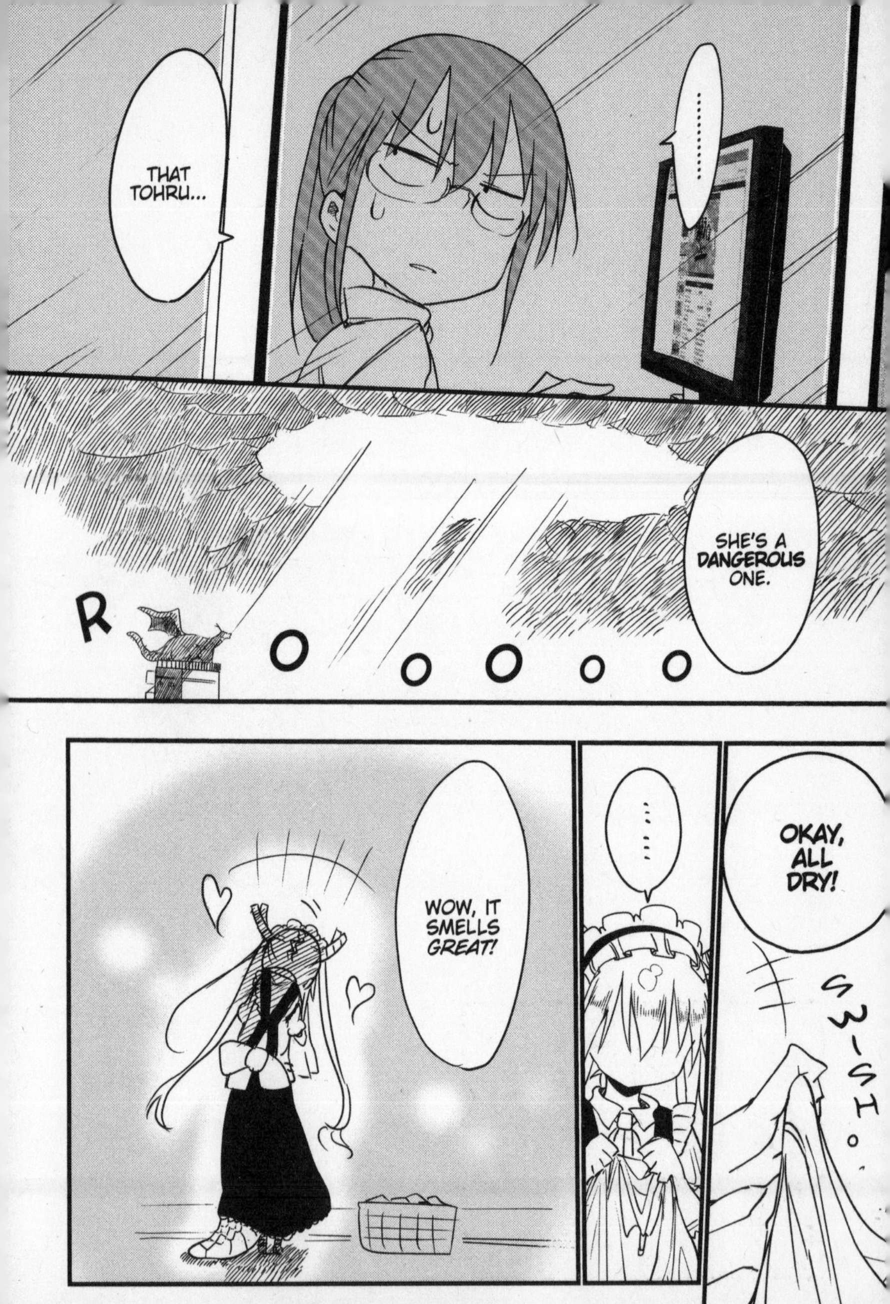
......
THAT TOHRU...
SHE'S A DANGEROUS ONE.
ROOOOOO
OKAY, ALL DRY!
SHI-SHI.
......
WOW, IT SMELLS *GREAT!*

**CHAPTER 3/END**

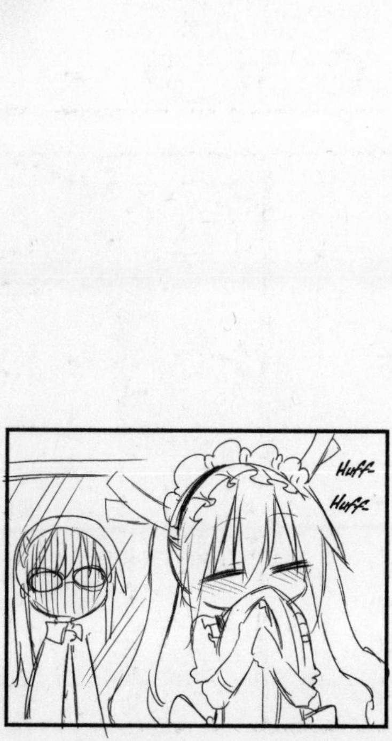
Huff
Huff

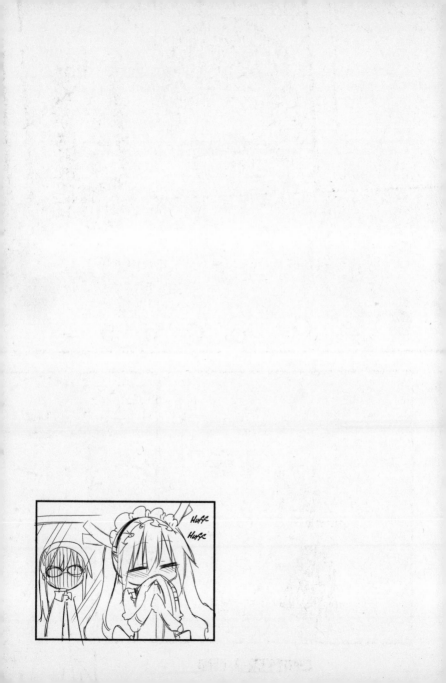

Miss Kobayashi's
DRAGON MAID

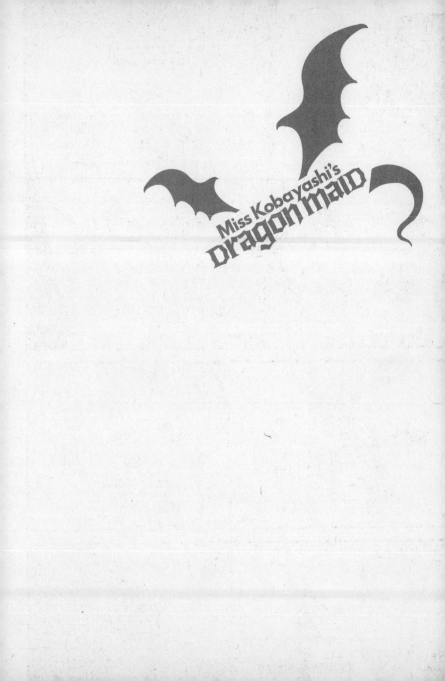

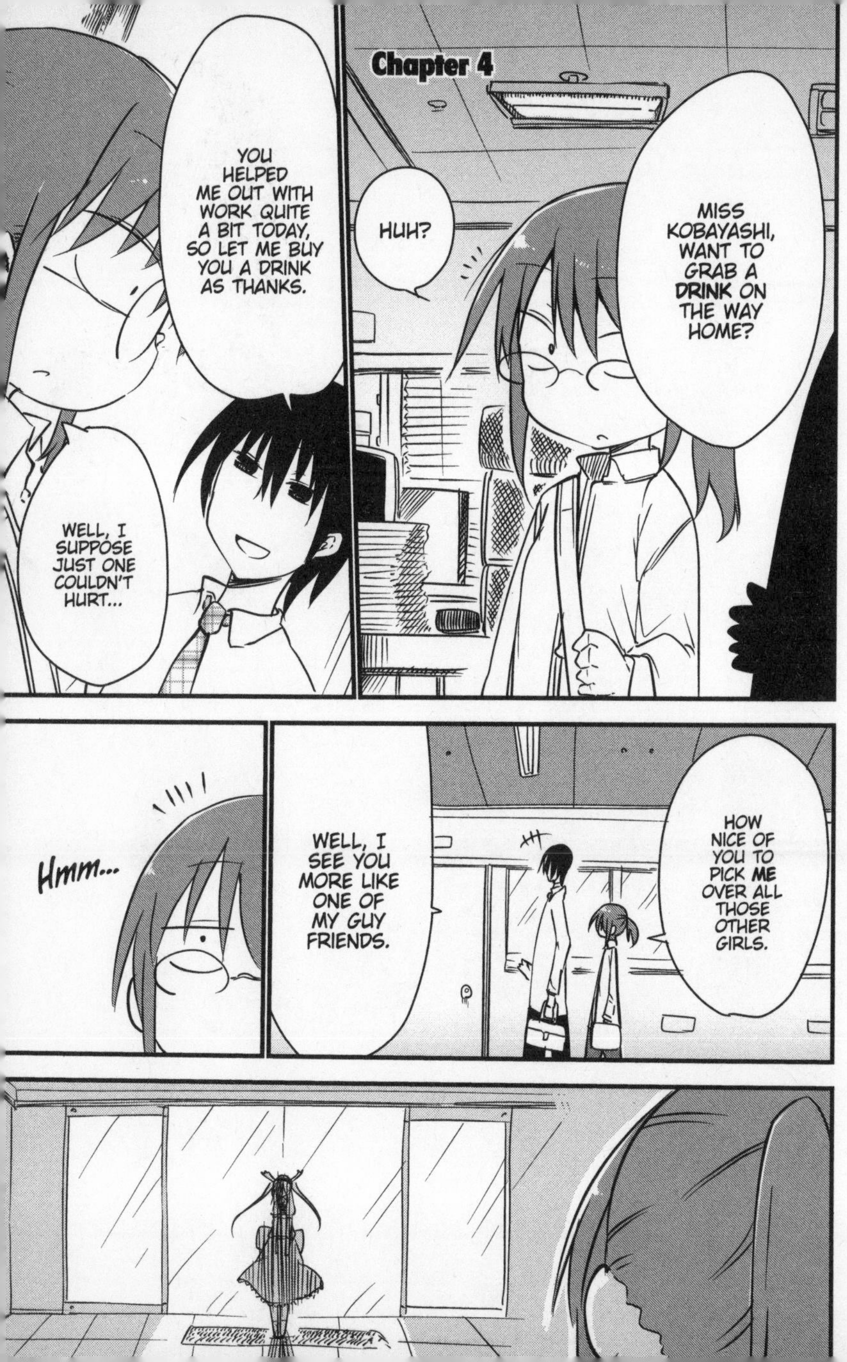
Chapter 4
MISS KOBAYASHI, WANT TO GRAB A DRINK ON THE WAY HOME?
HUH?
YOU HELPED ME OUT WITH WORK QUITE A BIT TODAY, SO LET ME BUY YOU A DRINK AS THANKS.
WELL, I SUPPOSE JUST ONE COULDN'T HURT...
HOW NICE OF YOU TO PICK ME OVER ALL THOSE OTHER GIRLS.
WELL, I SEE YOU MORE LIKE ONE OF MY GUY FRIENDS.
Hmm...

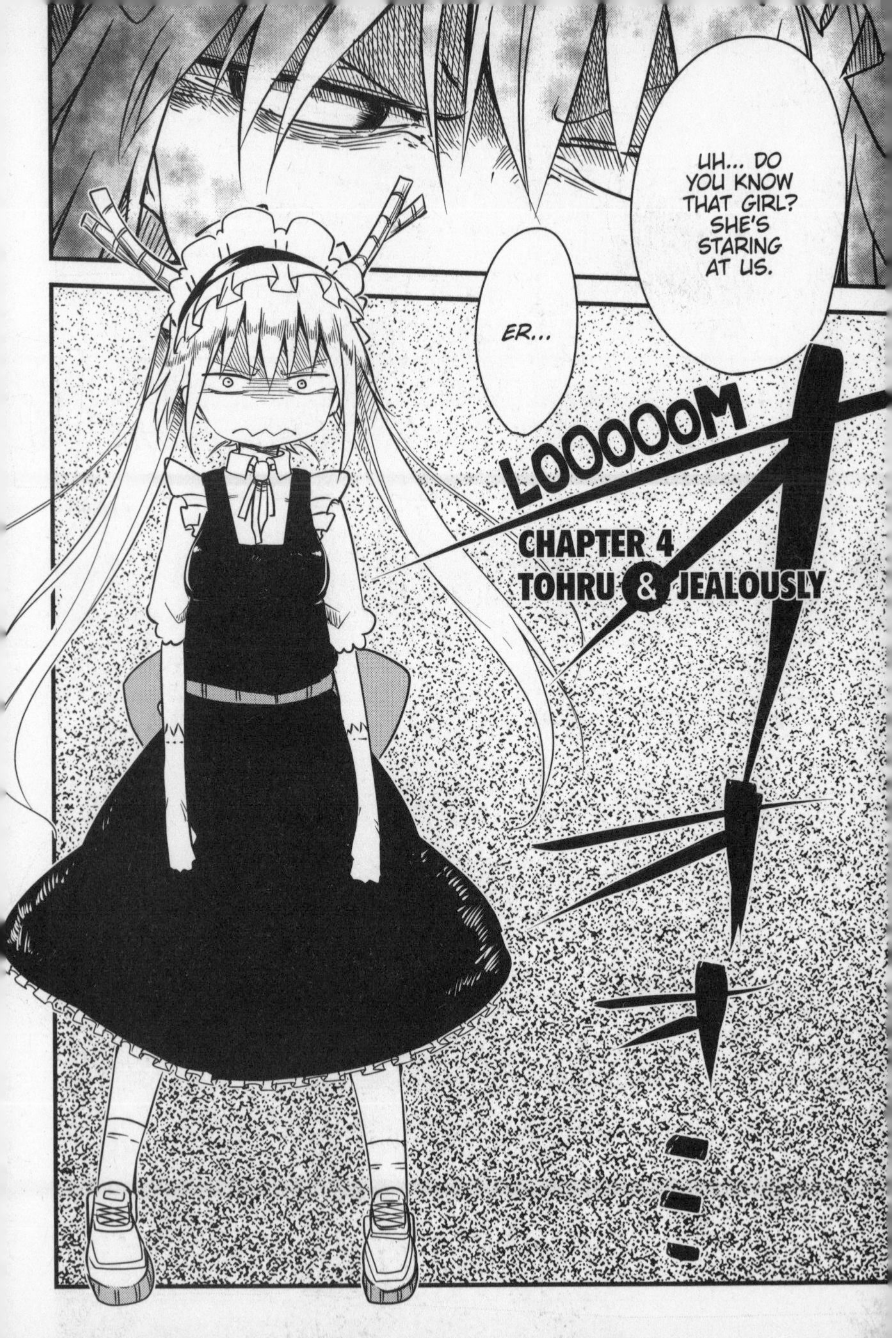
UH... DO YOU KNOW THAT GIRL? SHE'S STARING AT US.
ER...
LOOOOOM
CHAPTER 4
TOHRU & JEALOUSLY

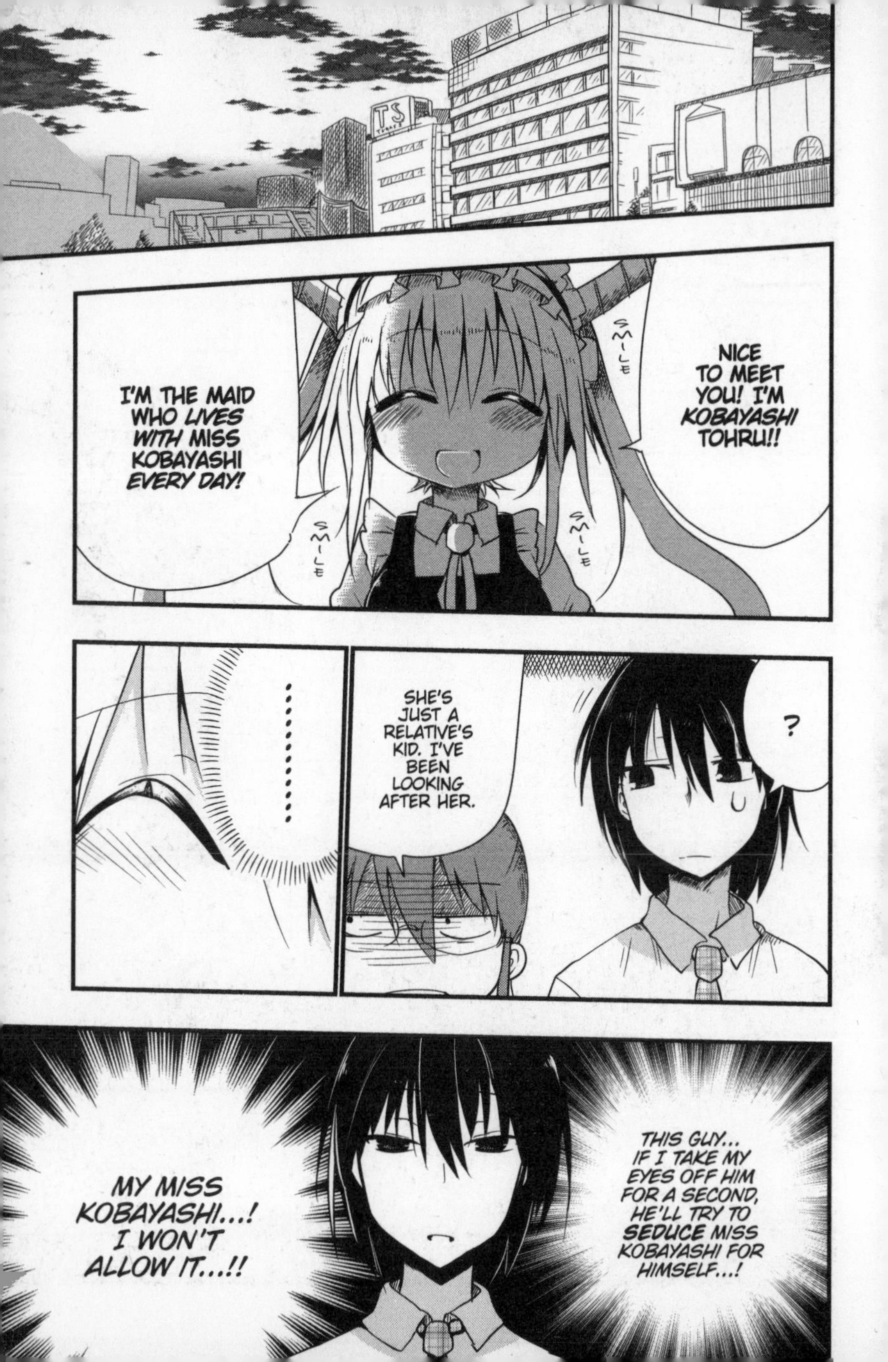
TS
NICE TO MEET YOU! I'M KOBAYASHI TOHRU!!
SMILE
SMILE
I'M THE MAID WHO *LIVES WITH* MISS KOBAYASHI *EVERY DAY!*
SMILE
?
SHE'S JUST A RELATIVE'S KID. I'VE BEEN LOOKING AFTER HER.
........
THIS GUY... IF I TAKE MY EYES OFF HIM FOR A SECOND, HE'LL TRY TO SEDUCE MISS KOBAYASHI FOR HIMSELF...!
MY MISS KOBAYASHI...! I WON'T ALLOW IT...!!

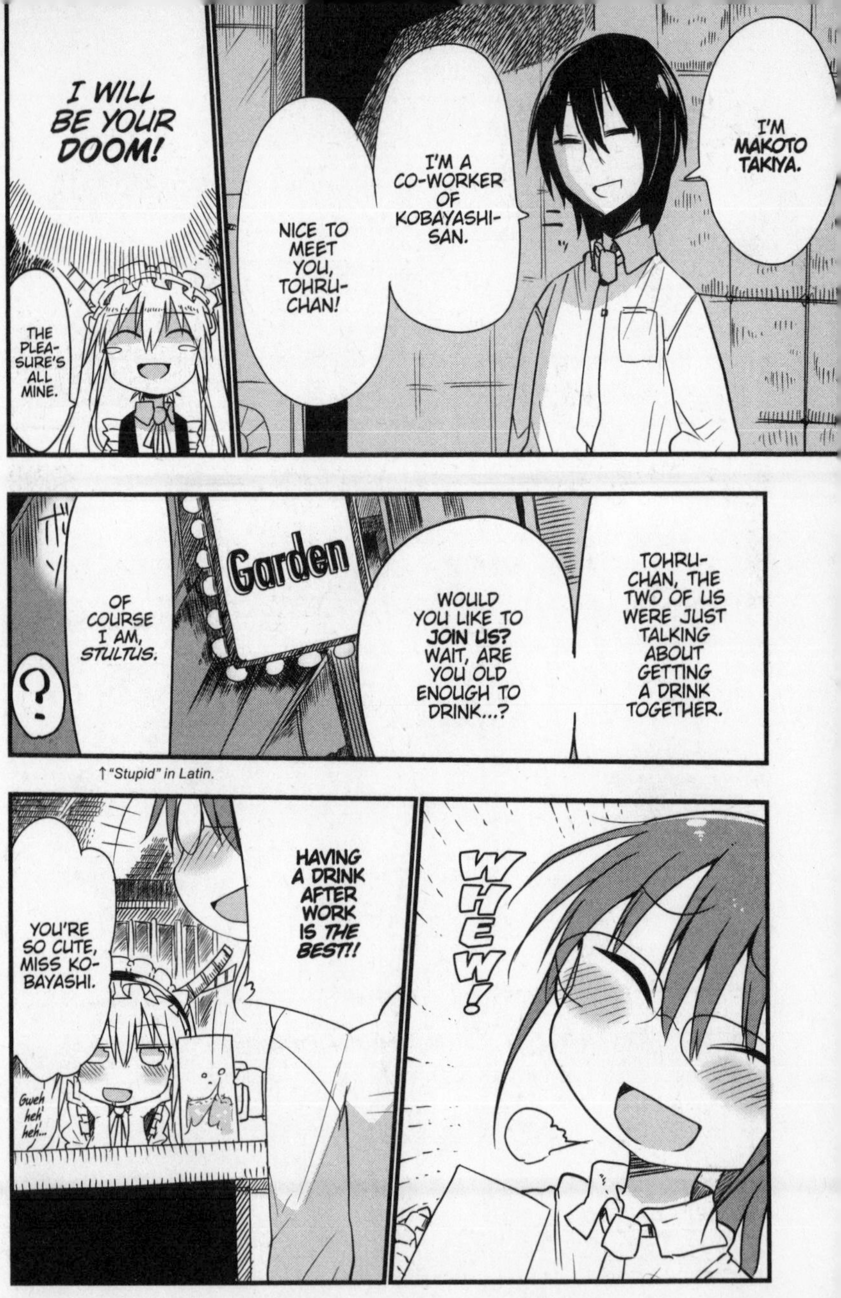
I'M MAKOTO TAKIYA.
I'M A CO-WORKER OF KOBAYASHI-SAN.
NICE TO MEET YOU, TOHRU-CHAN!
I WILL BE YOUR DOOM!
THE PLEASURE'S ALL MINE.
TOHRU-CHAN, THE TWO OF US WERE JUST TALKING ABOUT GETTING A DRINK TOGETHER.
WOULD YOU LIKE TO JOIN US? WAIT, ARE YOU OLD ENOUGH TO DRINK...?
Garden
OF COURSE I AM, STULTUS.
?
↑"Stupid" in Latin.
WHEW!
HAVING A DRINK AFTER WORK IS THE BEST!!
YOU'RE SO CUTE, MISS KOBAYASHI.
Gweh heh heh...

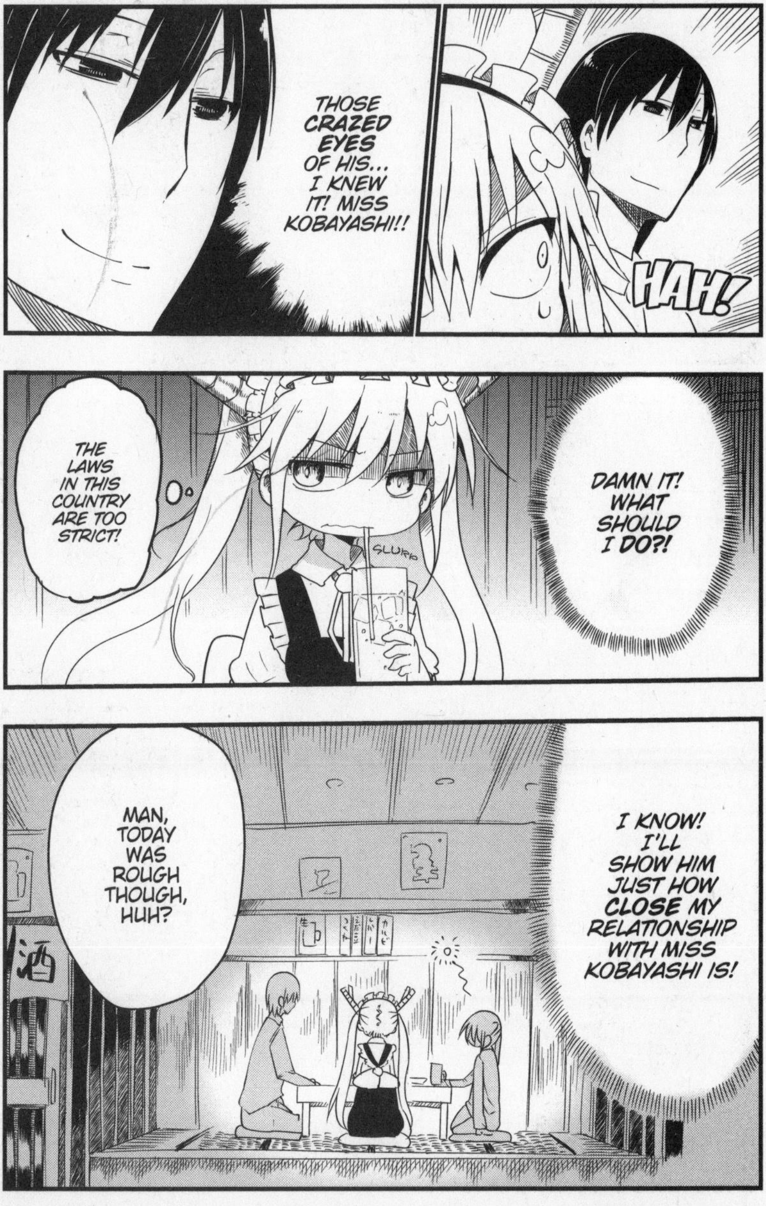
HAH!
THOSE CRAZED EYES OF HIS... I KNEW IT! MISS KOBAYASHI!!
DAMN IT! WHAT SHOULD I DO?!
THE LAWS IN THIS COUNTRY ARE TOO STRICT!
SLURP
I KNOW! I'LL SHOW HIM JUST HOW CLOSE MY RELATIONSHIP WITH MISS KOBAYASHI IS!
MAN, TODAY WAS ROUGH THOUGH, HUH?
酒

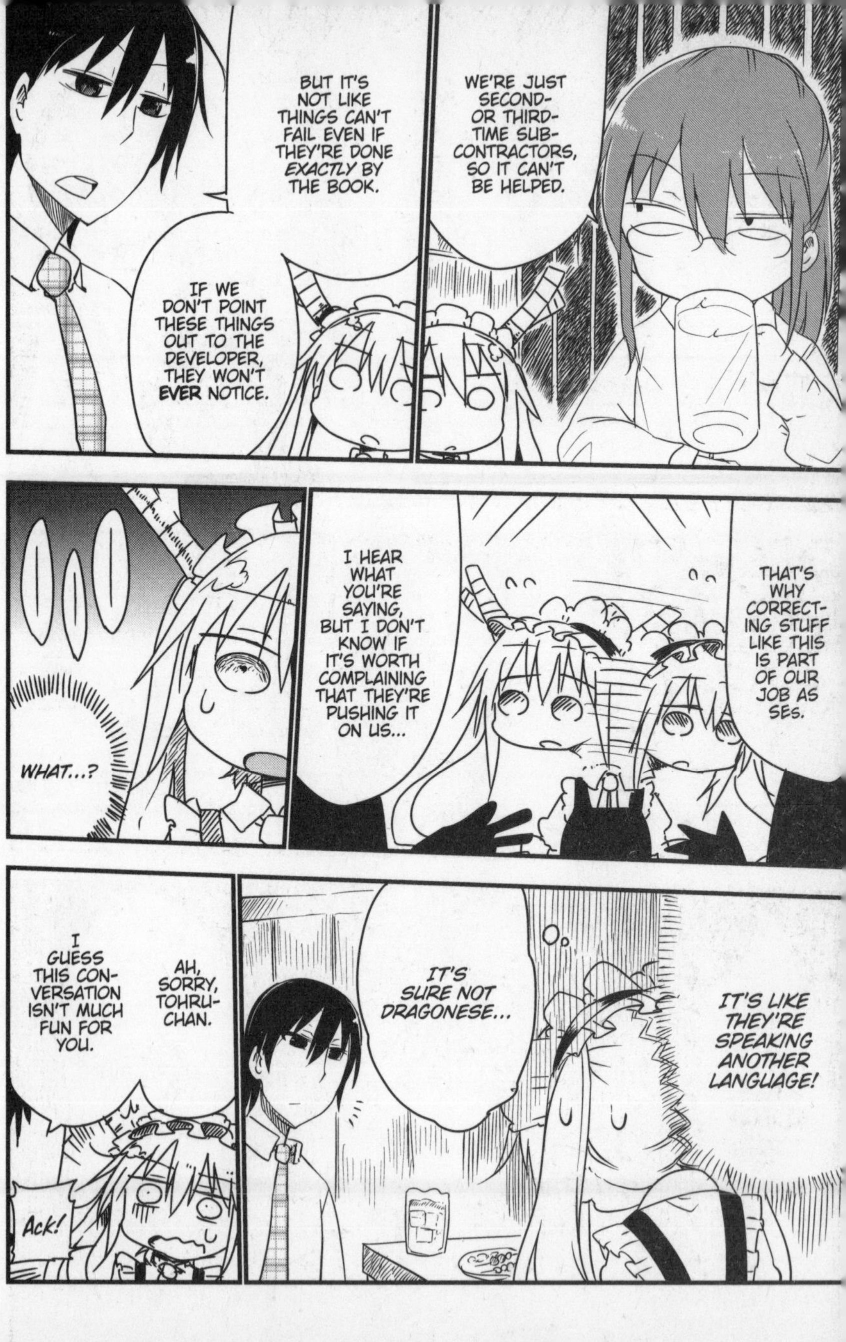
WE'RE JUST SECOND- OR THIRD-TIME SUB-CONTRACTORS, SO IT CAN'T BE HELPED.
BUT IT'S NOT LIKE THINGS CAN'T FAIL EVEN IF THEY'RE DONE *EXACTLY* BY THE BOOK.
IF WE DON'T POINT THESE THINGS OUT TO THE DEVELOPER, THEY WON'T **EVER** NOTICE.
THAT'S WHY CORRECTING STUFF LIKE THIS IS PART OF OUR JOB AS SES.
I HEAR WHAT YOU'RE SAYING, BUT I DON'T KNOW IF IT'S WORTH COMPLAINING THAT THEY'RE PUSHING IT ON US...
WHAT...?
IT'S LIKE THEY'RE SPEAKING ANOTHER LANGUAGE!
IT'S SURE NOT DRAGONESE...
AH, SORRY, TOHRU-CHAN.
I GUESS THIS CONVERSATION ISN'T MUCH FUN FOR YOU.
Ack!

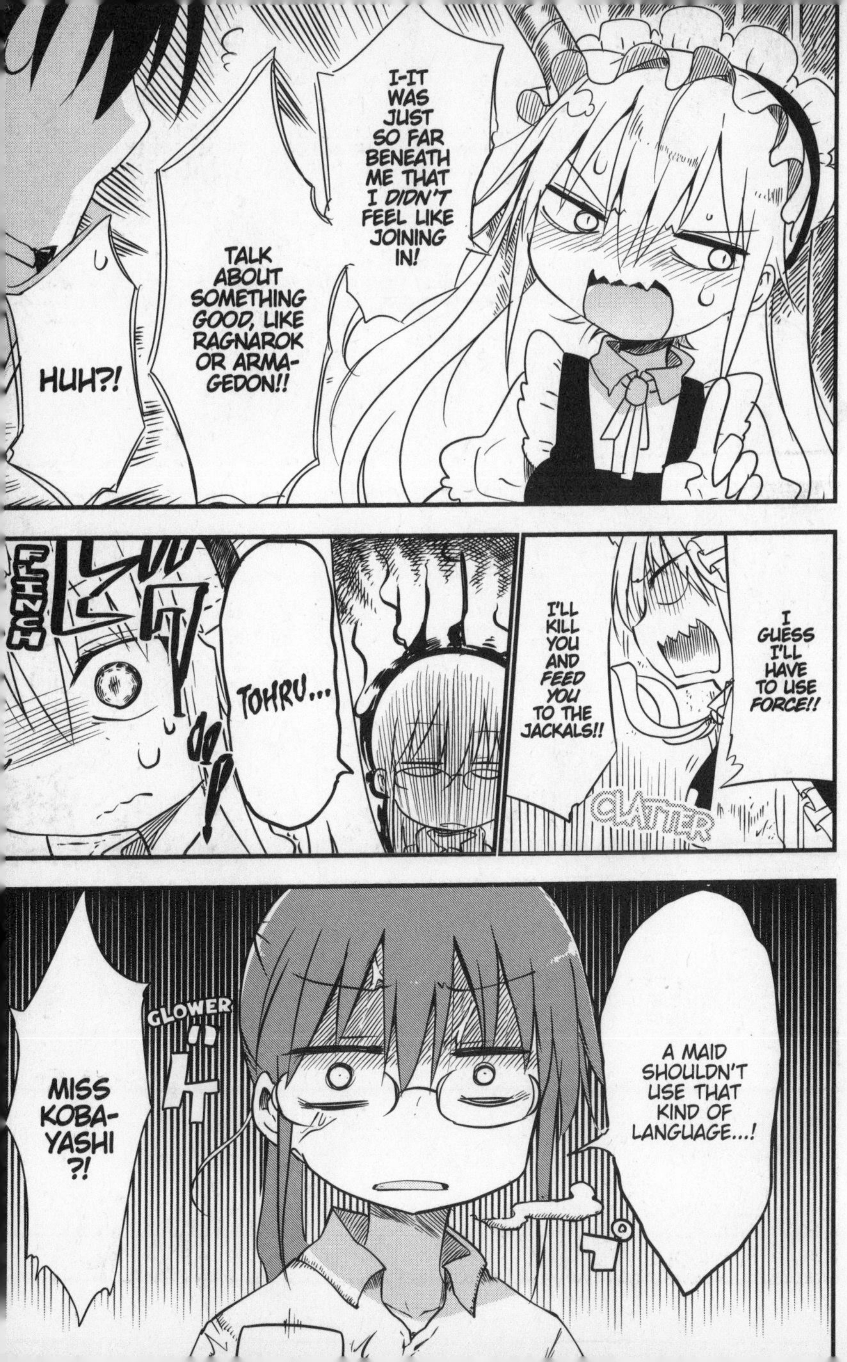
I-IT WAS JUST SO FAR BENEATH ME THAT I *DIDN'T* FEEL LIKE JOINING IN!
TALK ABOUT SOMETHING *GOOD*, LIKE RAGNAROK OR ARMA-GEDON!!
HUH?!
I GUESS I'LL HAVE TO USE FORCE!!
I'LL KILL YOU AND *FEED* YOU TO THE JACKALS!!
CLATTER
TOHRU...
FLINCH
A MAID SHOULDN'T USE THAT KIND OF LANGUAGE...!
GLOWER
MISS KOBA-YASHI ?!

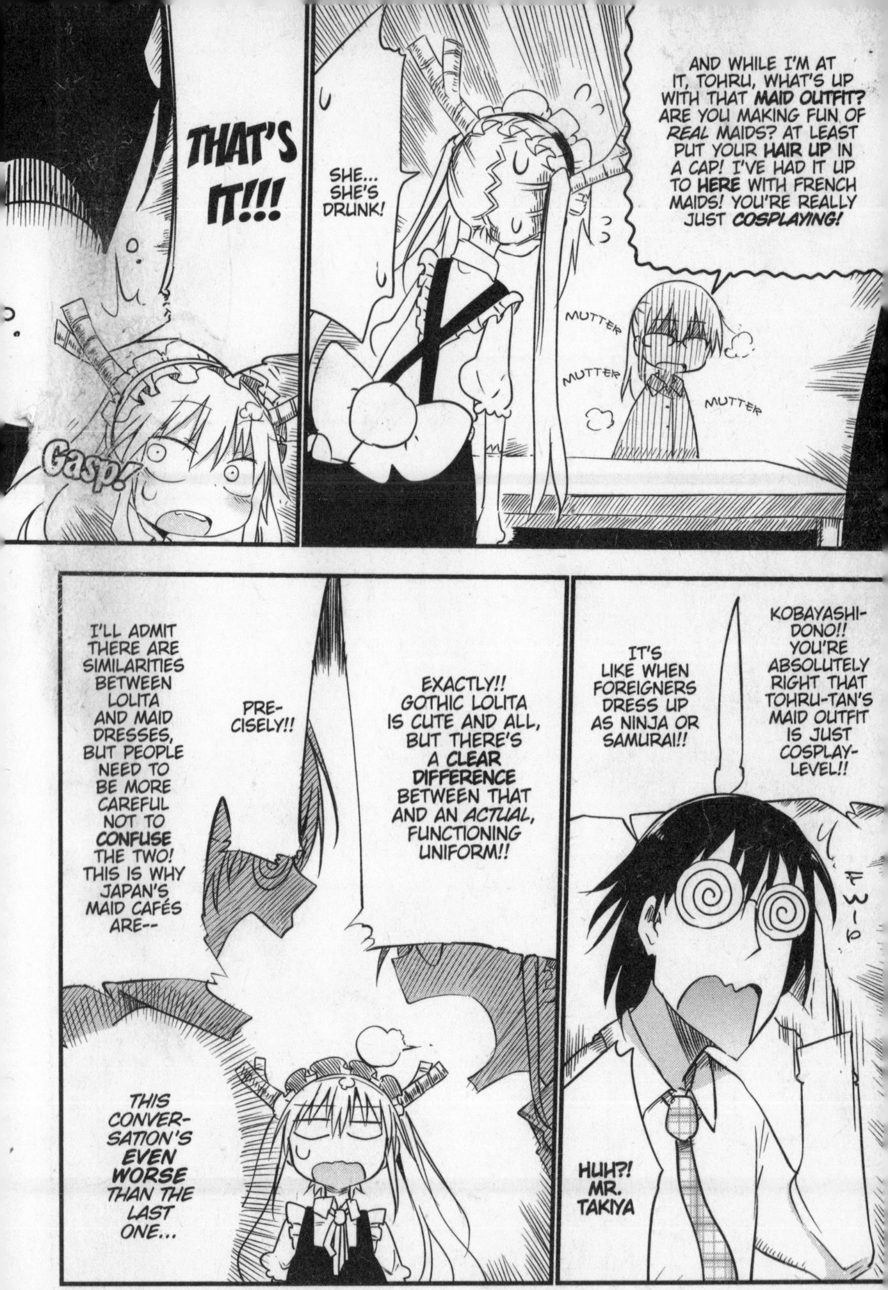
AND WHILE I'M AT IT, TOHRU, WHAT'S UP WITH THAT **MAID OUTFIT?** ARE YOU MAKING FUN OF *REAL* MAIDS? AT LEAST PUT YOUR **HAIR UP** IN A CAP! I'VE HAD IT UP TO **HERE** WITH FRENCH MAIDS! YOU'RE REALLY JUST ***COSPLAYING!***
MUTTER
MUTTER
MUTTER
SHE... SHE'S DRUNK!
THAT'S IT!!!
Gasp!
KOBAYASHI-DONO!! YOU'RE ABSOLUTELY RIGHT THAT TOHRU-TAN'S MAID OUTFIT IS JUST COSPLAY-LEVEL!!
IT'S LIKE WHEN FOREIGNERS DRESS UP AS NINJA OR SAMURAI!!
HUH?! MR. TAKIYA
EXACTLY!! GOTHIC LOLITA IS CUTE AND ALL, BUT THERE'S A **CLEAR DIFFERENCE** BETWEEN THAT AND AN *ACTUAL*, FUNCTIONING UNIFORM!!
PRE-CISELY!!
I'LL ADMIT THERE ARE SIMILARITIES BETWEEN LOLITA AND MAID DRESSES, BUT PEOPLE NEED TO BE MORE CAREFUL NOT TO **CONFUSE** THE TWO! THIS IS WHY JAPAN'S MAID CAFÉS ARE--
*THIS CONVER-SATION'S* ***EVEN WORSE*** *THAN THE LAST ONE...*

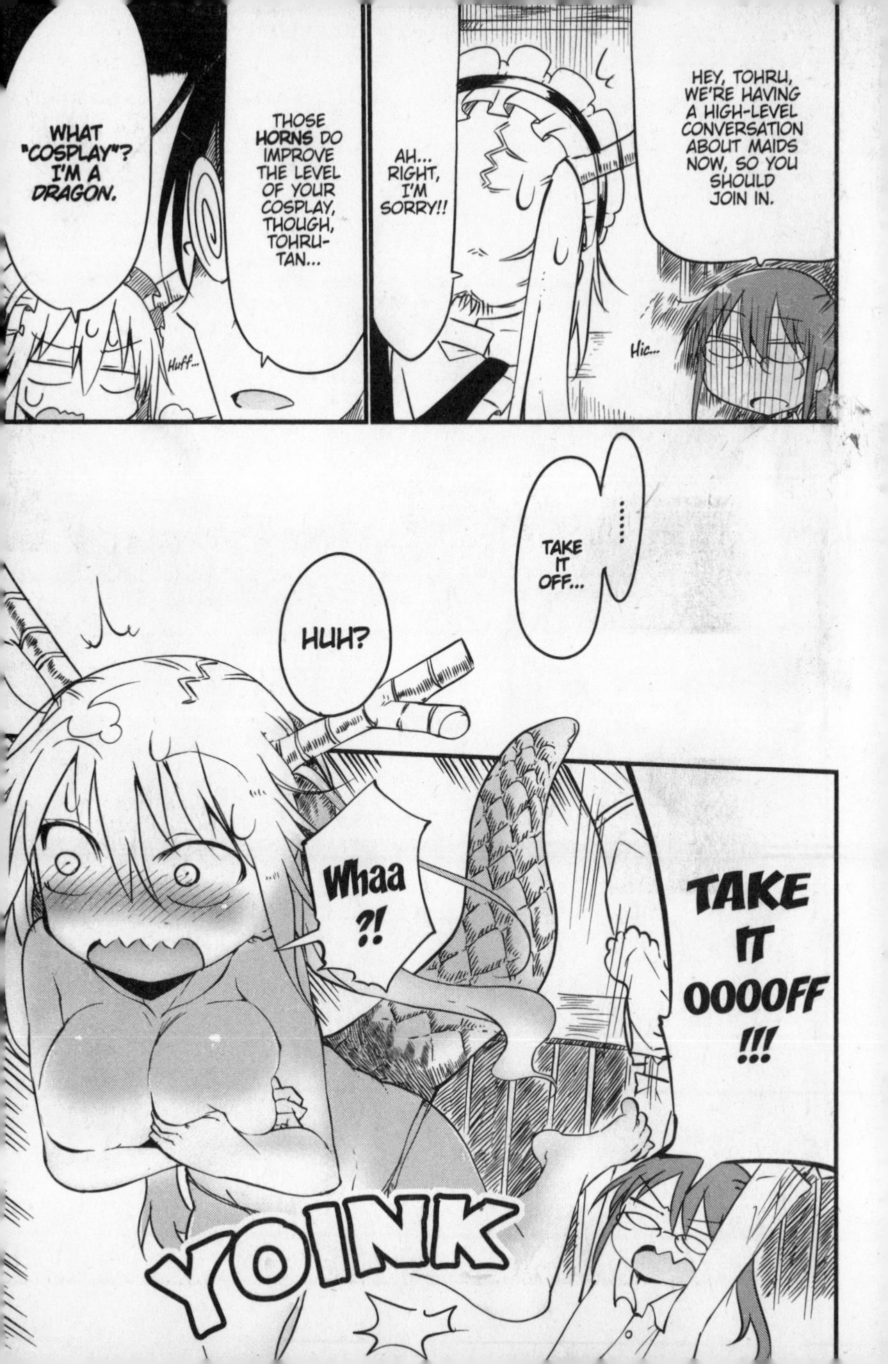
HEY, TOHRU, WE'RE HAVING A HIGH-LEVEL CONVERSATION ABOUT MAIDS NOW, SO YOU SHOULD JOIN IN.
Hic...
AH... RIGHT, I'M SORRY!!
THOSE HORNS DO IMPROVE THE LEVEL OF YOUR COSPLAY, THOUGH, TOHRU-TAN...
WHAT "COSPLAY"? I'M A DRAGON.
Huff...
......
TAKE IT OFF...
HUH?
TAKE IT OOOOFF!!!
Whaa?!
YOINK

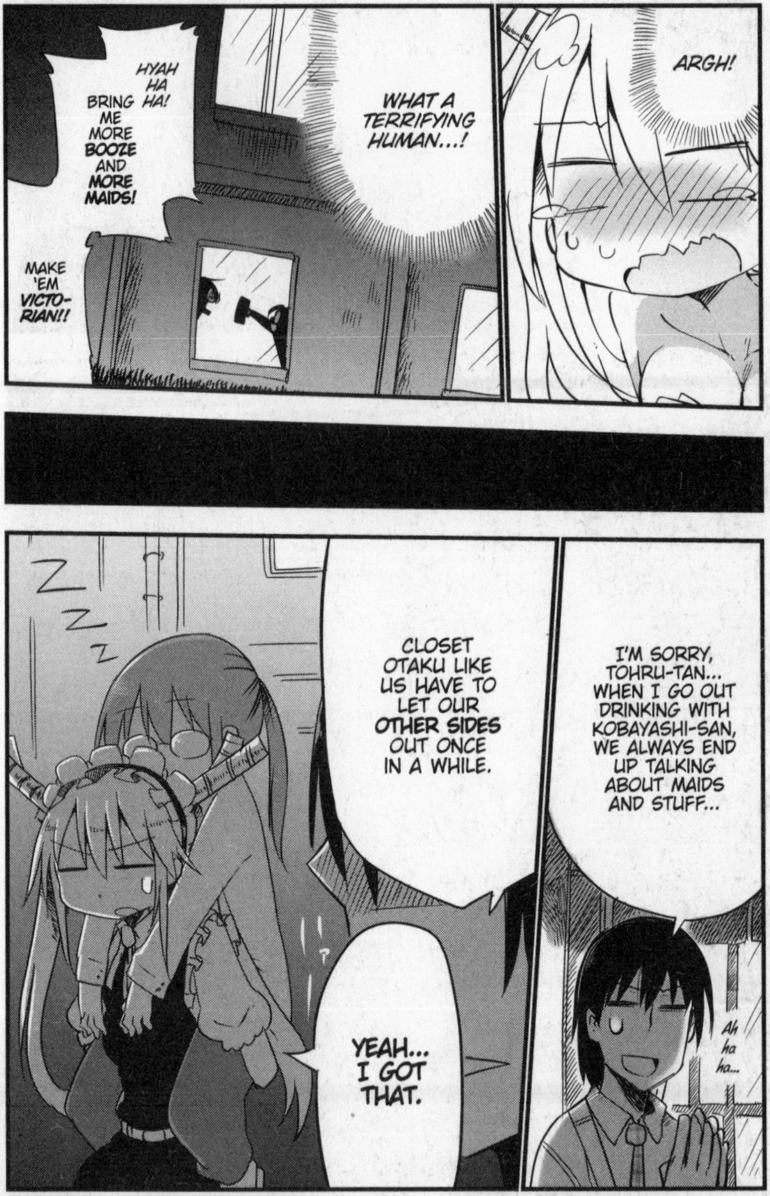
ARGH!
HYAH HA HA!
BRING ME MORE BOOZE AND MORE MAIDS!
MAKE 'EM VICTORIAN!!
WHAT A TERRIFYING HUMAN...!
I'M SORRY, TOHRU-TAN... WHEN I GO OUT DRINKING WITH KOBAYASHI-SAN, WE ALWAYS END UP TALKING ABOUT MAIDS AND STUFF...
Ah ha ha...
CLOSET OTAKU LIKE US HAVE TO LET OUR OTHER SIDES OUT ONCE IN A WHILE.
YEAH... I GOT THAT.

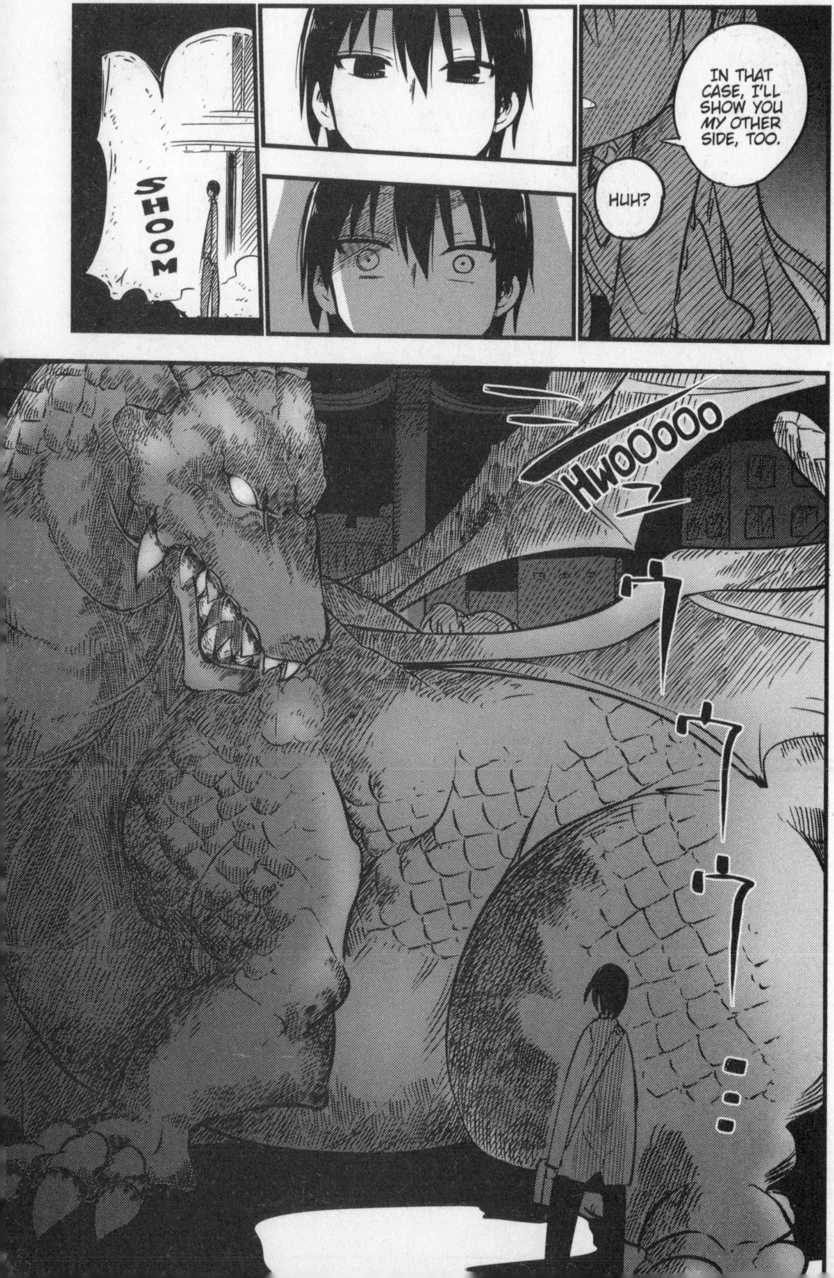
IN THAT CASE, I'LL SHOW YOU MY OTHER SIDE, TOO.
HUH?
SHOOM
HWOOOOO

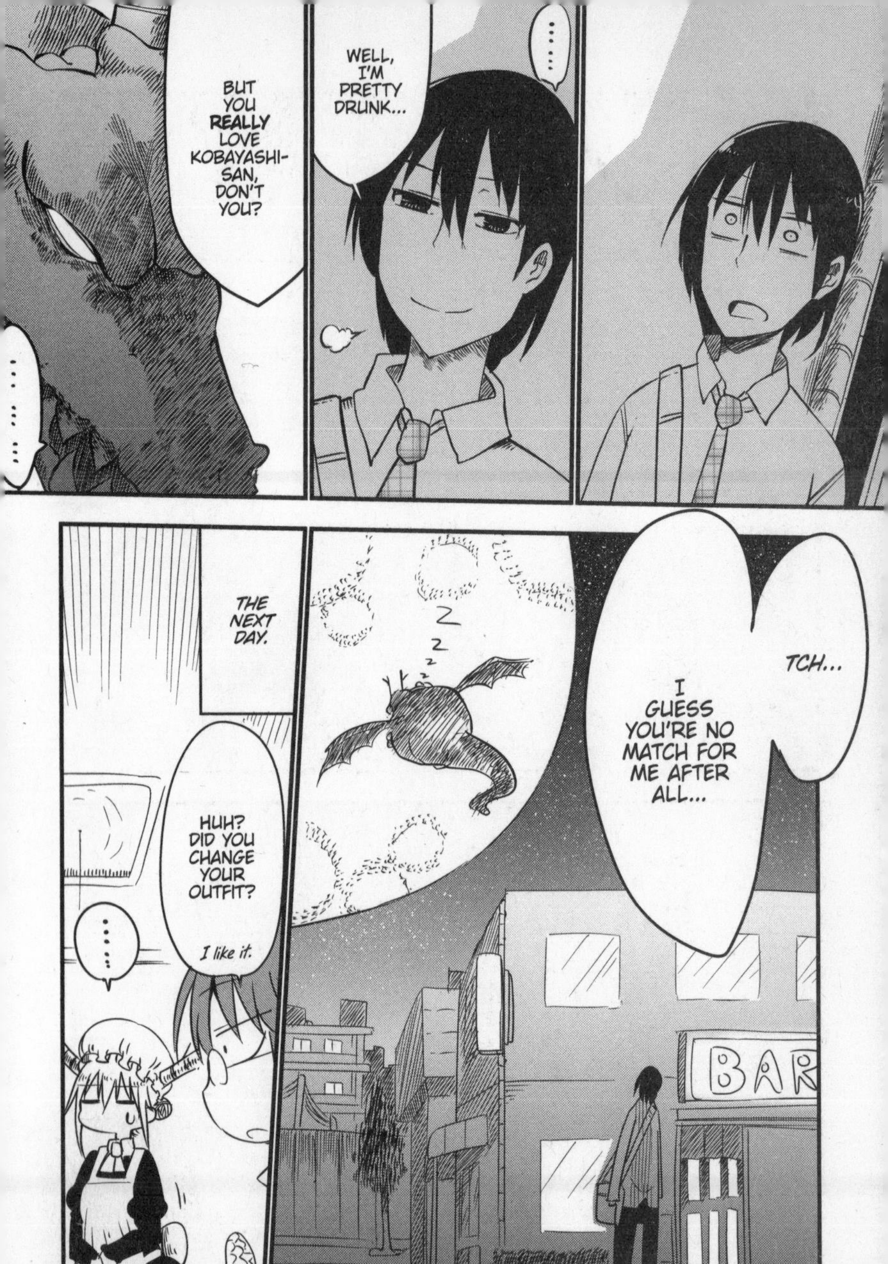
......
WELL, I'M PRETTY DRUNK...
BUT YOU **REALLY** LOVE KOBAYASHI-SAN, DON'T YOU?
......
TCH... I GUESS YOU'RE NO MATCH FOR ME AFTER ALL...
Z z z
BAR
THE NEXT DAY.
HUH? DID YOU CHANGE YOUR OUTFIT?
I like it.
......

**CHAPTER 4/END**

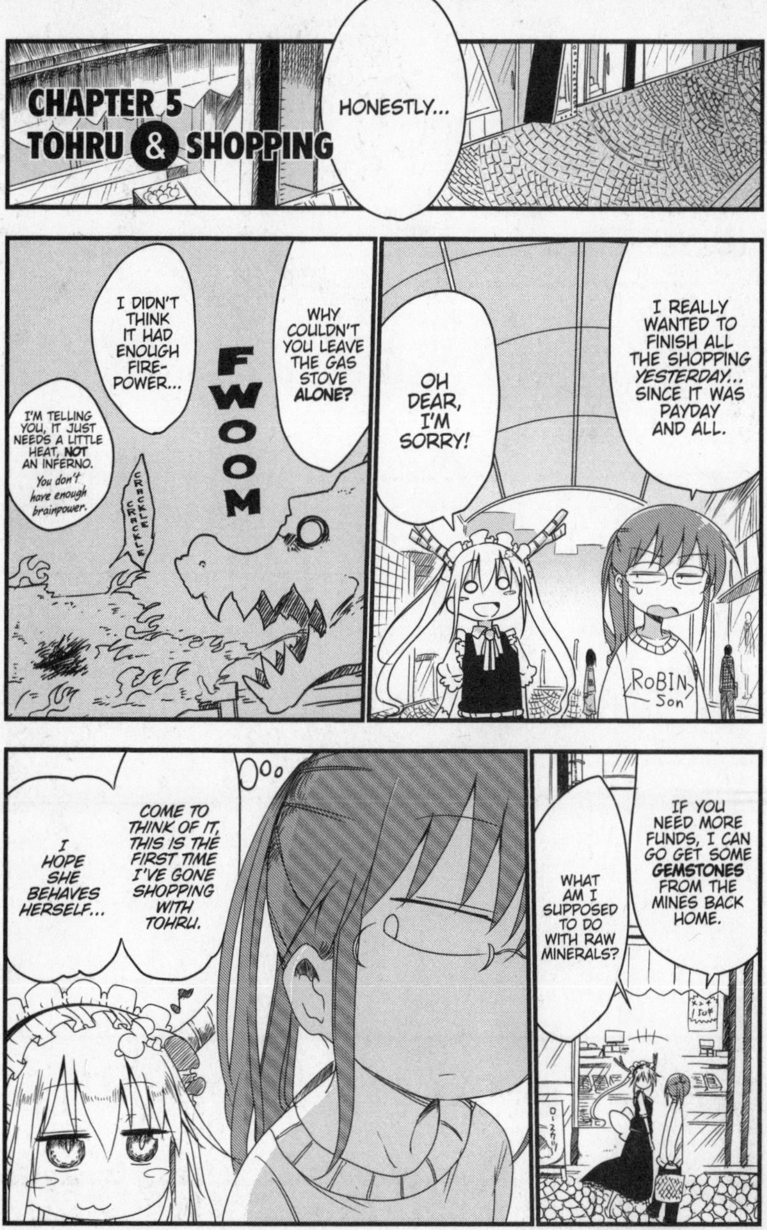
CHAPTER 5
TOHRU & SHOPPING
HONESTLY...
I REALLY WANTED TO FINISH ALL THE SHOPPING YESTERDAY... SINCE IT WAS PAYDAY AND ALL.
OH DEAR, I'M SORRY!
ROBIN Son
WHY COULDN'T YOU LEAVE THE GAS STOVE ALONE?
I DIDN'T THINK IT HAD ENOUGH FIRE-POWER...
FWOOM
I'M TELLING YOU, IT JUST NEEDS A LITTLE HEAT, NOT AN INFERNO. You don't have enough brainpower.
CRACKLE CRACKLE
IF YOU NEED MORE FUNDS, I CAN GO GET SOME GEMSTONES FROM THE MINES BACK HOME.
WHAT AM I SUPPOSED TO DO WITH RAW MINERALS?
COME TO THINK OF IT, THIS IS THE FIRST TIME I'VE GONE SHOPPING WITH TOHRU.
I HOPE SHE BEHAVES HERSELF...

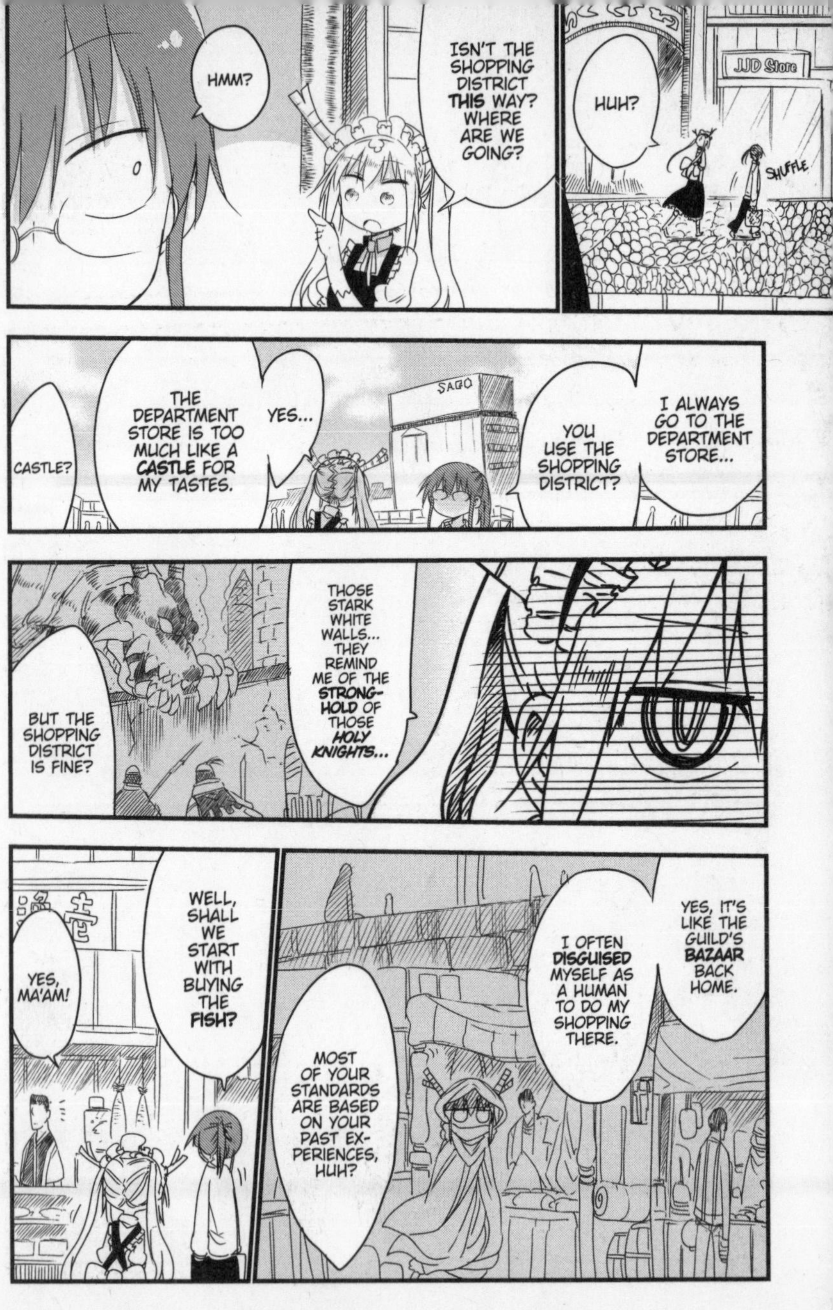
JJD Store
HUH?
SHUFFLE
ISN'T THE SHOPPING DISTRICT **THIS** WAY? WHERE ARE WE GOING?
HMM?
I ALWAYS GO TO THE DEPARTMENT STORE...
YOU USE THE SHOPPING DISTRICT?
SAGO
YES...
THE DEPARTMENT STORE IS TOO MUCH LIKE A **CASTLE** FOR MY TASTES.
CASTLE?
THOSE STARK WHITE WALLS... THEY REMIND ME OF THE **STRONGHOLD** OF THOSE ***HOLY KNIGHTS...***
BUT THE SHOPPING DISTRICT IS FINE?
YES, IT'S LIKE THE GUILD'S **BAZAAR** BACK HOME.
I OFTEN **DISGUISED** MYSELF AS A HUMAN TO DO MY SHOPPING THERE.
MOST OF YOUR STANDARDS ARE BASED ON YOUR PAST EXPERIENCES, HUH?
WELL, SHALL WE START WITH BUYING THE **FISH?**
YES, MA'AM!

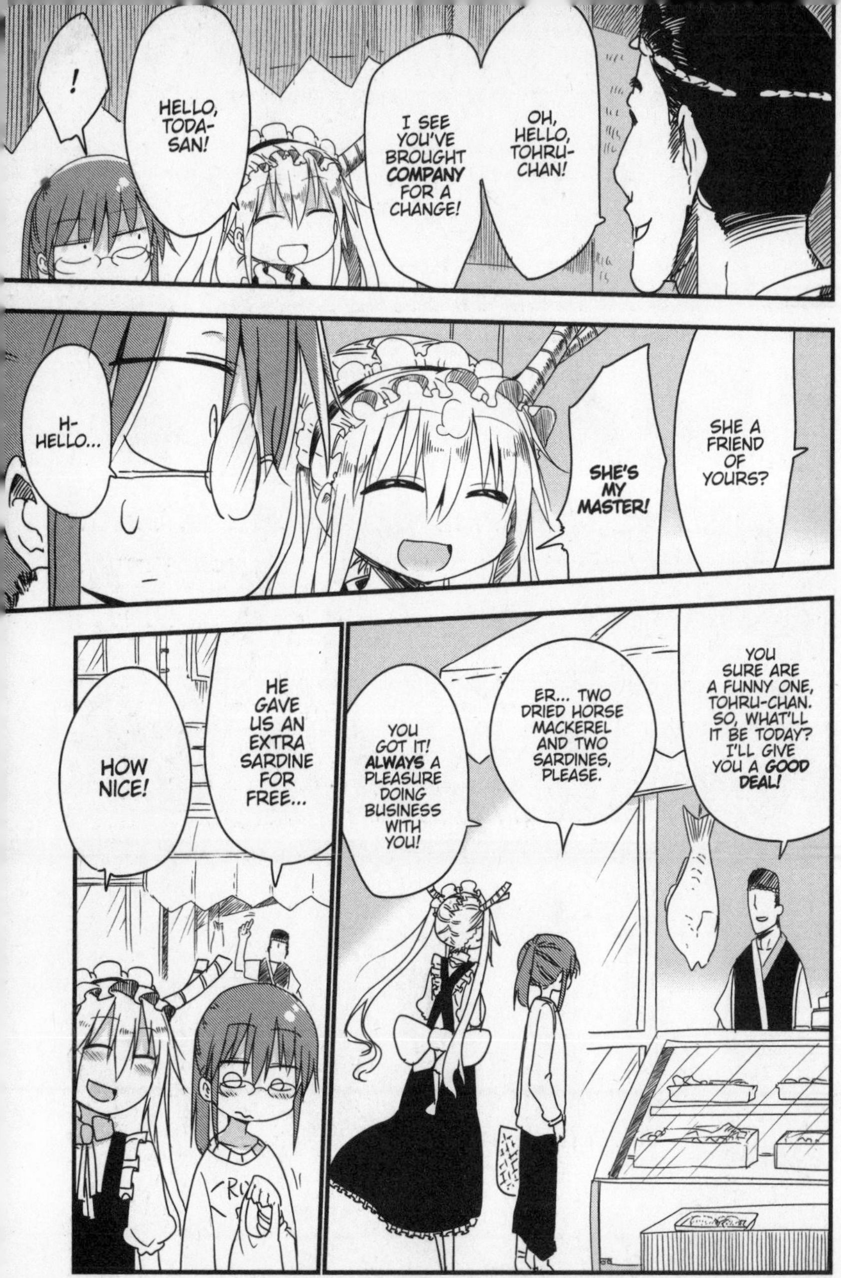
OH, HELLO, TOHRU-CHAN!
I SEE YOU'VE BROUGHT **COMPANY** FOR A CHANGE!
HELLO, TODA-SAN!
!
SHE A FRIEND OF YOURS?
**SHE'S MY MASTER!**
H-HELLO...
YOU SURE ARE A FUNNY ONE, TOHRU-CHAN. SO, WHAT'LL IT BE TODAY? I'LL GIVE YOU A **GOOD DEAL!**
ER... TWO DRIED HORSE MACKEREL AND TWO SARDINES, PLEASE.
YOU GOT IT! **ALWAYS** A PLEASURE DOING BUSINESS WITH YOU!
HE GAVE US AN EXTRA SARDINE FOR FREE...
HOW NICE!

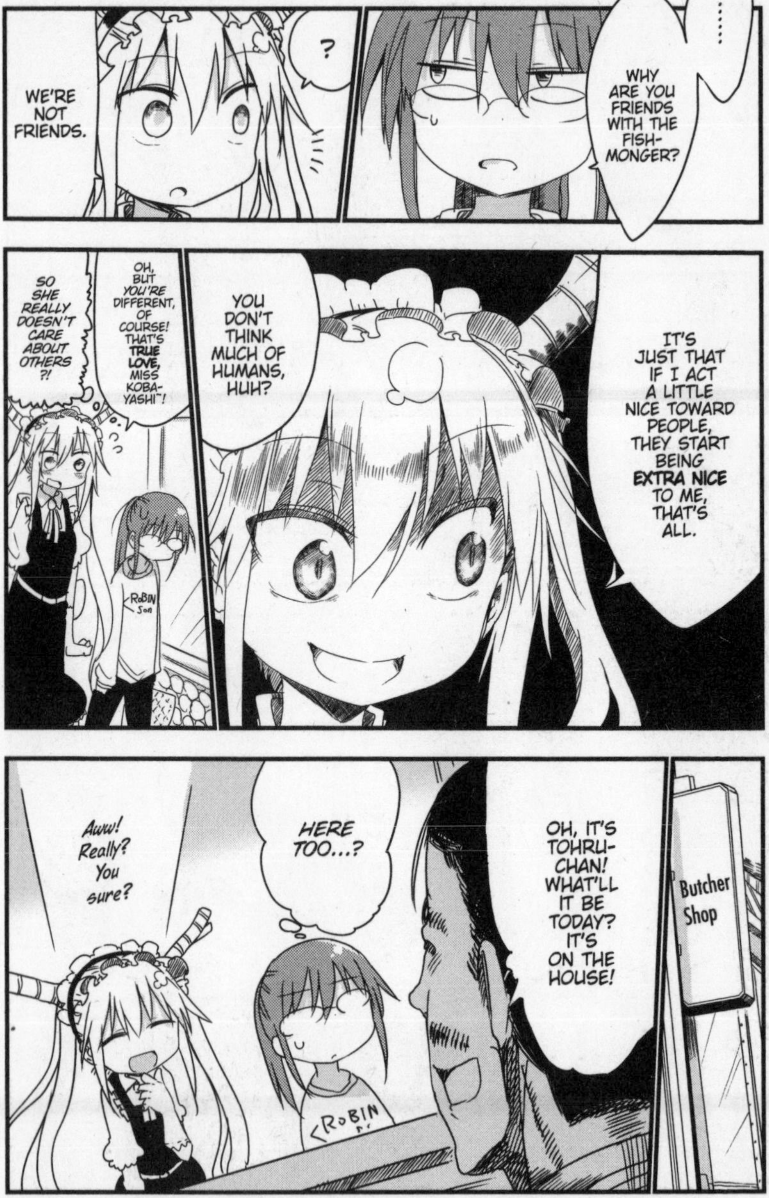
……
WHY ARE YOU FRIENDS WITH THE FISH-MONGER?
?
WE'RE NOT FRIENDS.
IT'S JUST THAT IF I ACT A LITTLE NICE TOWARD PEOPLE, THEY START BEING EXTRA NICE TO ME, THAT'S ALL.
YOU DON'T THINK MUCH OF HUMANS, HUH?
OH, BUT YOU'RE DIFFERENT, OF COURSE! THAT'S TRUE LOVE, MISS KOBA-YASHI~!
SO SHE REALLY DOESN'T CARE ABOUT OTHERS?!
RoBIN Son
Butcher Shop
OH, IT'S TOHRU-CHAN! WHAT'LL IT BE TODAY? IT'S ON THE HOUSE!
HERE TOO...?
Aww! Really? You sure?

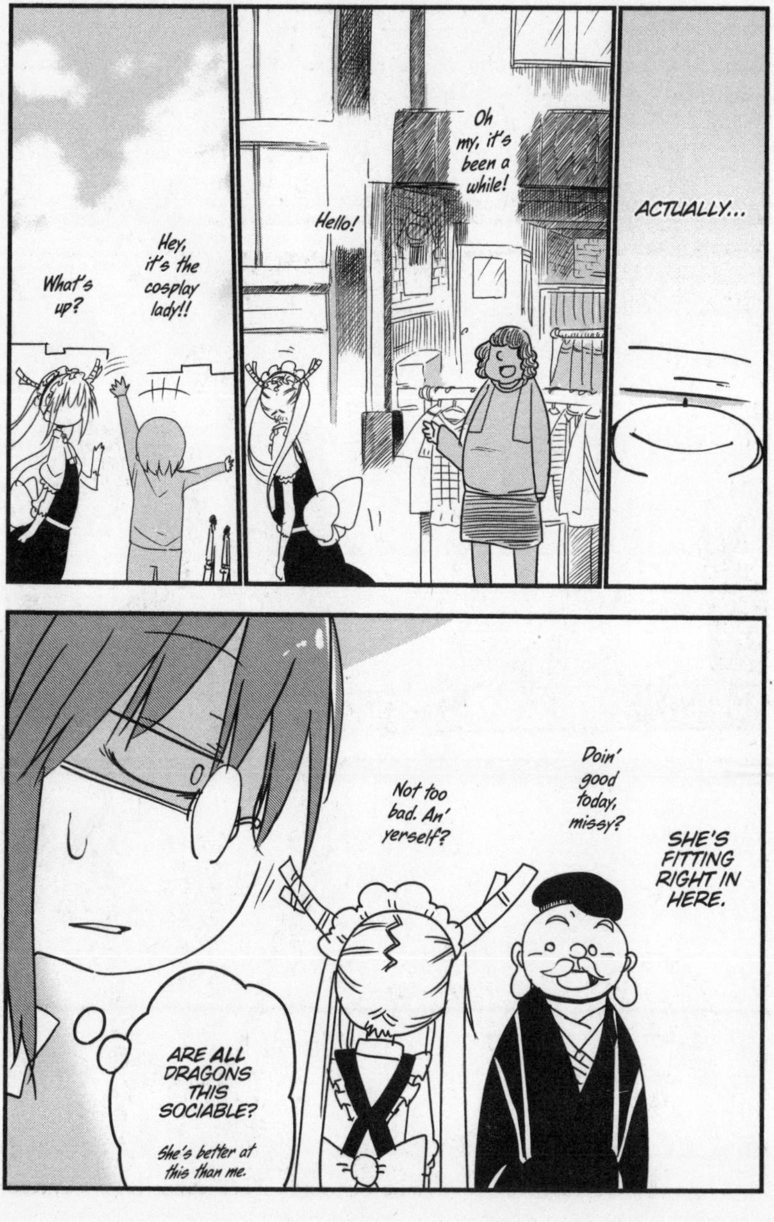
ACTUALLY...
Oh my, it's been a while!
Hello!
Hey, it's the cosplay lady!!
What's up?
SHE'S FITTING RIGHT IN HERE.
Doin' good today, missy?
Not too bad. An' yerself?
ARE ALL DRAGONS THIS SOCIABLE?
She's better at this than me.

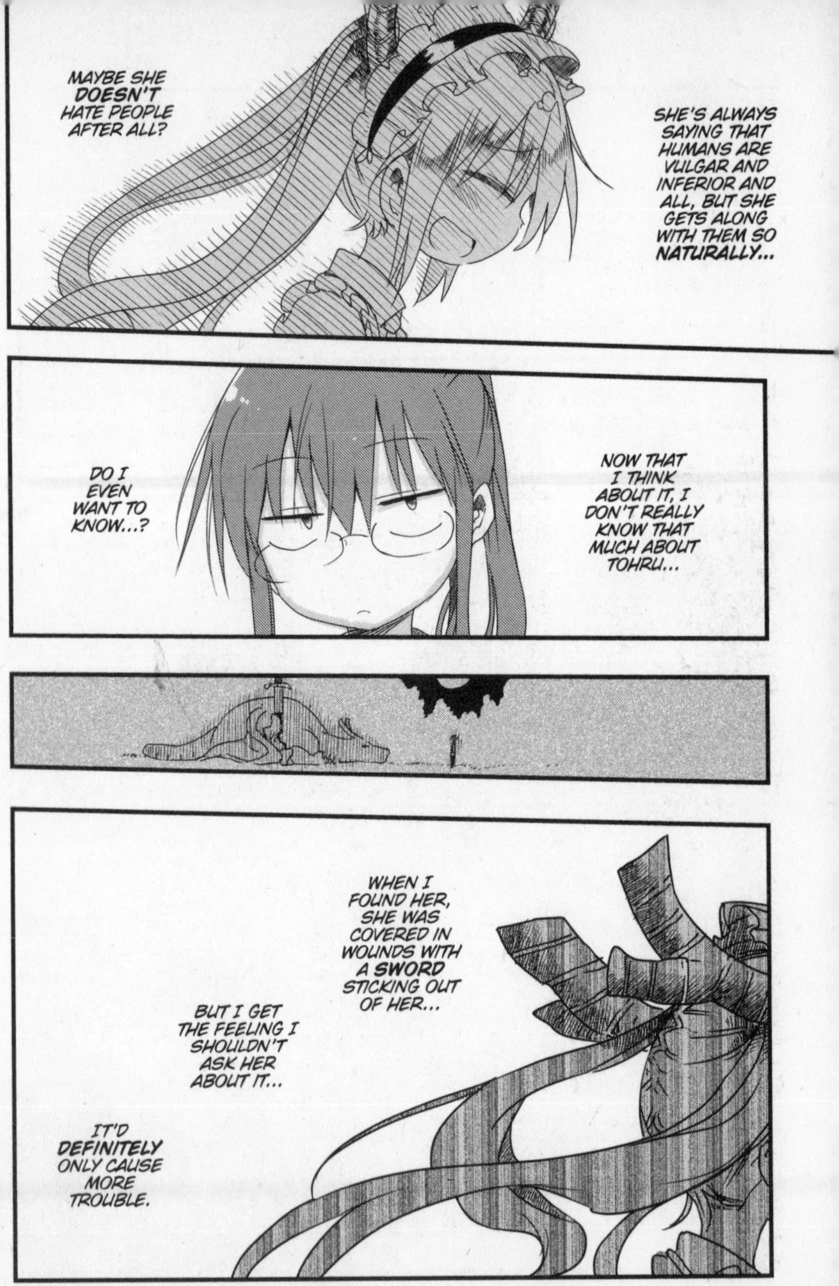
SHE'S ALWAYS SAYING THAT HUMANS ARE VULGAR AND INFERIOR AND ALL, BUT SHE GETS ALONG WITH THEM SO **NATURALLY**...
MAYBE SHE **DOESN'T** HATE PEOPLE AFTER ALL?
NOW THAT I THINK ABOUT IT, I DON'T REALLY KNOW THAT MUCH ABOUT TOHRU...
DO I EVEN WANT TO KNOW...?
WHEN I FOUND HER, SHE WAS COVERED IN WOUNDS WITH A **SWORD** STICKING OUT OF HER...
BUT I GET THE FEELING I SHOULDN'T ASK HER ABOUT IT...
IT'D **DEFINITELY** ONLY CAUSE MORE TROUBLE.

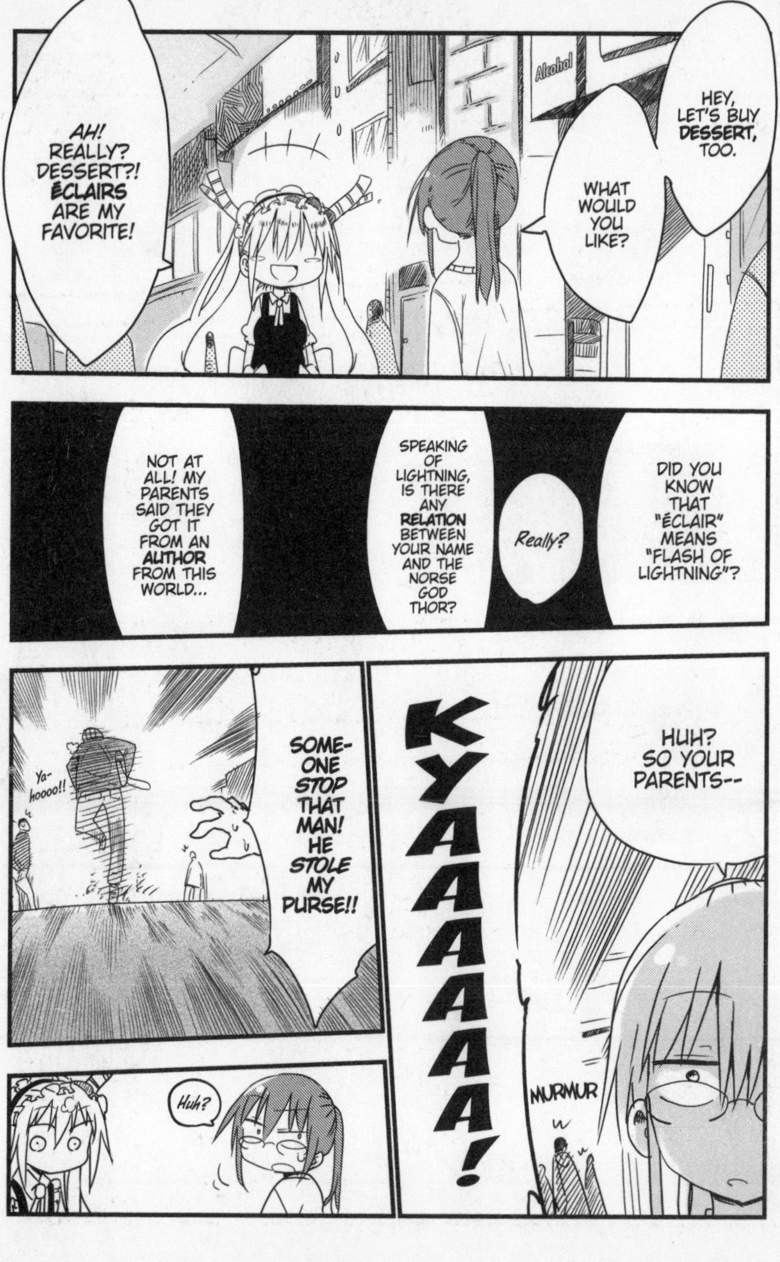

Alcohol
HEY, LET'S BUY DESSERT, TOO.
WHAT WOULD YOU LIKE?
AH! REALLY? DESSERT?! ÉCLAIRS ARE MY FAVORITE!
DID YOU KNOW THAT "ÉCLAIR" MEANS "FLASH OF LIGHTNING"?
Really?
SPEAKING OF LIGHTNING, IS THERE ANY RELATION BETWEEN YOUR NAME AND THE NORSE GOD THOR?
NOT AT ALL! MY PARENTS SAID THEY GOT IT FROM AN AUTHOR FROM THIS WORLD...
HUH? SO YOUR PARENTS--
KYAAAAAA!
MURMUR
SOME-ONE STOP THAT MAN! HE STOLE MY PURSE!!
Ya-hoooo!!
Huh?

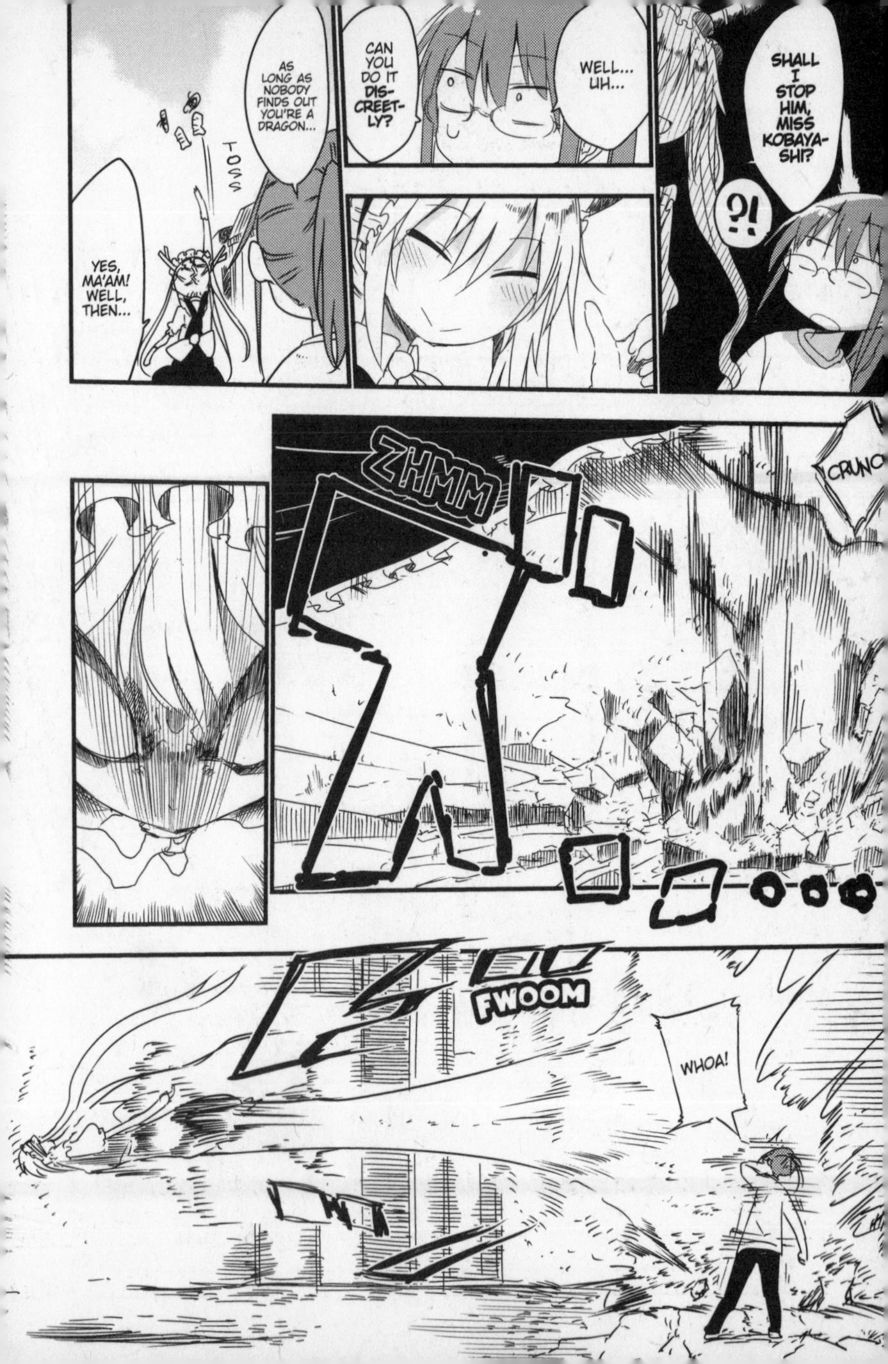
SHALL I STOP HIM, MISS KOBAYASHI?
?!
WELL... UH...
CAN YOU DO IT DIS-CREET-LY?
...
AS LONG AS NOBODY FINDS OUT YOU'RE A DRAGON...
TOSS
YES, MA'AM! WELL, THEN...
CRUNC
ZHMM
FWOOM
WHOA!

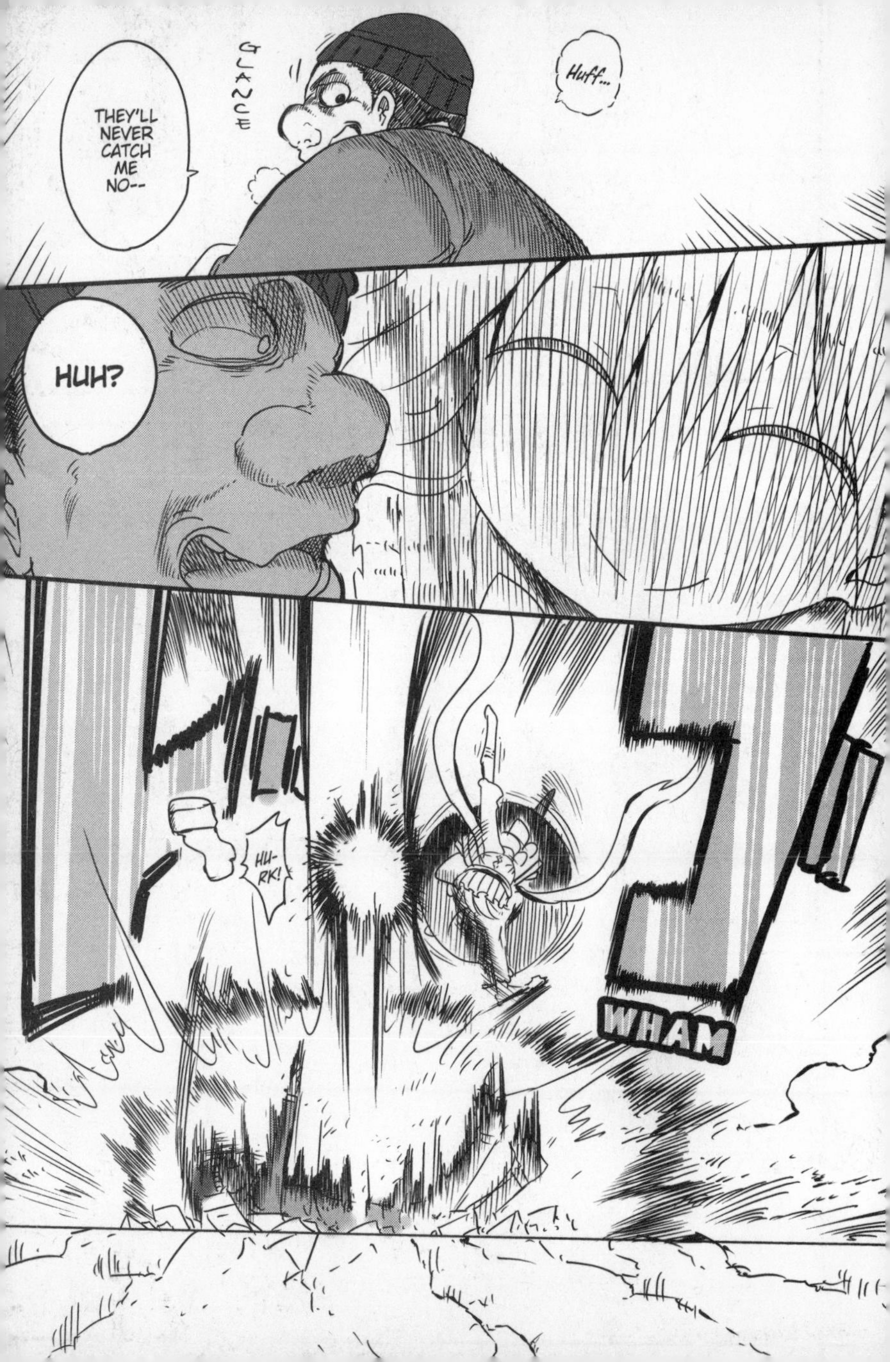
Huff...
GLANCE
THEY'LL NEVER CATCH ME NO--
HUH?
WHAM
HU-RK!

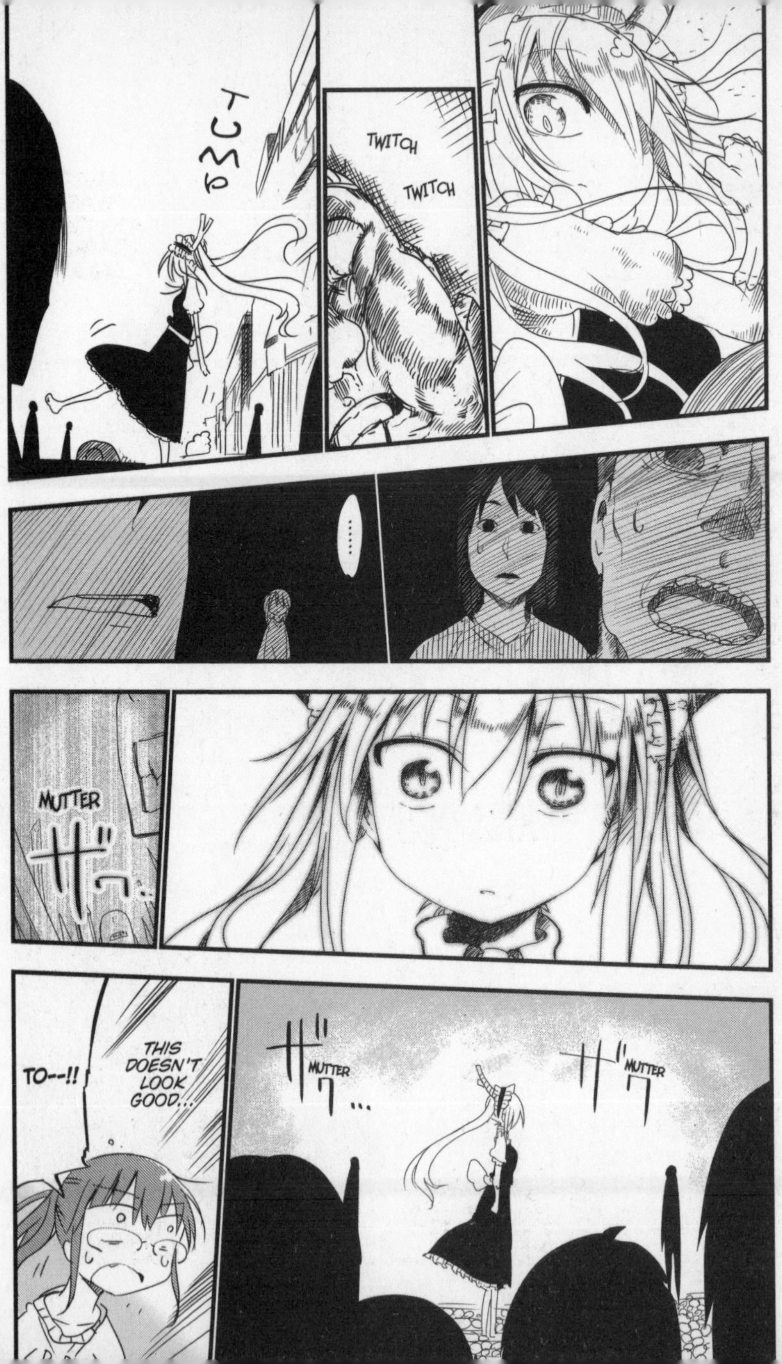
TWITCH
TWITCH
TUMP
......
MUTTER
ザワ…
MUTTER
ザワ
MUTTER
ザワ…
THIS DOESN'T LOOK GOOD...
TO--!!

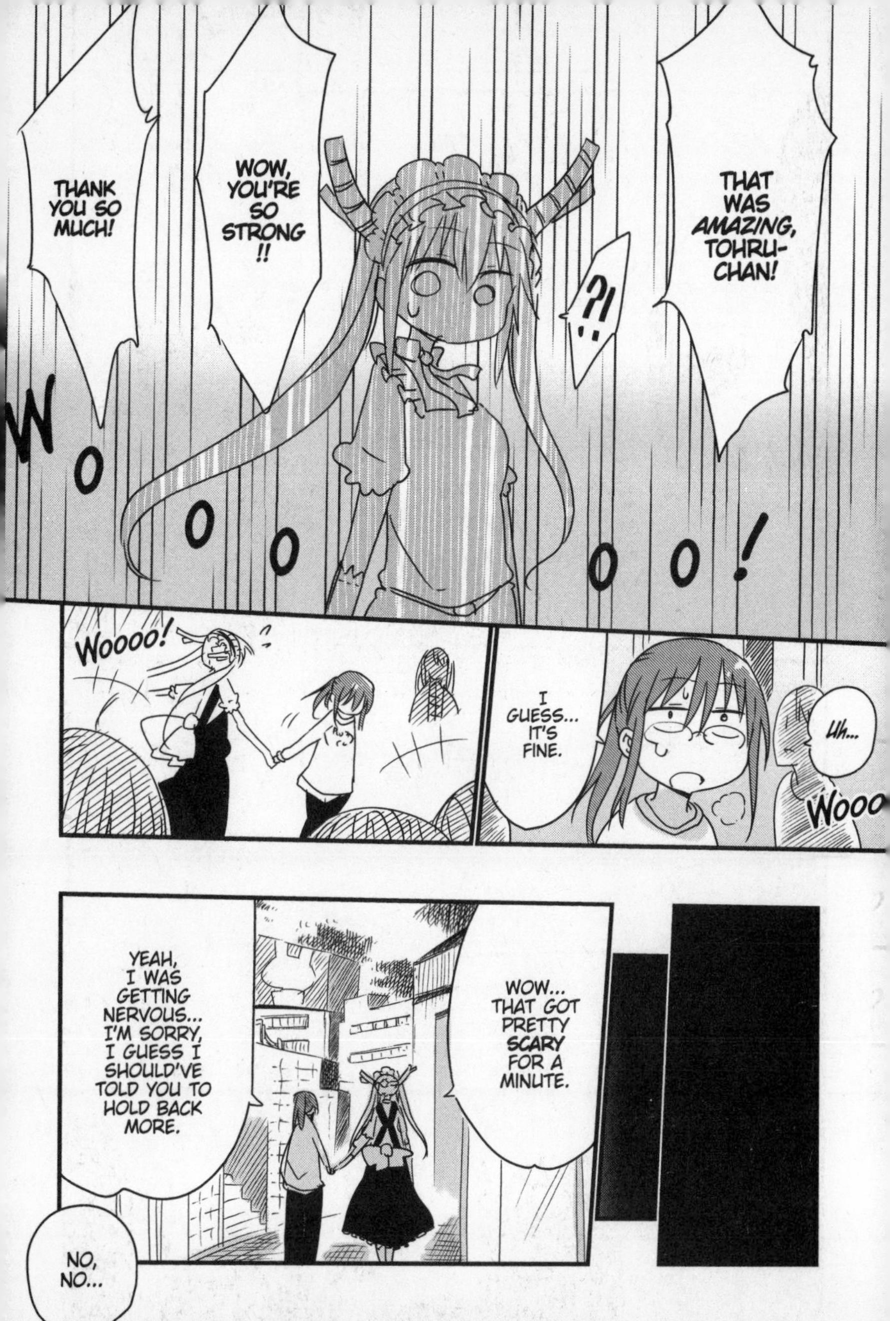
THAT WAS AMAZING, TOHRU-CHAN!
?!
WOW, YOU'RE SO STRONG!!
THANK YOU SO MUCH!
WOOOOOO!
Uh...
Wooo
I GUESS... IT'S FINE.
Woooo!
WOW... THAT GOT PRETTY SCARY FOR A MINUTE.
YEAH, I WAS GETTING NERVOUS... I'M SORRY, I GUESS I SHOULD'VE TOLD YOU TO HOLD BACK MORE.
NO, NO...

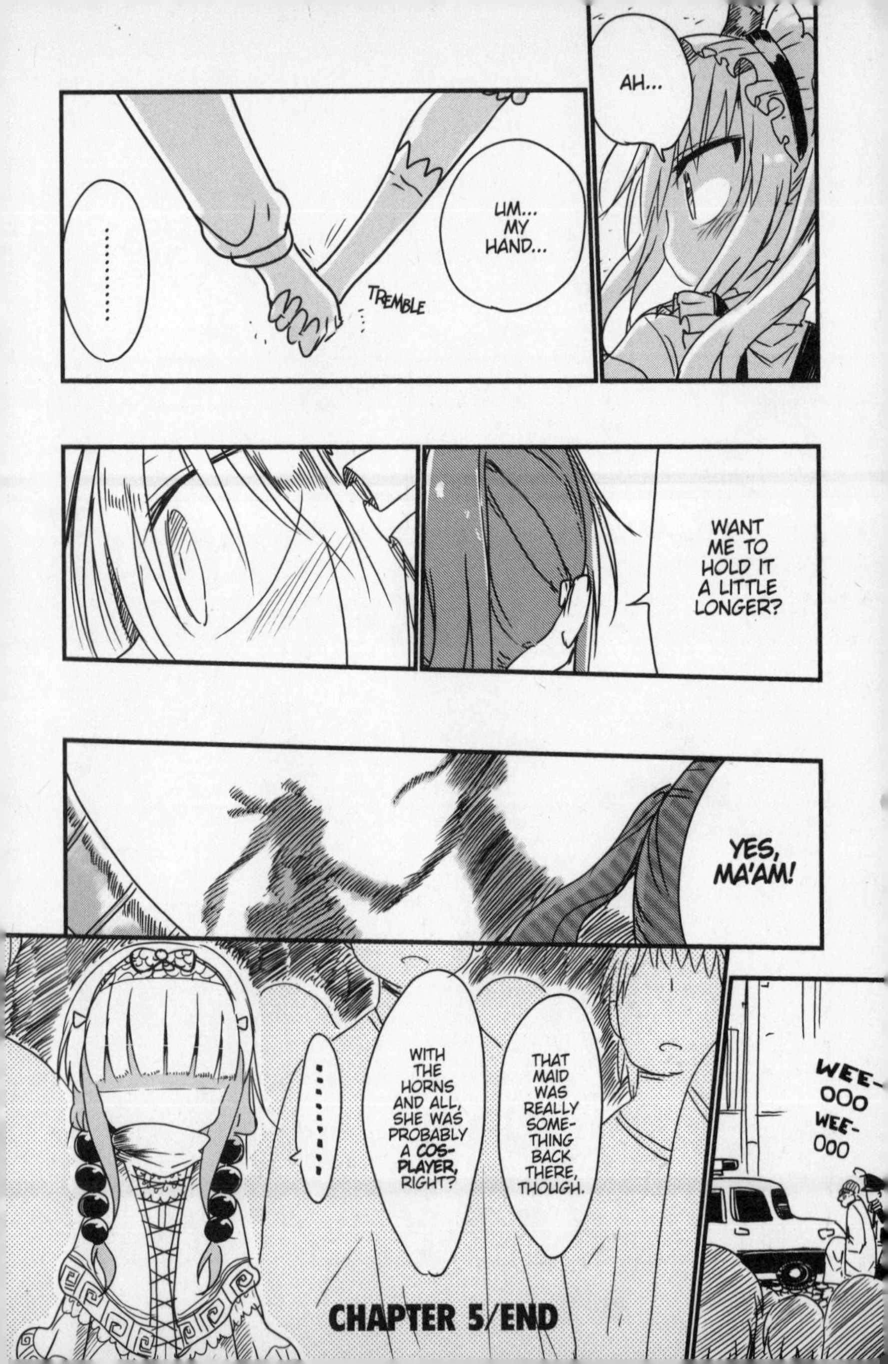
AH...
UM... MY HAND...
TREMBLE
......
WANT ME TO HOLD IT A LITTLE LONGER?
YES, MA'AM!
WEE-OOO WEE-OOO
THAT MAID WAS REALLY SOMETHING BACK THERE, THOUGH.
WITH THE HORNS AND ALL, SHE WAS PROBABLY A COS-PLAYER, RIGHT?
......
CHAPTER 5/END

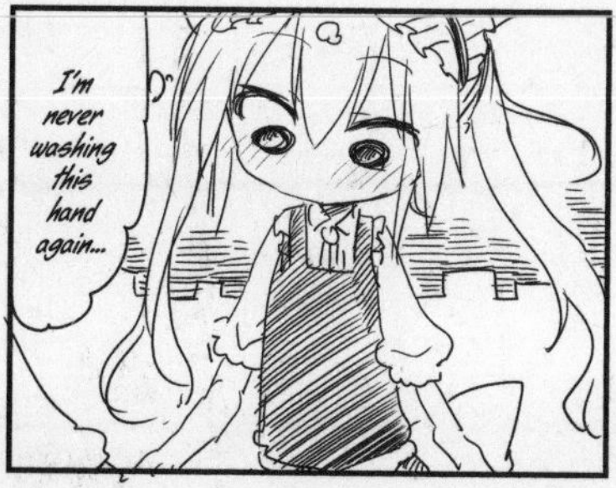
I'm never washing this hand again...

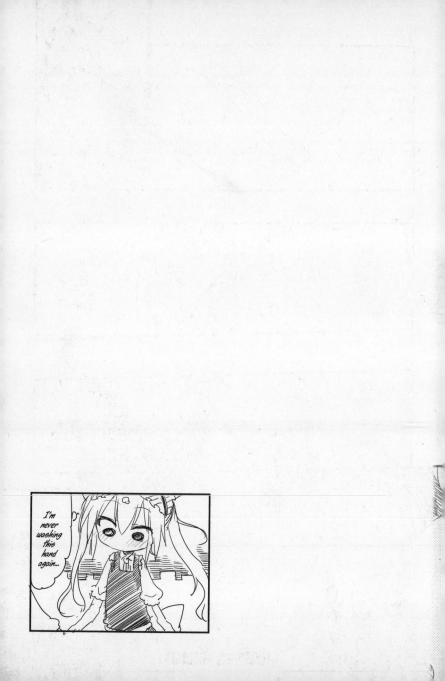

Miss Kobayashi's
Dragon Maid

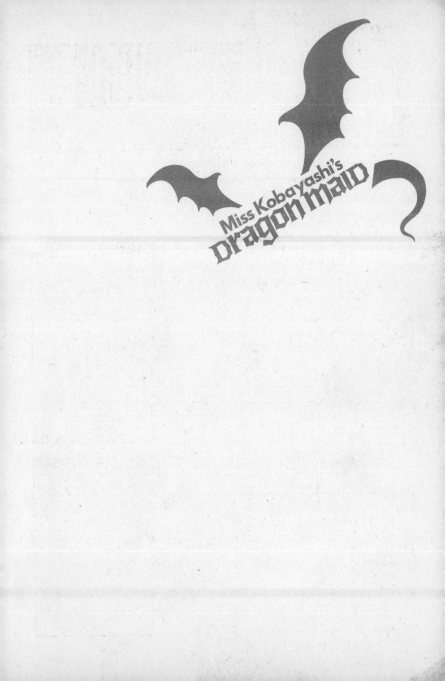

# Chapter 6

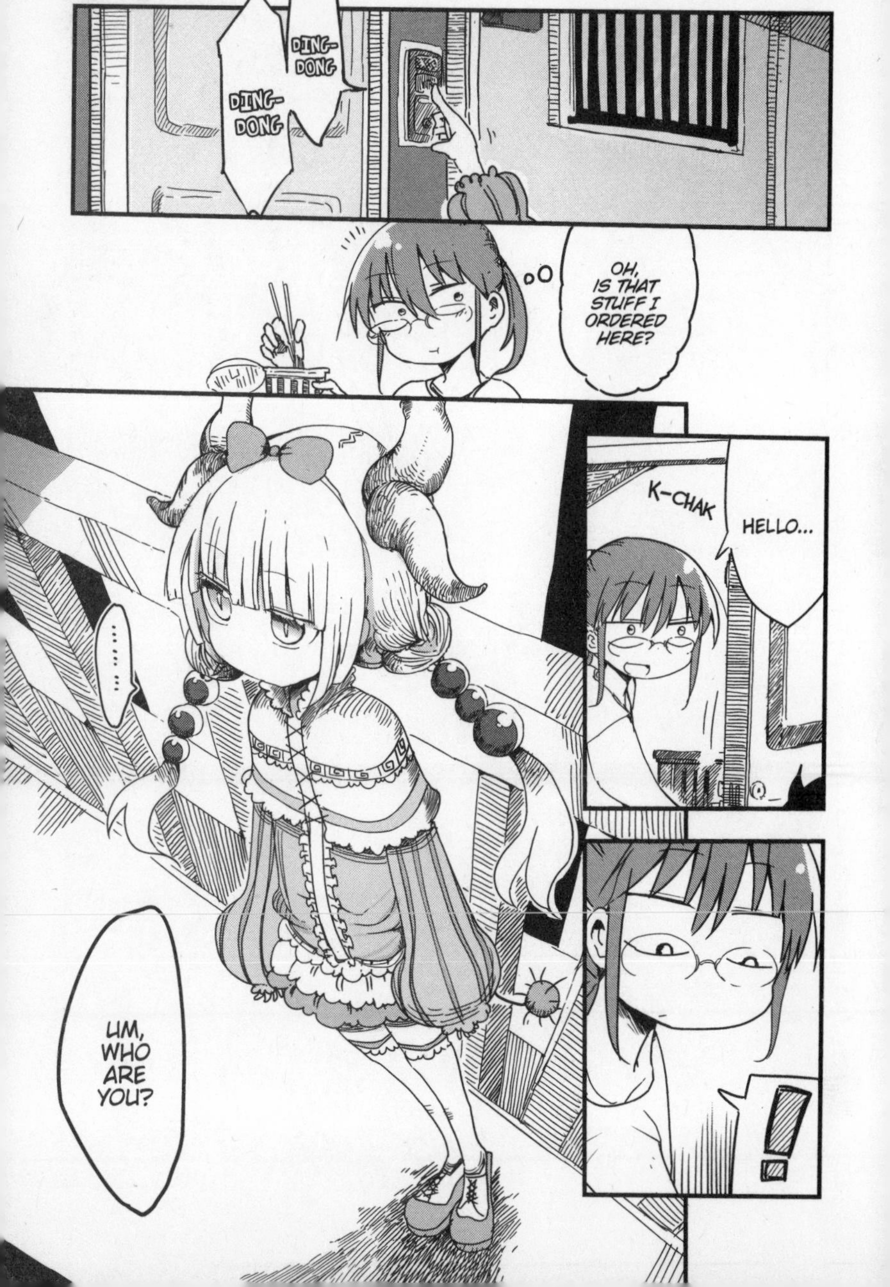

DING-DONG
DING-DONG
OH, IS THAT STUFF I ORDERED HERE?
K-CHAK
HELLO...
!
......
UM, WHO ARE YOU?

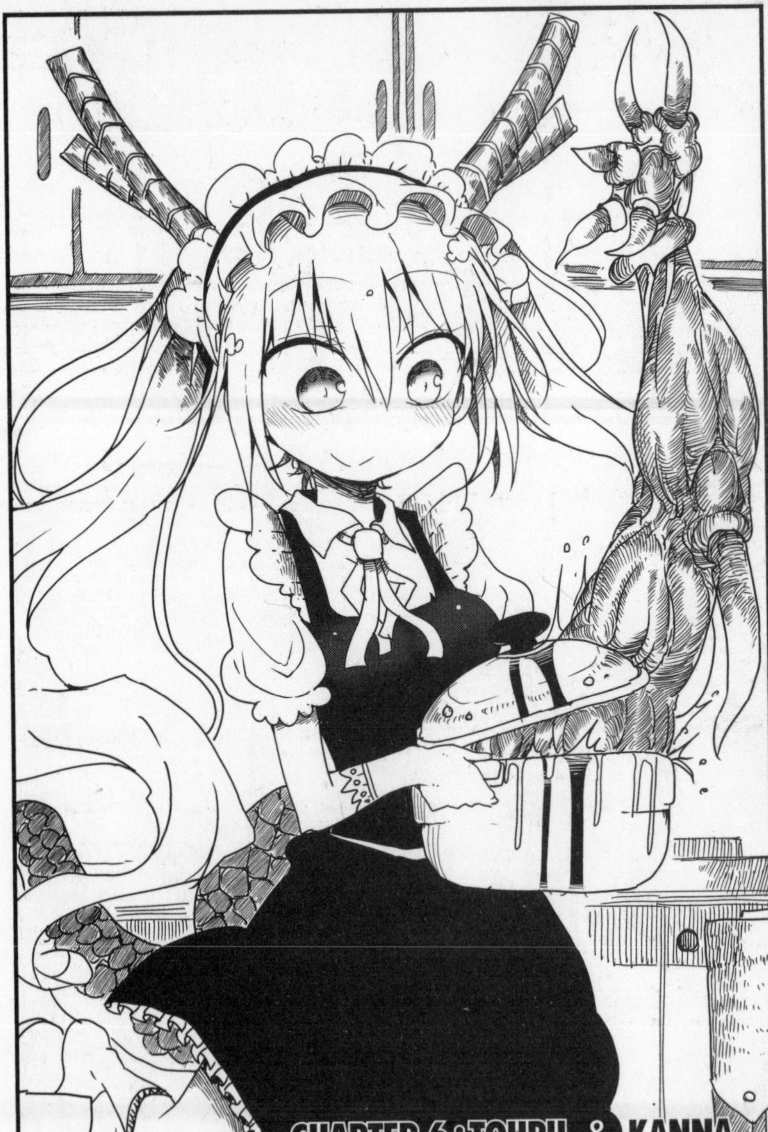
CHAPTER 6: TOHRU & KANNA

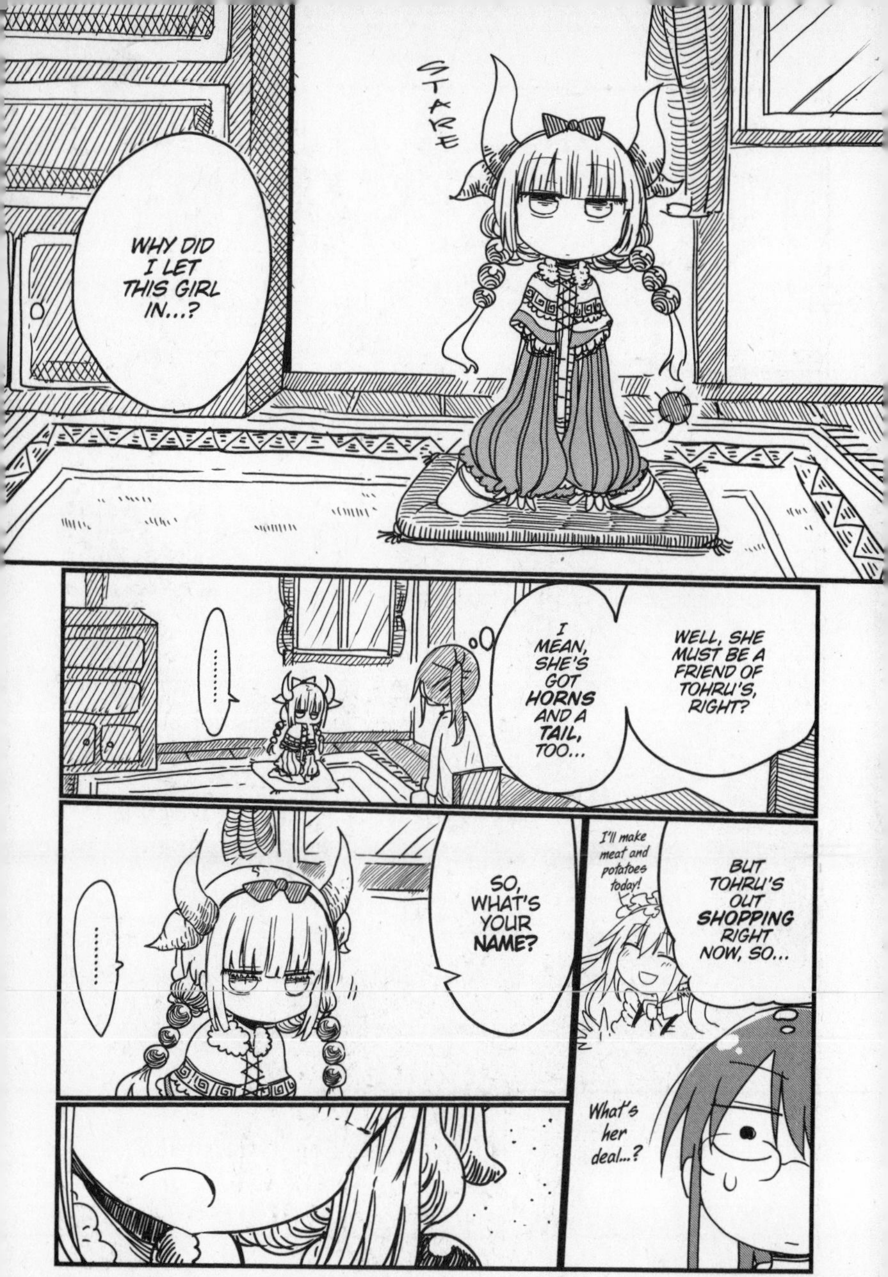
STARE
WHY DID I LET THIS GIRL IN...?
WELL, SHE MUST BE A FRIEND OF TOHRU'S, RIGHT?
I MEAN, SHE'S GOT HORNS AND A TAIL, TOO...
......
BUT TOHRU'S OUT SHOPPING RIGHT NOW, SO...
I'll make meat and potatoes today!
What's her deal...?
SO, WHAT'S YOUR NAME?
......

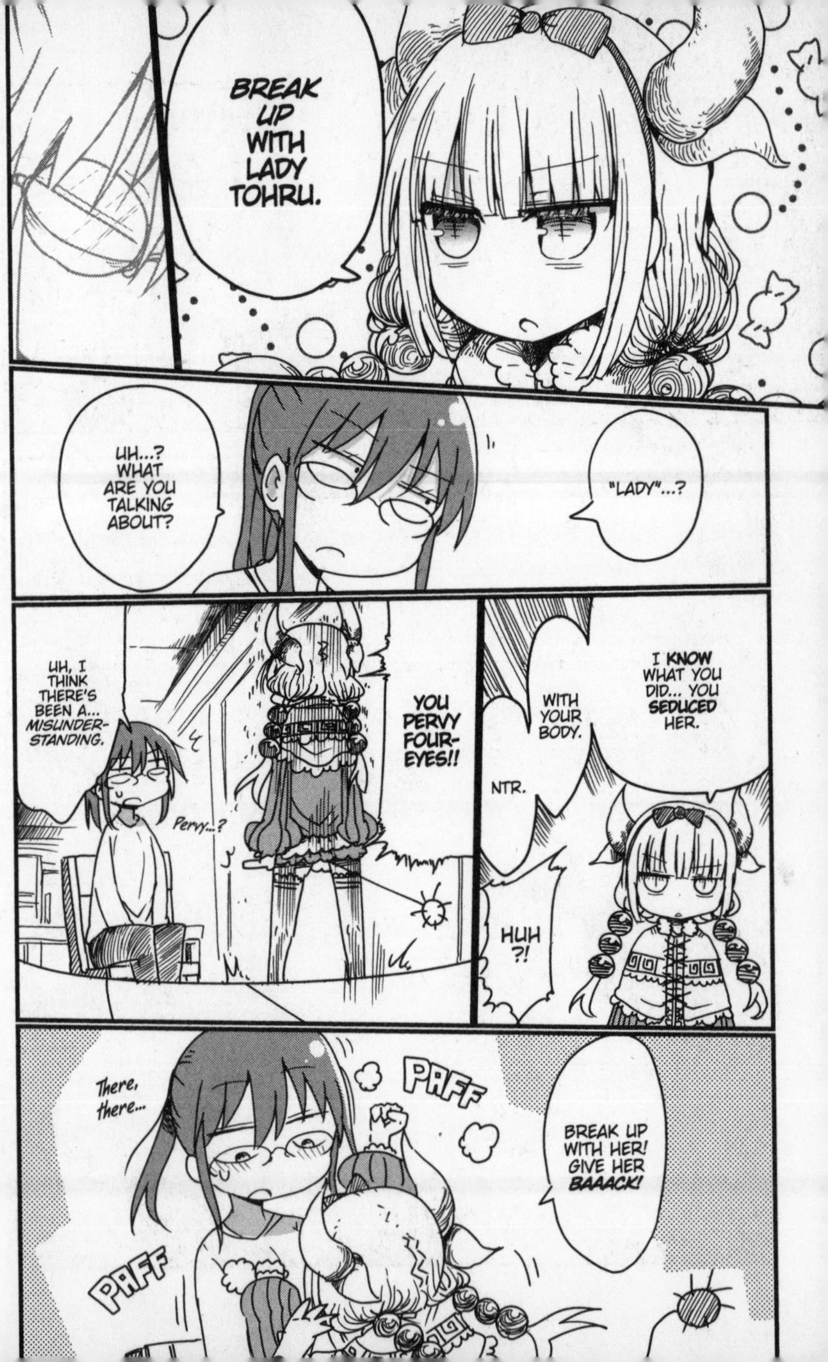
BREAK UP WITH LADY TOHRU.
"LADY"...?
UH...? WHAT ARE YOU TALKING ABOUT?
I KNOW WHAT YOU DID... YOU SEDUCED HER.
WITH YOUR BODY.
NTR.
HUH ?!
YOU PERVY FOUR-EYES!!
Pervy...?
UH, I THINK THERE'S BEEN A... MISUNDERSTANDING.
BREAK UP WITH HER! GIVE HER BAAACK!
PAFF
There, there...
PAFF

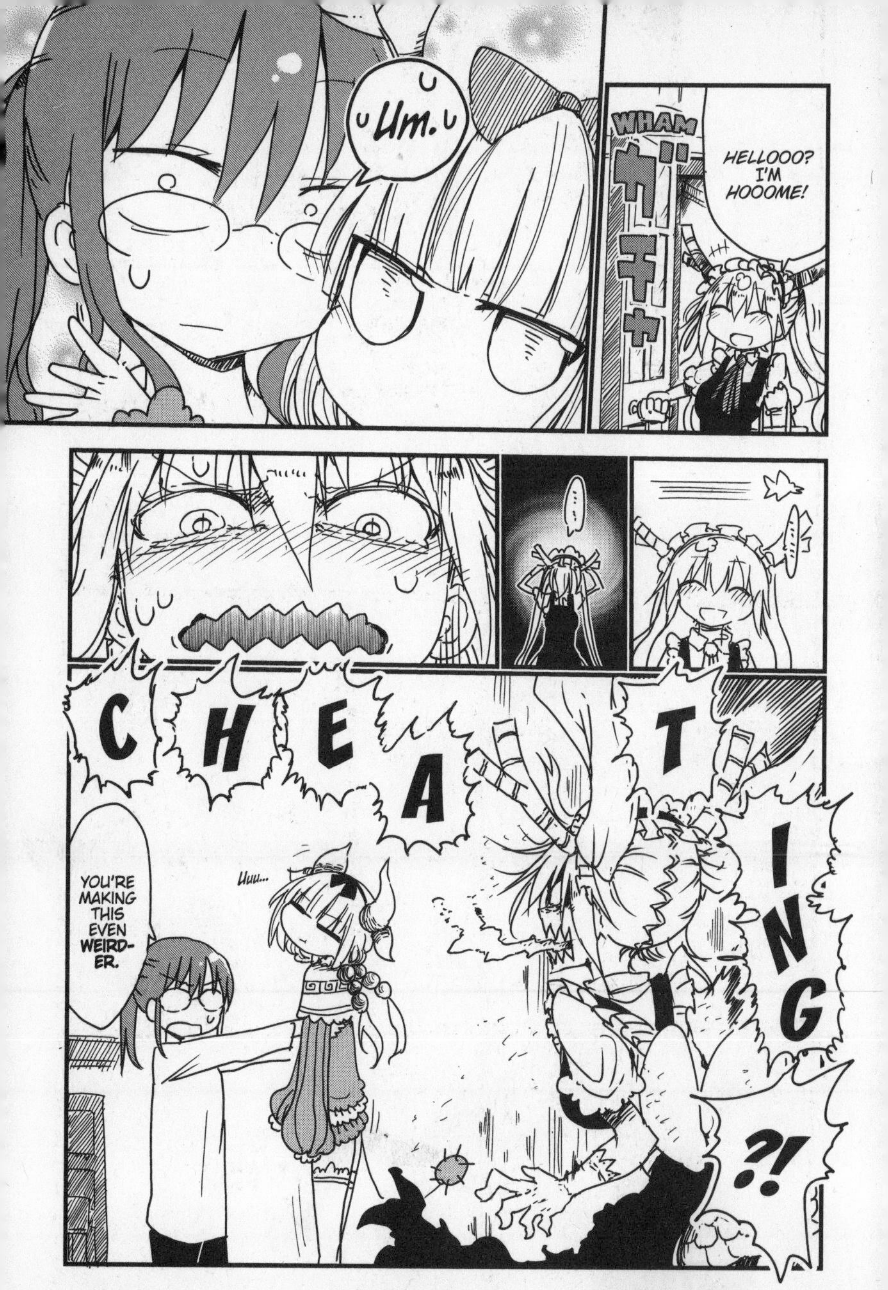
WHAM
ガチャ
HELLOOO? I'M HOOOME!
Um.
...
...
CHEATING
?!
Uuu...
YOU'RE MAKING THIS EVEN WEIRD-ER.

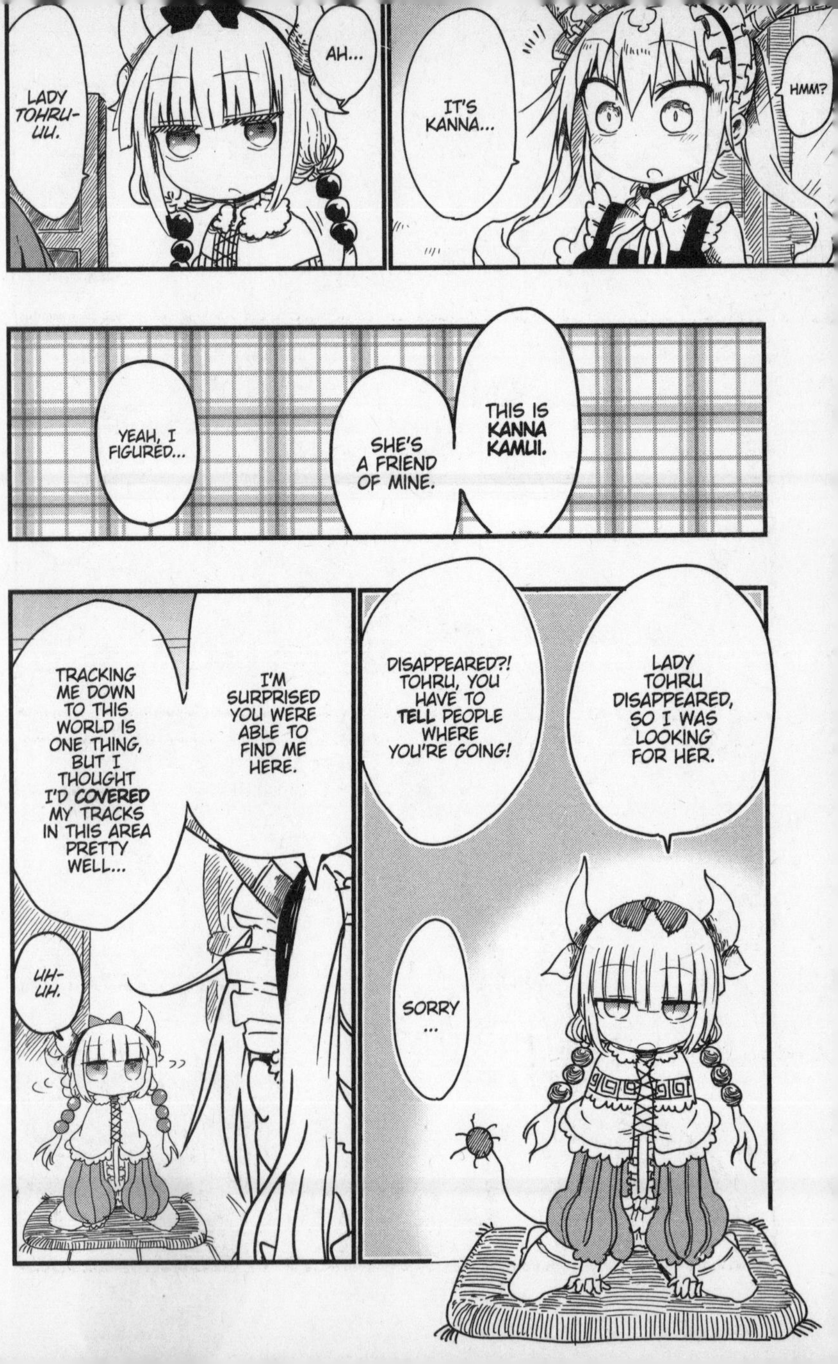
HMM?
IT'S KANNA...
AH...
LADY TOHRU-UU.
THIS IS KANNA KAMUI.
SHE'S A FRIEND OF MINE.
YEAH, I FIGURED...
LADY TOHRU DISAPPEARED, SO I WAS LOOKING FOR HER.
DISAPPEARED?! TOHRU, YOU HAVE TO TELL PEOPLE WHERE YOU'RE GOING!
SORRY ...
I'M SURPRISED YOU WERE ABLE TO FIND ME HERE.
TRACKING ME DOWN TO THIS WORLD IS ONE THING, BUT I THOUGHT I'D COVERED MY TRACKS IN THIS AREA PRETTY WELL...
UH-UH.

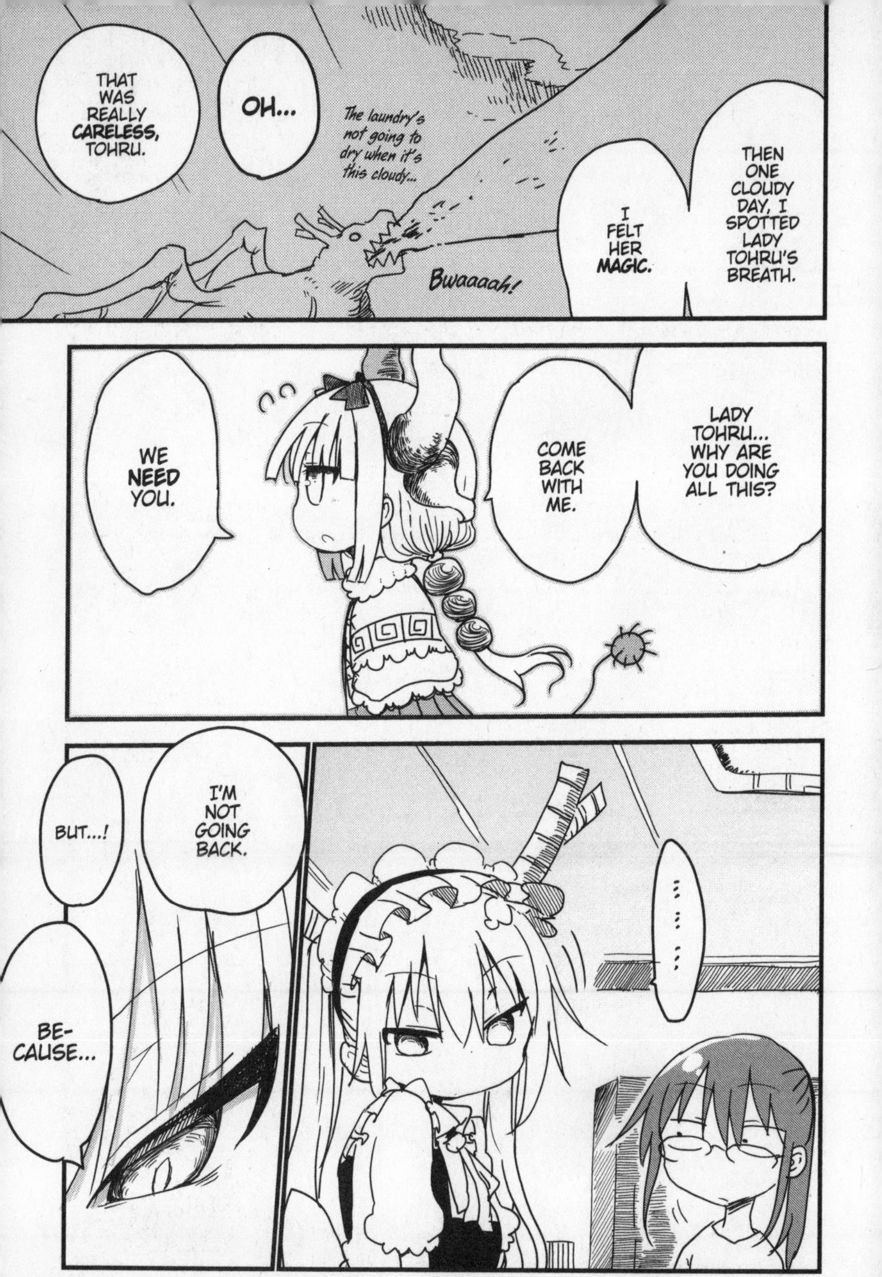
THEN ONE CLOUDY DAY, I SPOTTED LADY TOHRU'S BREATH.
I FELT HER MAGIC.
Bwaaaah!
The laundry's not going to dry when it's this cloudy...
OH...
THAT WAS REALLY CARELESS, TOHRU.
LADY TOHRU... WHY ARE YOU DOING ALL THIS?
COME BACK WITH ME.
WE NEED YOU.
......
I'M NOT GOING BACK.
BUT...!
BE-CAUSE...

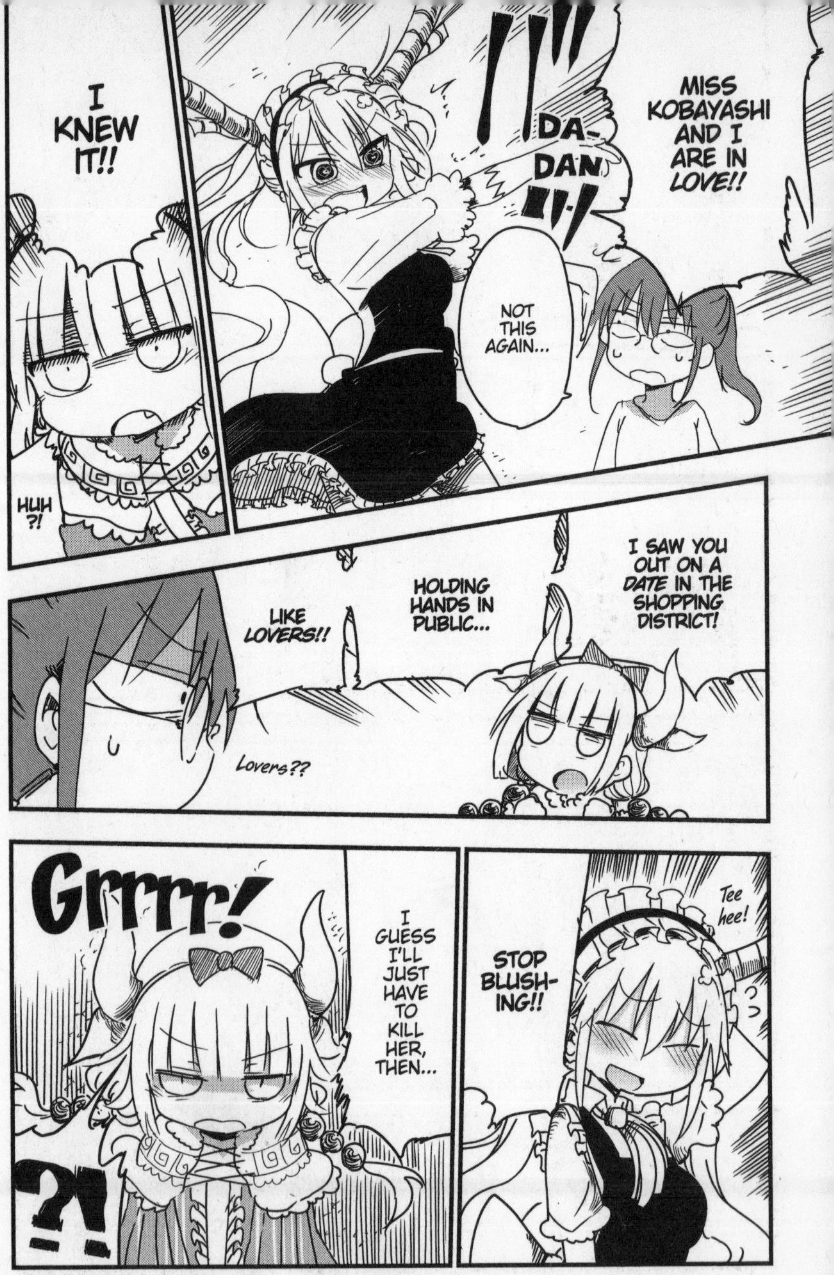
MISS KOBAYASHI AND I ARE IN LOVE!!
DA-DAN
NOT THIS AGAIN...
I KNEW IT!!
HUH ?!
I SAW YOU OUT ON A DATE IN THE SHOPPING DISTRICT!
HOLDING HANDS IN PUBLIC...
LIKE LOVERS!!
Lovers??
Tee hee!
STOP BLUSH-ING!!
Grrrr!
I GUESS I'LL JUST HAVE TO KILL HER, THEN...
?!

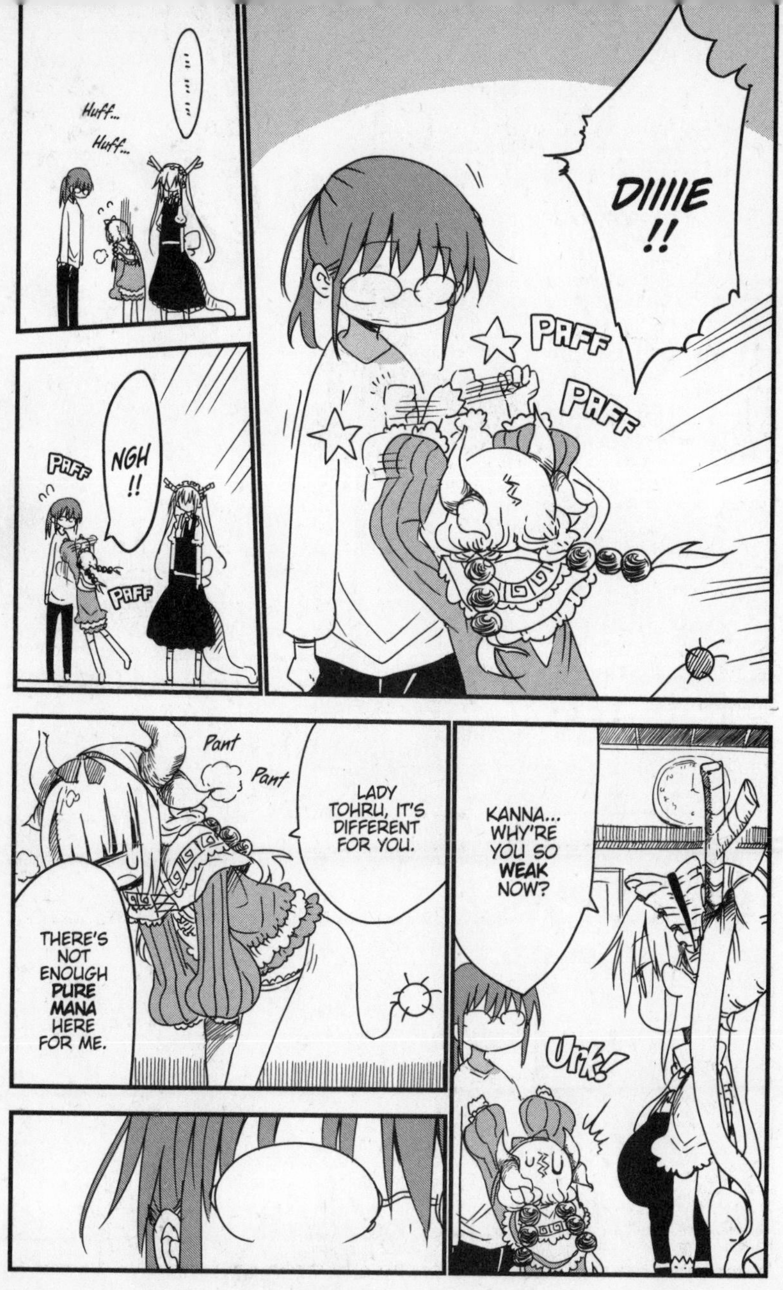
DIIIIE !!
PAFF
PAFF
Huff...
Huff...
......
PAFF
NGH !!
PAFF
KANNA... WHY'RE YOU SO WEAK NOW?
Urk!
Pant
Pant
LADY TOHRU, IT'S DIFFERENT FOR YOU.
THERE'S NOT ENOUGH PURE MANA HERE FOR ME.

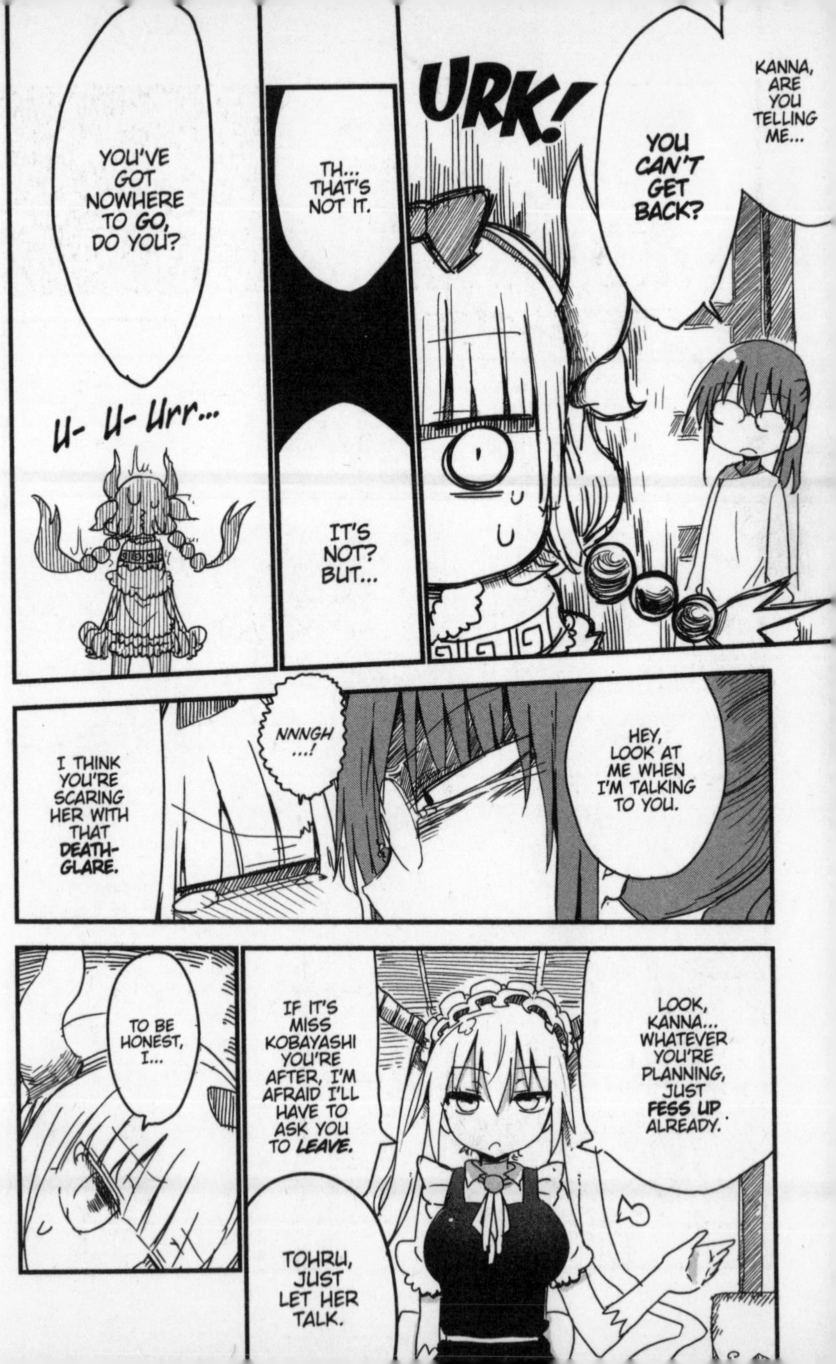
KANNA, ARE YOU TELLING ME...
YOU CAN'T GET BACK?
URK!
TH... THAT'S NOT IT.
IT'S NOT? BUT...
YOU'VE GOT NOWHERE TO GO, DO YOU?
U- U- Urr...
HEY, LOOK AT ME WHEN I'M TALKING TO YOU.
NNNGH ...!
I THINK YOU'RE SCARING HER WITH THAT DEATH-GLARE.
LOOK, KANNA... WHATEVER YOU'RE PLANNING, JUST FESS UP ALREADY.
IF IT'S MISS KOBAYASHI YOU'RE AFTER, I'M AFRAID I'LL HAVE TO ASK YOU TO LEAVE.
TOHRU, JUST LET HER TALK.
TO BE HONEST, I...

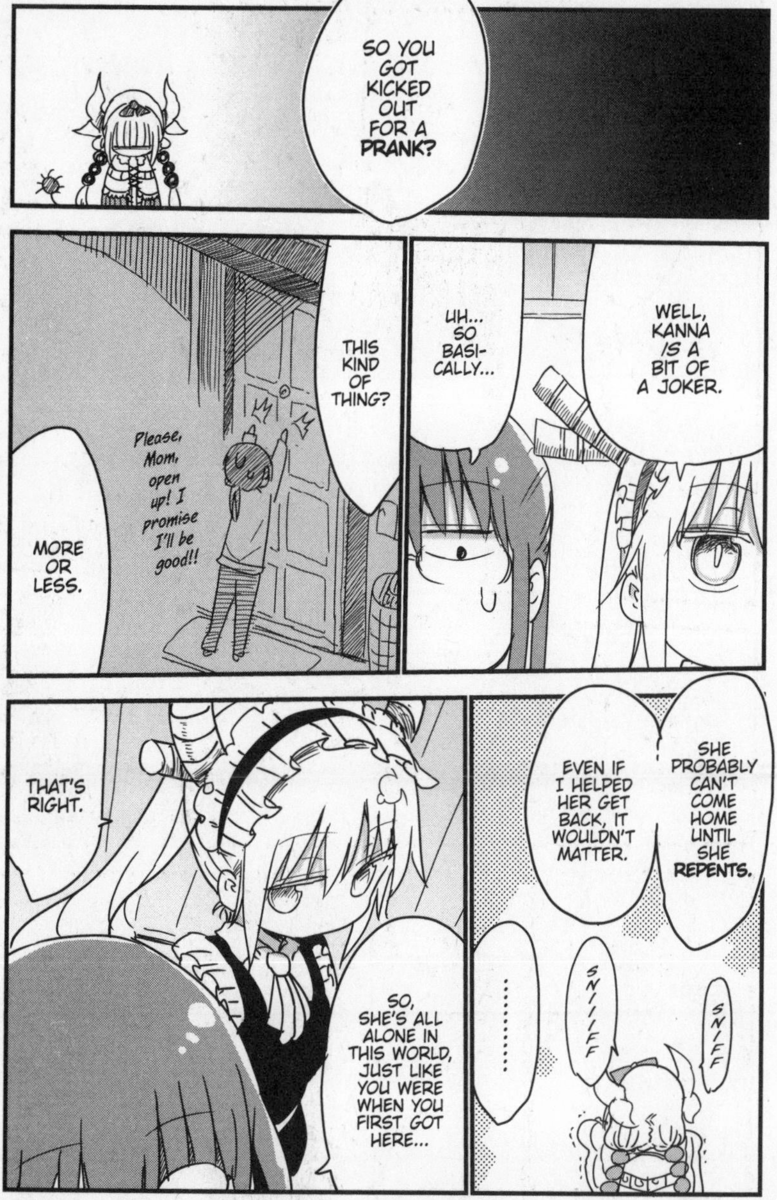
SO YOU GOT KICKED OUT FOR A PRANK?
WELL, KANNA IS A BIT OF A JOKER.
UH... SO BASI-CALLY...
THIS KIND OF THING?
Please, Mom, open up! I promise I'll be good!!
MORE OR LESS.
SHE PROBABLY CAN'T COME HOME UNTIL SHE REPENTS.
EVEN IF I HELPED HER GET BACK, IT WOULDN'T MATTER.
SNIFF
SNIIIFF
........
THAT'S RIGHT.
SO, SHE'S ALL ALONE IN THIS WORLD, JUST LIKE YOU WERE WHEN YOU FIRST GOT HERE...

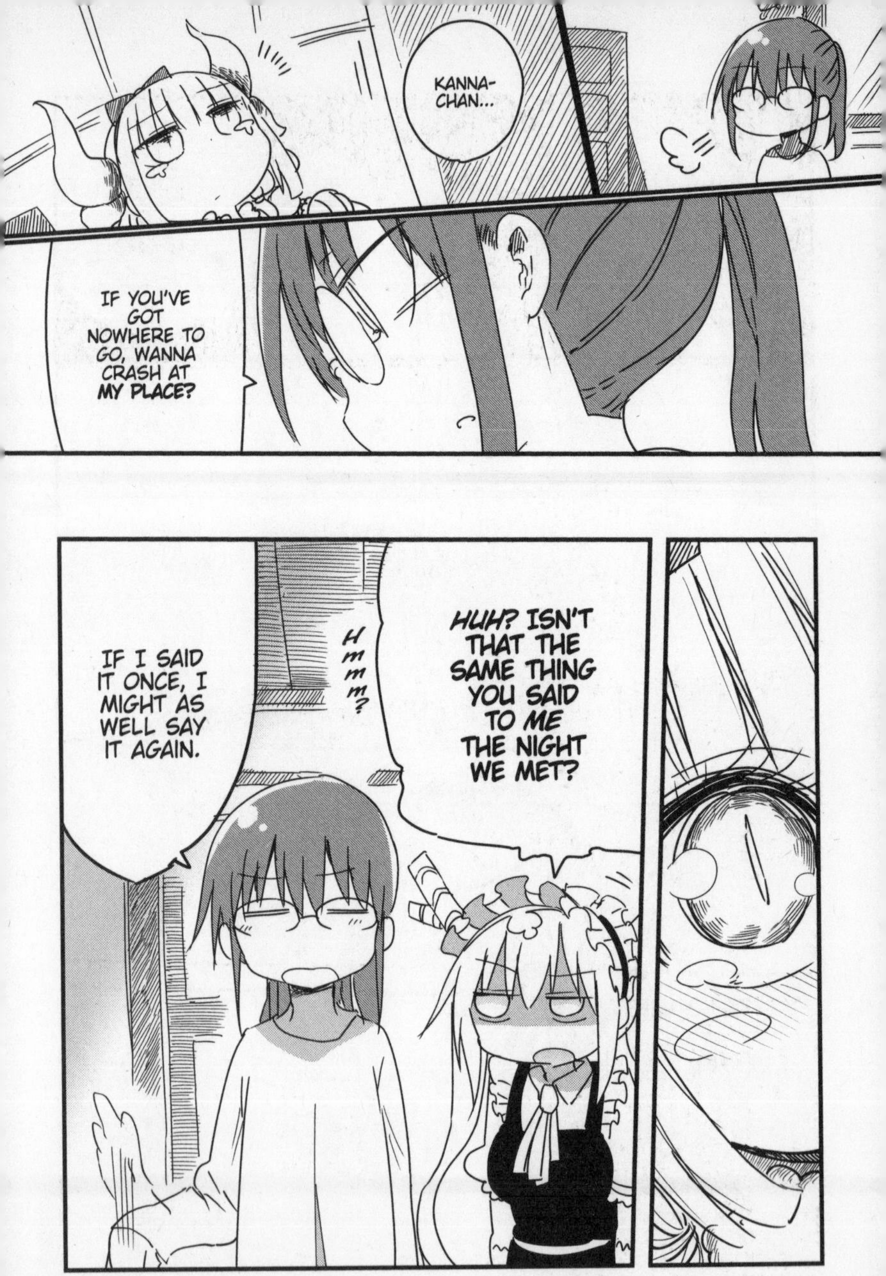
KANNA-CHAN...
IF YOU'VE GOT NOWHERE TO GO, WANNA CRASH AT MY PLACE?
HUH? ISN'T THAT THE SAME THING YOU SAID TO ME THE NIGHT WE MET?
Hmmm?
IF I SAID IT ONCE, I MIGHT AS WELL SAY IT AGAIN.

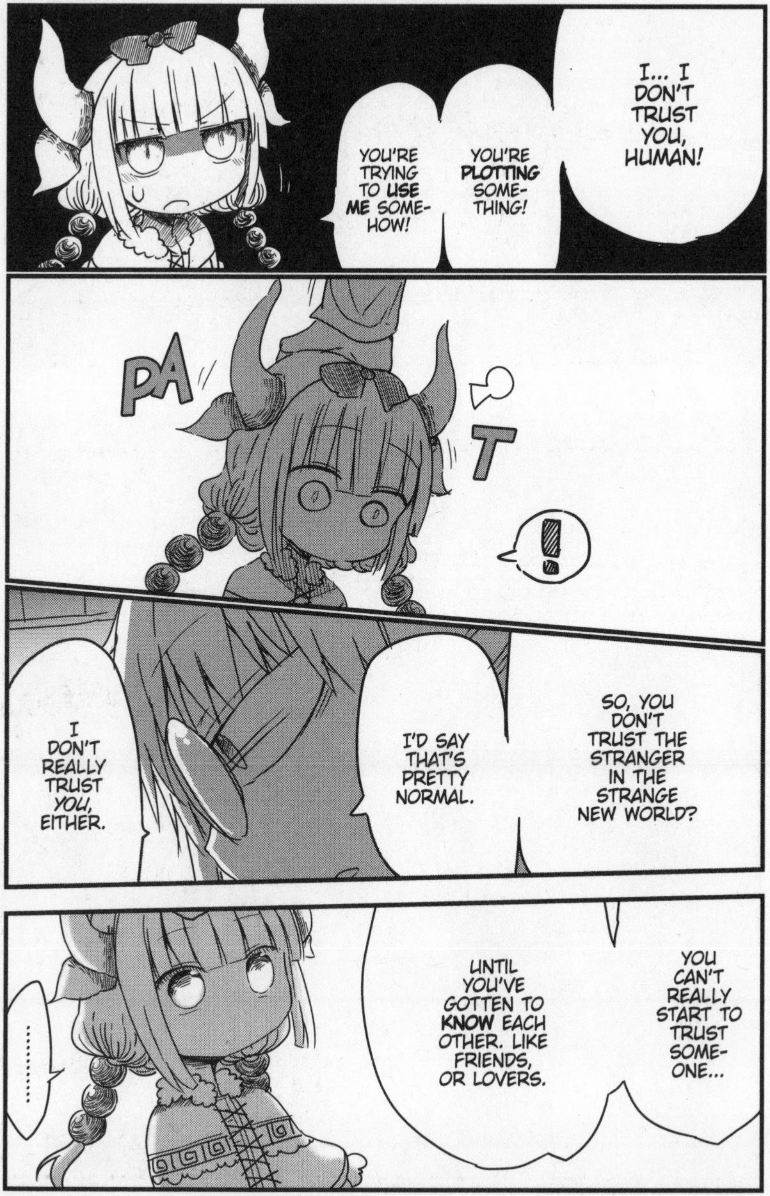
I... I DON'T TRUST YOU, HUMAN!
YOU'RE **PLOTTING** SOME-THING!
YOU'RE TRYING TO **USE ME** SOME-HOW!
PAT
!
SO, YOU DON'T TRUST THE STRANGER IN THE STRANGE NEW WORLD?
I'D SAY THAT'S PRETTY NORMAL.
I DON'T REALLY TRUST *YOU*, EITHER.
YOU CAN'T REALLY START TO TRUST SOME-ONE...
UNTIL YOU'VE GOTTEN TO **KNOW** EACH OTHER. LIKE FRIENDS, OR LOVERS.
......

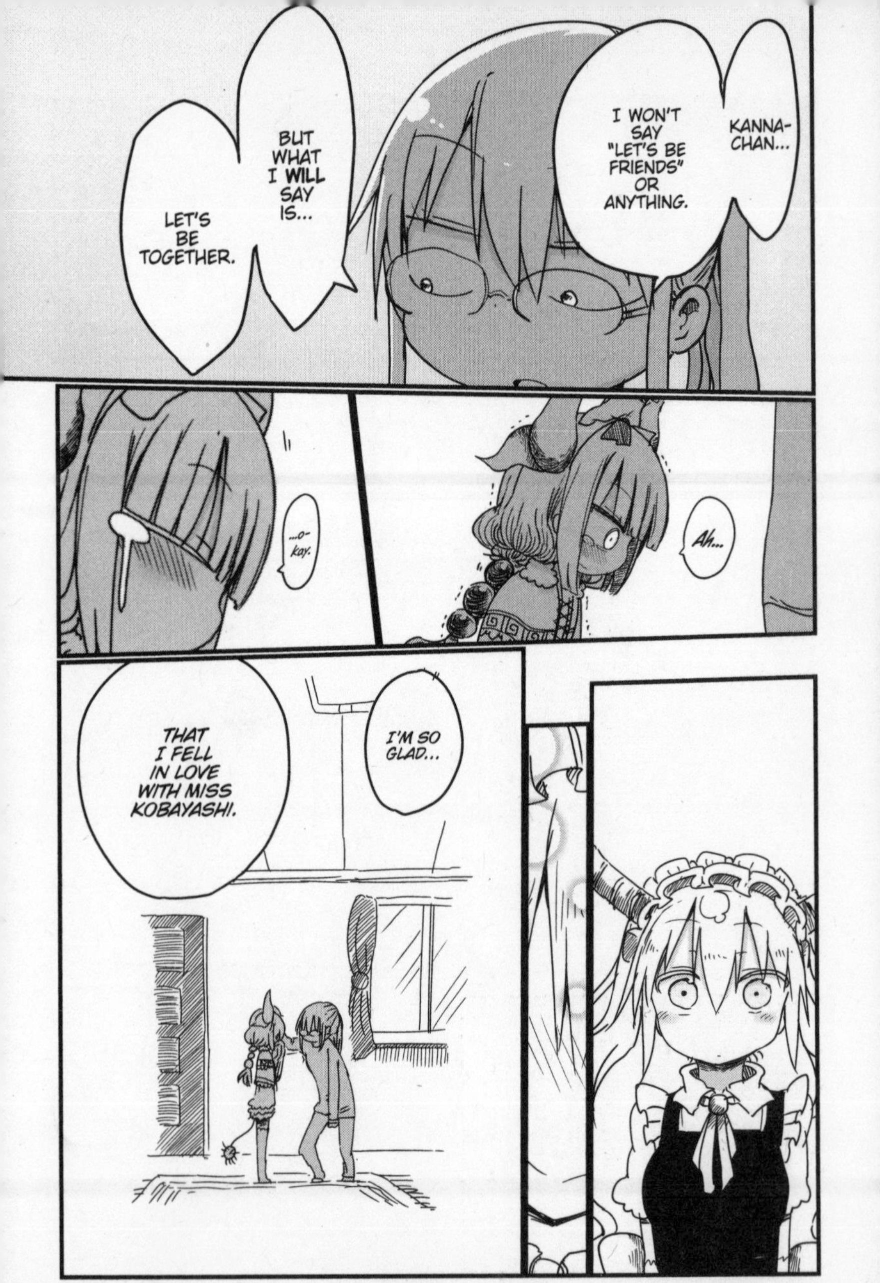
KANNA-CHAN...
I WON'T SAY "LET'S BE FRIENDS" OR ANYTHING.
BUT WHAT I WILL SAY IS...
LET'S BE TOGETHER.
Ah...
...o-kay.
I'M SO GLAD...
THAT I FELL IN LOVE WITH MISS KOBAYASHI.

**CHAPTER 6/END**

This is okay, right? I won't get arrested for kid-napping, right...?

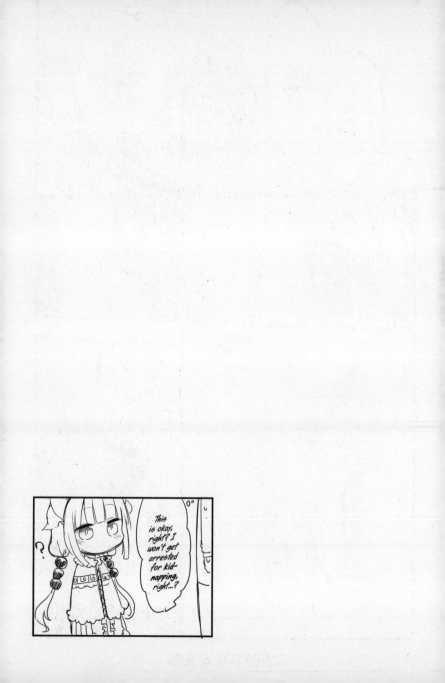

Miss Kobayashi's
DRAGON MAID

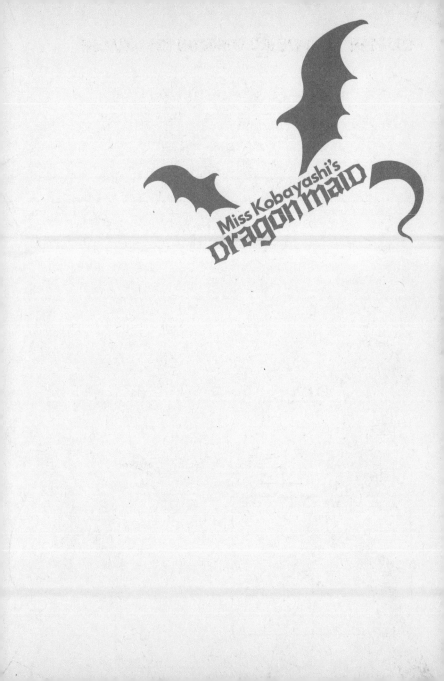

# CHAPTER 7 : TOHRU & COMMON KNOWLEDGE

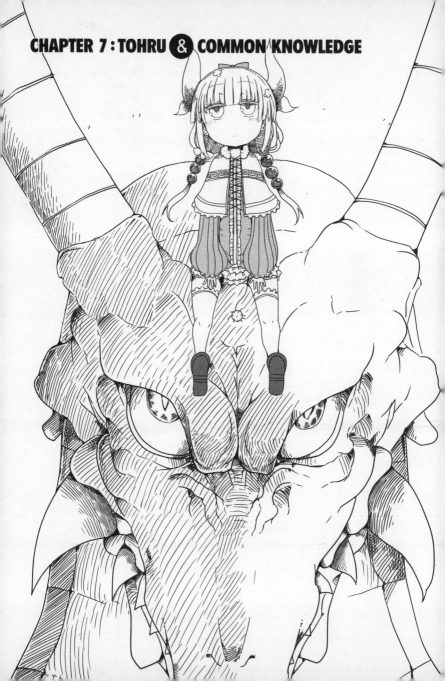

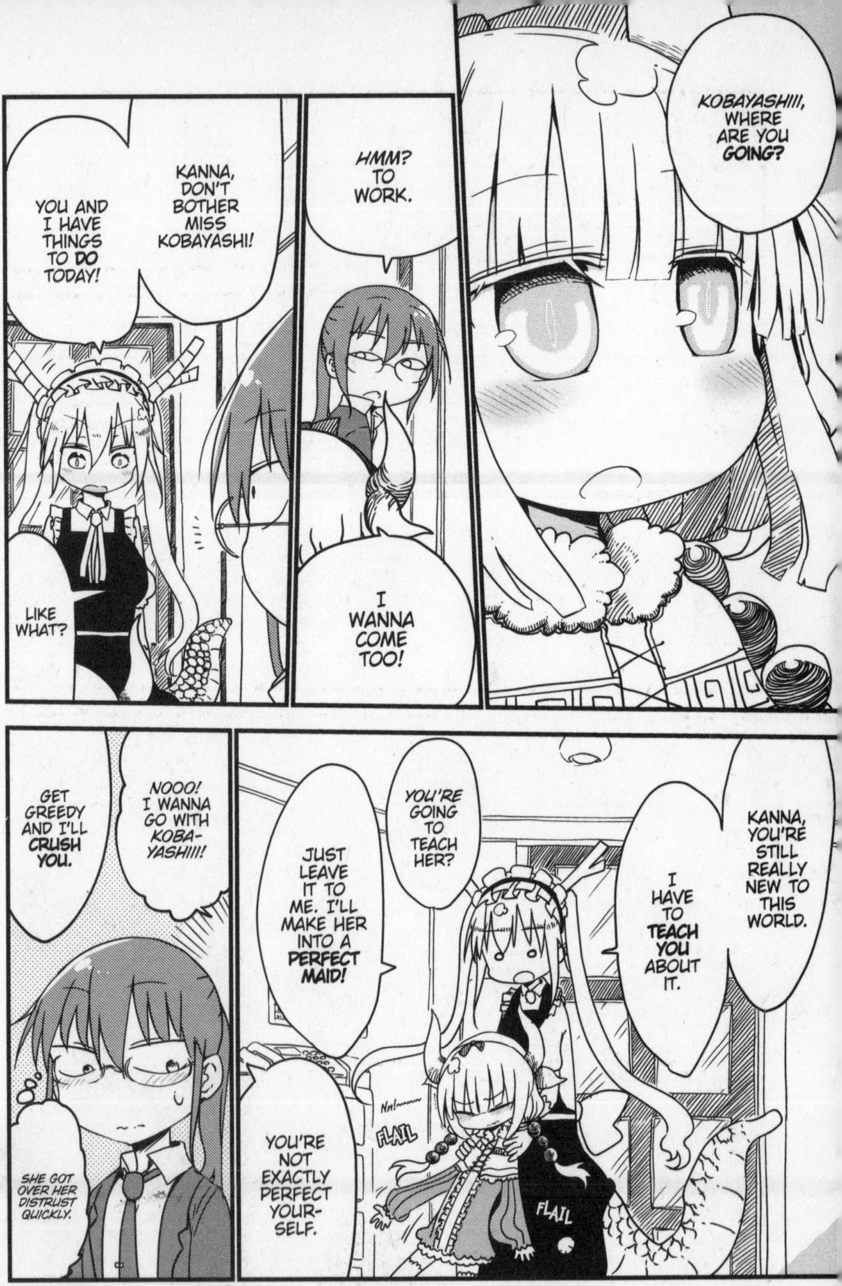
KOBAYASHIII, WHERE ARE YOU GOING?
HMM? TO WORK.
I WANNA COME TOO!
KANNA, DON'T BOTHER MISS KOBAYASHI!
YOU AND I HAVE THINGS TO DO TODAY!
LIKE WHAT?
KANNA, YOU'RE STILL REALLY NEW TO THIS WORLD.
I HAVE TO TEACH YOU ABOUT IT.
YOU'RE GOING TO TEACH HER?
JUST LEAVE IT TO ME. I'LL MAKE HER INTO A PERFECT MAID!
FLAIL
FLAIL
YOU'RE NOT EXACTLY PERFECT YOURSELF.
NOOO! I WANNA GO WITH KOBAYASHIII!
GET GREEDY AND I'LL CRUSH YOU.
SHE GOT OVER HER DISTRUST QUICKLY.

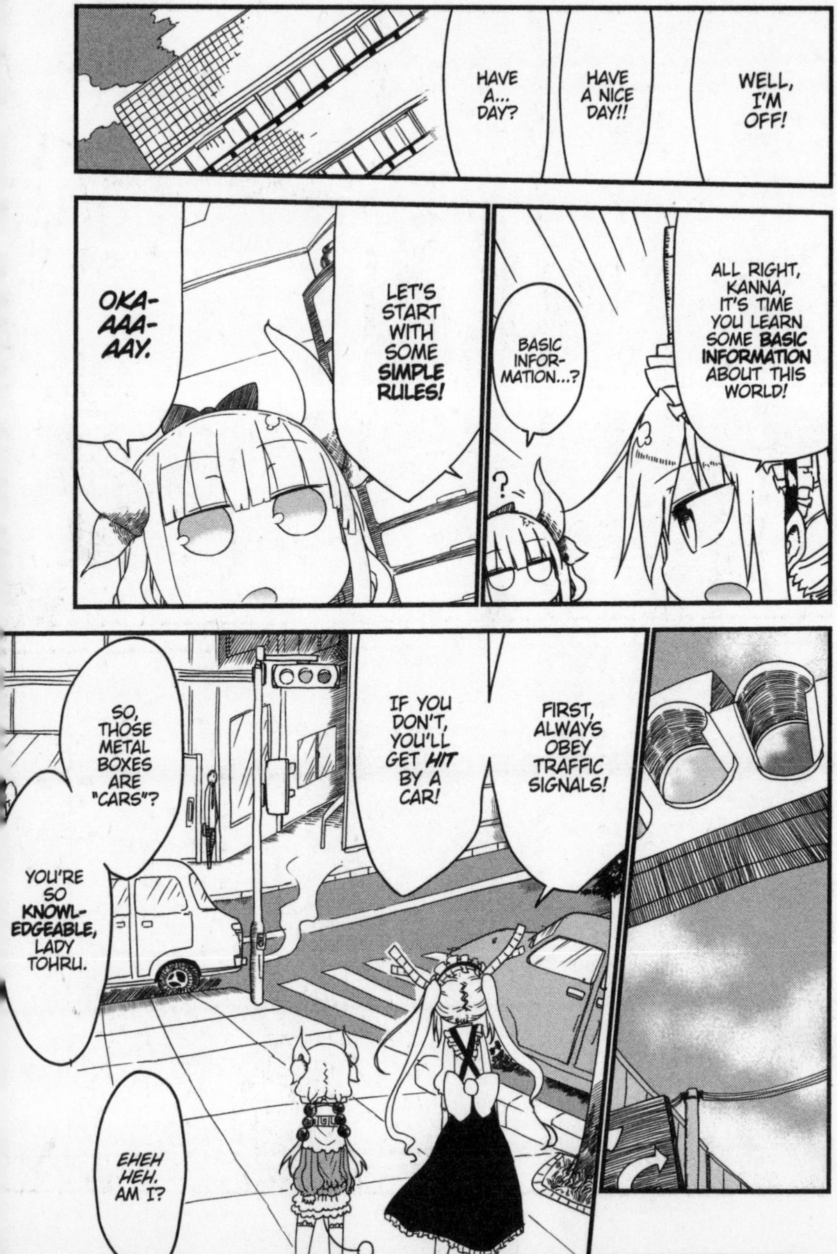
WELL, I'M OFF!
HAVE A NICE DAY!!
HAVE A... DAY?
ALL RIGHT, KANNA, IT'S TIME YOU LEARN SOME **BASIC INFORMATION** ABOUT THIS WORLD!
BASIC INFOR-MATION...?
LET'S START WITH SOME **SIMPLE RULES!**
OKA-AAAA-AAY.
FIRST, ALWAYS OBEY TRAFFIC SIGNALS!
IF YOU DON'T, YOU'LL GET *HIT* BY A CAR!
SO, THOSE METAL BOXES ARE "CARS"?
YOU'RE SO KNOWL-EDGEABLE, LADY TOHRU.
EHEH HEH. AM I?

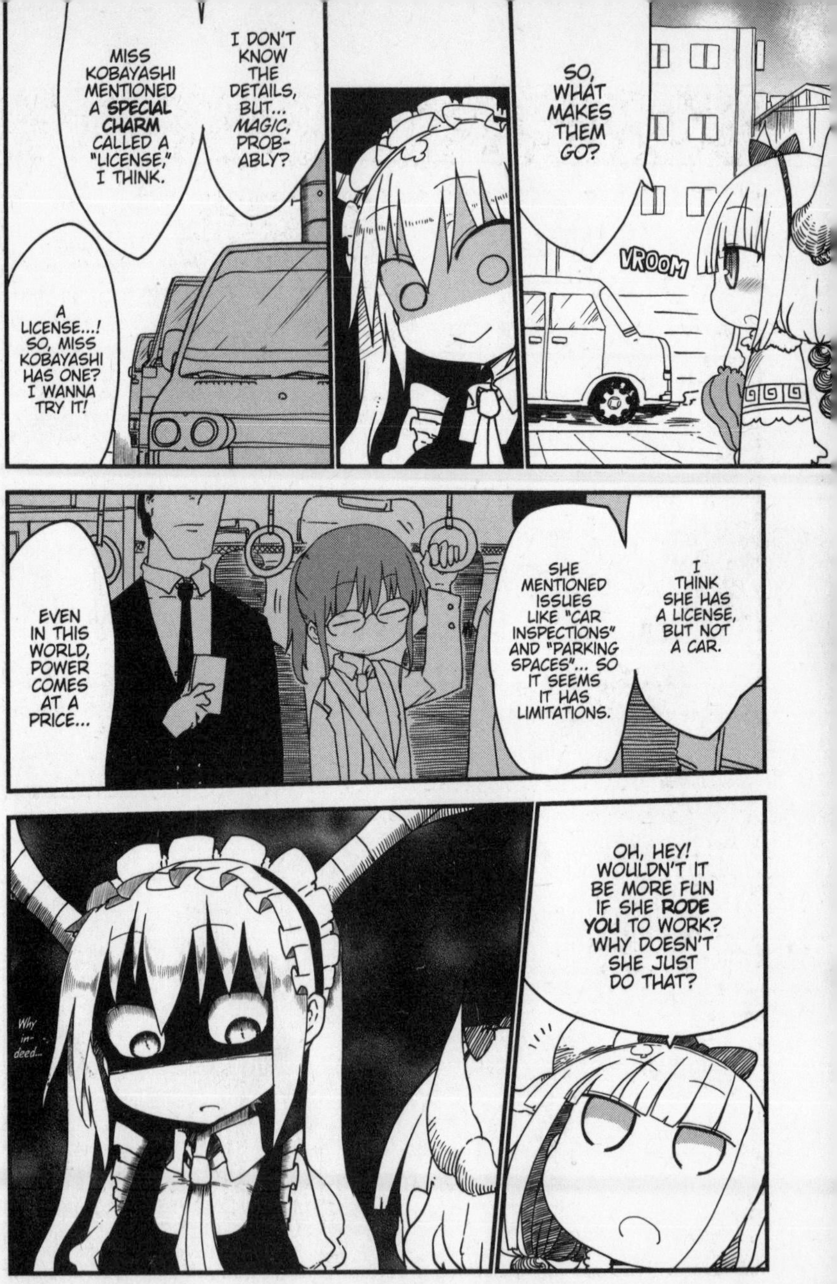
SO, WHAT MAKES THEM GO?
VROOM
I DON'T KNOW THE DETAILS, BUT... *MAGIC*, PROBABLY?
MISS KOBAYASHI MENTIONED A **SPECIAL CHARM** CALLED A "LICENSE," I THINK.
A LICENSE...! SO, MISS KOBAYASHI HAS ONE? I WANNA TRY IT!
I THINK SHE HAS A LICENSE, BUT NOT A CAR.
SHE MENTIONED ISSUES LIKE "CAR INSPECTIONS" AND "PARKING SPACES"... SO IT SEEMS IT HAS LIMITATIONS.
EVEN IN THIS WORLD, POWER COMES AT A PRICE...
OH, HEY! WOULDN'T IT BE MORE FUN IF SHE **RODE YOU** TO WORK? WHY DOESN'T SHE JUST DO THAT?
Why indeed...

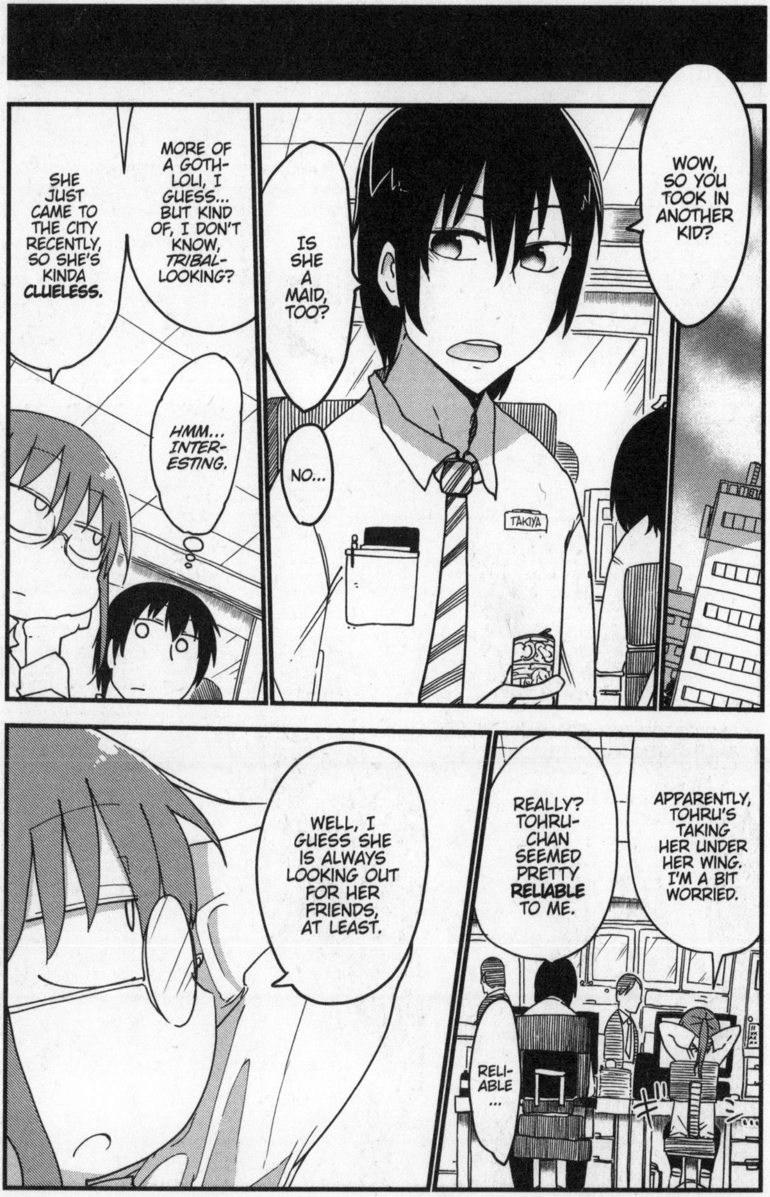
WOW, SO YOU TOOK IN ANOTHER KID?
IS SHE A MAID, TOO?
NO...
TAKIYA
MORE OF A GOTH-LOLI, I GUESS... BUT KIND OF, I DON'T KNOW, *TRIBAL*-LOOKING?
SHE JUST CAME TO THE CITY RECENTLY, SO SHE'S KINDA **CLUELESS.**
*HMM... INTER-ESTING.*
APPARENTLY, TOHRU'S TAKING HER UNDER HER WING. I'M A BIT WORRIED.
REALLY? TOHRU-CHAN SEEMED PRETTY **RELIABLE** TO ME.
RELI-ABLE ...
WELL, I GUESS SHE IS ALWAYS LOOKING OUT FOR HER FRIENDS, AT LEAST.

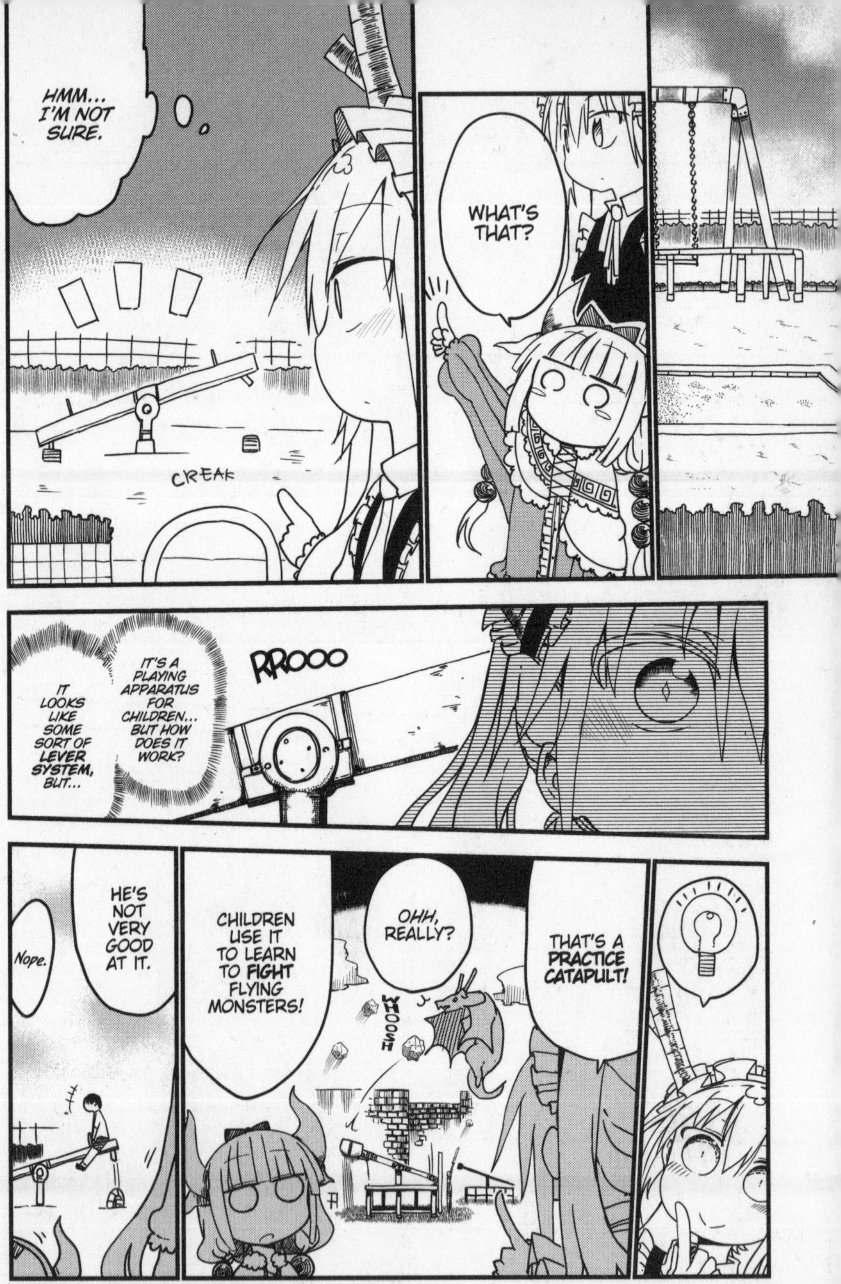
WHAT'S THAT?
HMM... I'M NOT SURE.
CREAK
RROOO
IT'S A PLAYING APPARATUS FOR CHILDREN... BUT HOW DOES IT WORK?
IT LOOKS LIKE SOME SORT OF **LEVER SYSTEM**, BUT...
THAT'S A **PRACTICE CATAPULT!**
OHH, REALLY?
CHILDREN USE IT TO LEARN TO **FIGHT** FLYING MONSTERS!
WHOOSH
HE'S NOT VERY GOOD AT IT.
Nope.

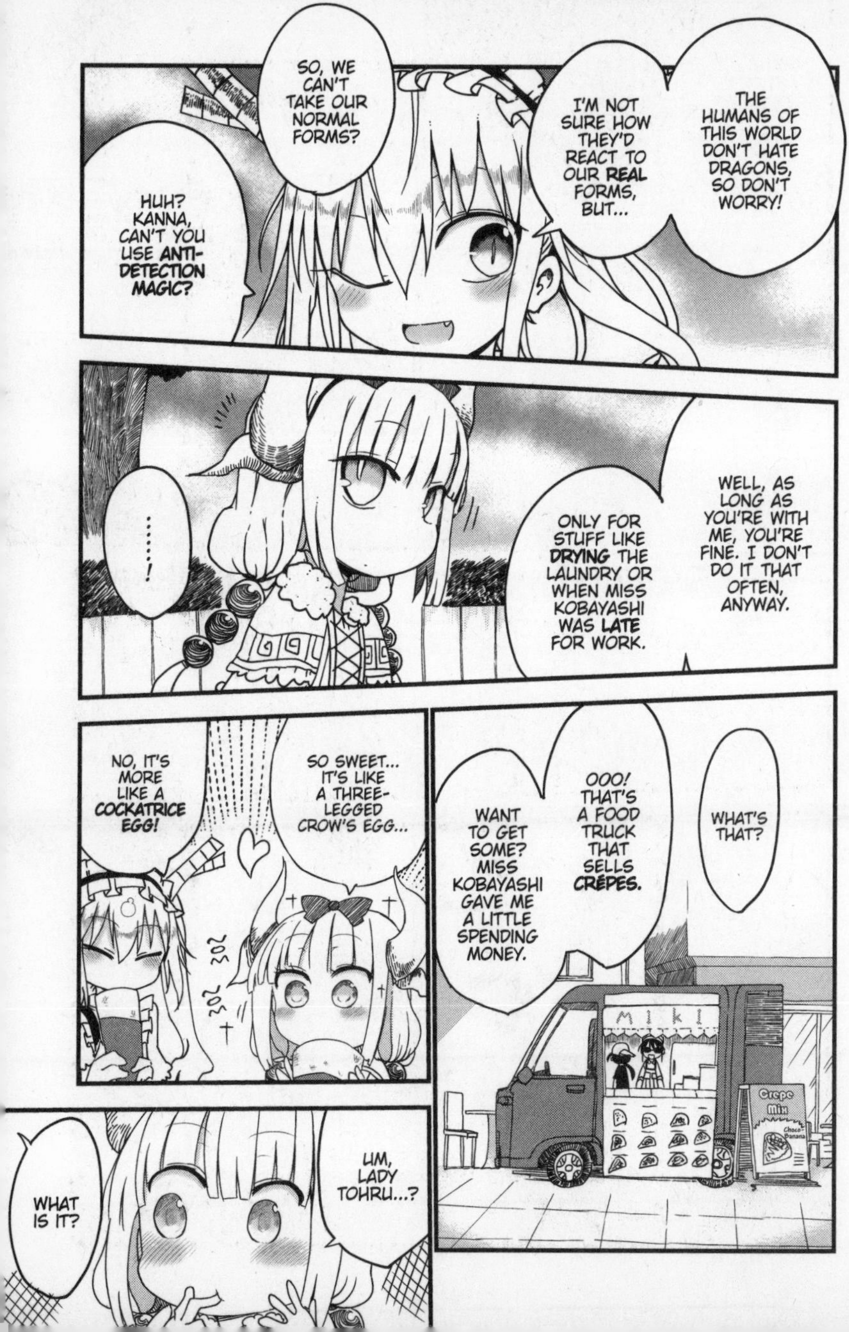
THE HUMANS OF THIS WORLD DON'T HATE DRAGONS, SO DON'T WORRY!
I'M NOT SURE HOW THEY'D REACT TO OUR **REAL** FORMS, BUT...
SO, WE CAN'T TAKE OUR NORMAL FORMS?
HUH? KANNA, CAN'T YOU USE **ANTI-DETECTION MAGIC?**
WELL, AS LONG AS YOU'RE WITH ME, YOU'RE FINE. I DON'T DO IT THAT OFTEN, ANYWAY.
ONLY FOR STUFF LIKE **DRYING** THE LAUNDRY OR WHEN MISS KOBAYASHI WAS **LATE** FOR WORK.
......!
WHAT'S THAT?
OOO! THAT'S A FOOD TRUCK THAT SELLS **CRÊPES.**
WANT TO GET SOME? MISS KOBAYASHI GAVE ME A LITTLE SPENDING MONEY.
miki
Crepe Mix
Choco Banana
SO SWEET... IT'S LIKE A THREE-LEGGED CROW'S EGG...
NO, IT'S MORE LIKE A **COCKATRICE EGG!**
UM, LADY TOHRU...?
WHAT IS IT?

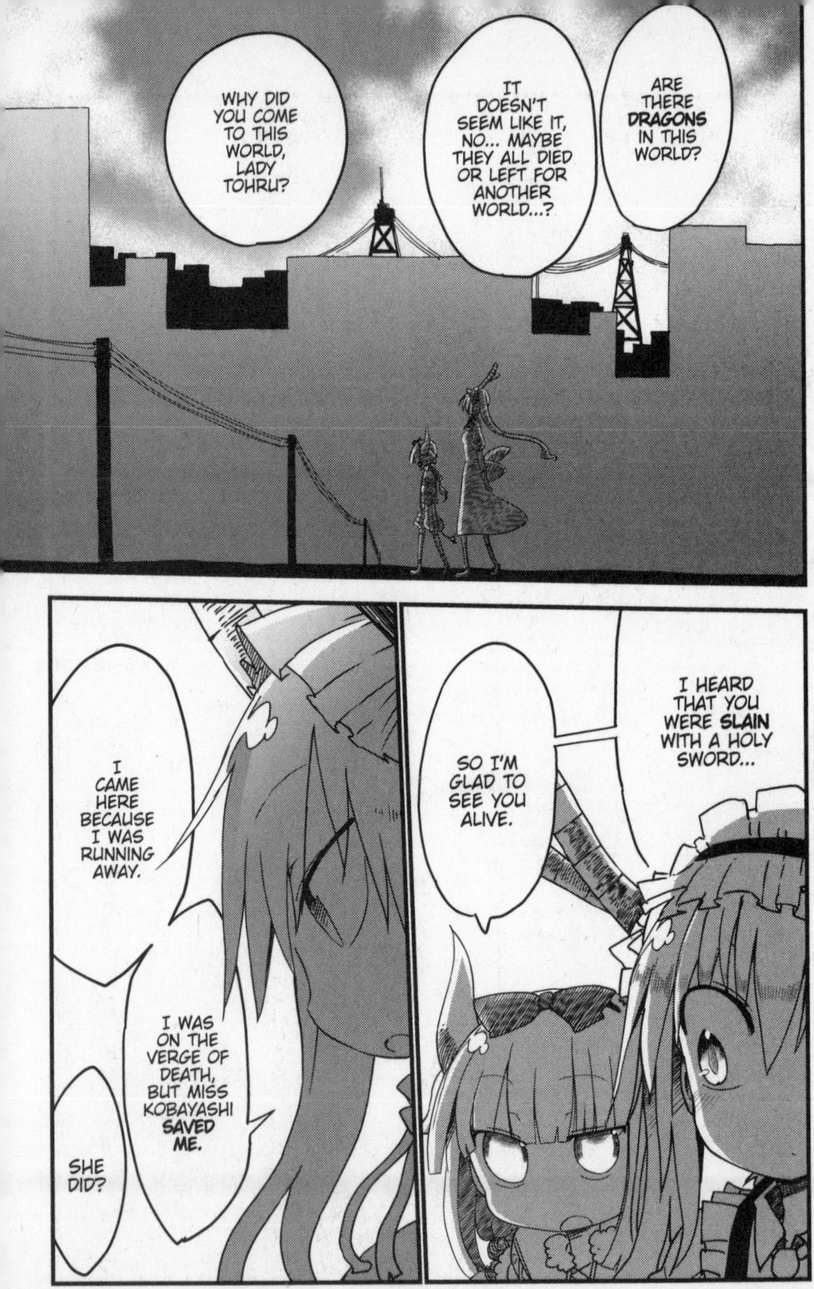
ARE THERE DRAGONS IN THIS WORLD?
IT DOESN'T SEEM LIKE IT, NO... MAYBE THEY ALL DIED OR LEFT FOR ANOTHER WORLD...?
WHY DID YOU COME TO THIS WORLD, LADY TOHRU?
I HEARD THAT YOU WERE SLAIN WITH A HOLY SWORD...
SO I'M GLAD TO SEE YOU ALIVE.
I CAME HERE BECAUSE I WAS RUNNING AWAY.
I WAS ON THE VERGE OF DEATH, BUT MISS KOBAYASHI SAVED ME.
SHE DID?

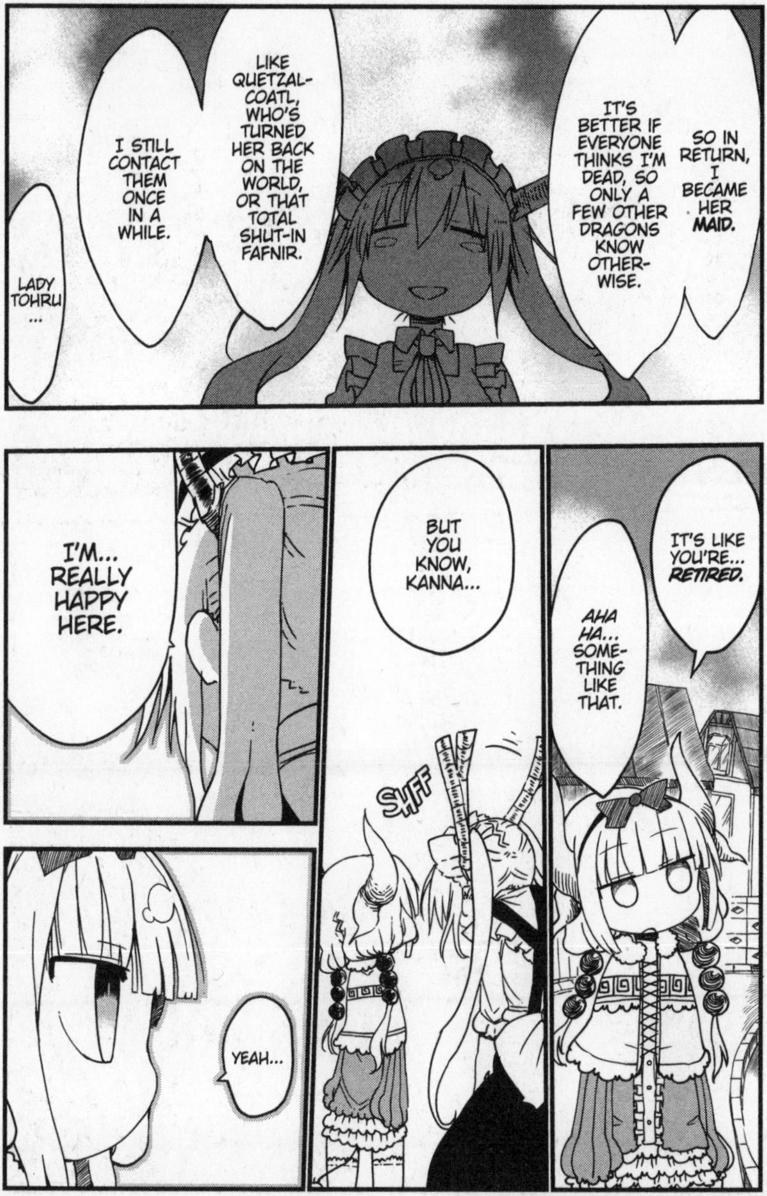
SO IN RETURN, I BECAME HER **MAID.**
IT'S BETTER IF EVERYONE THINKS I'M DEAD, SO ONLY A FEW OTHER DRAGONS KNOW OTHERWISE.
LIKE QUETZALCOATL, WHO'S TURNED HER BACK ON THE WORLD, OR THAT TOTAL SHUT-IN FAFNIR.
I STILL CONTACT THEM ONCE IN A WHILE.
LADY TOHRU ...
IT'S LIKE YOU'RE... ***RETIRED.***
*AHA HA...* SOMETHING LIKE THAT.
BUT YOU KNOW, KANNA...
SHFF
I'M... REALLY HAPPY HERE.
YEAH...

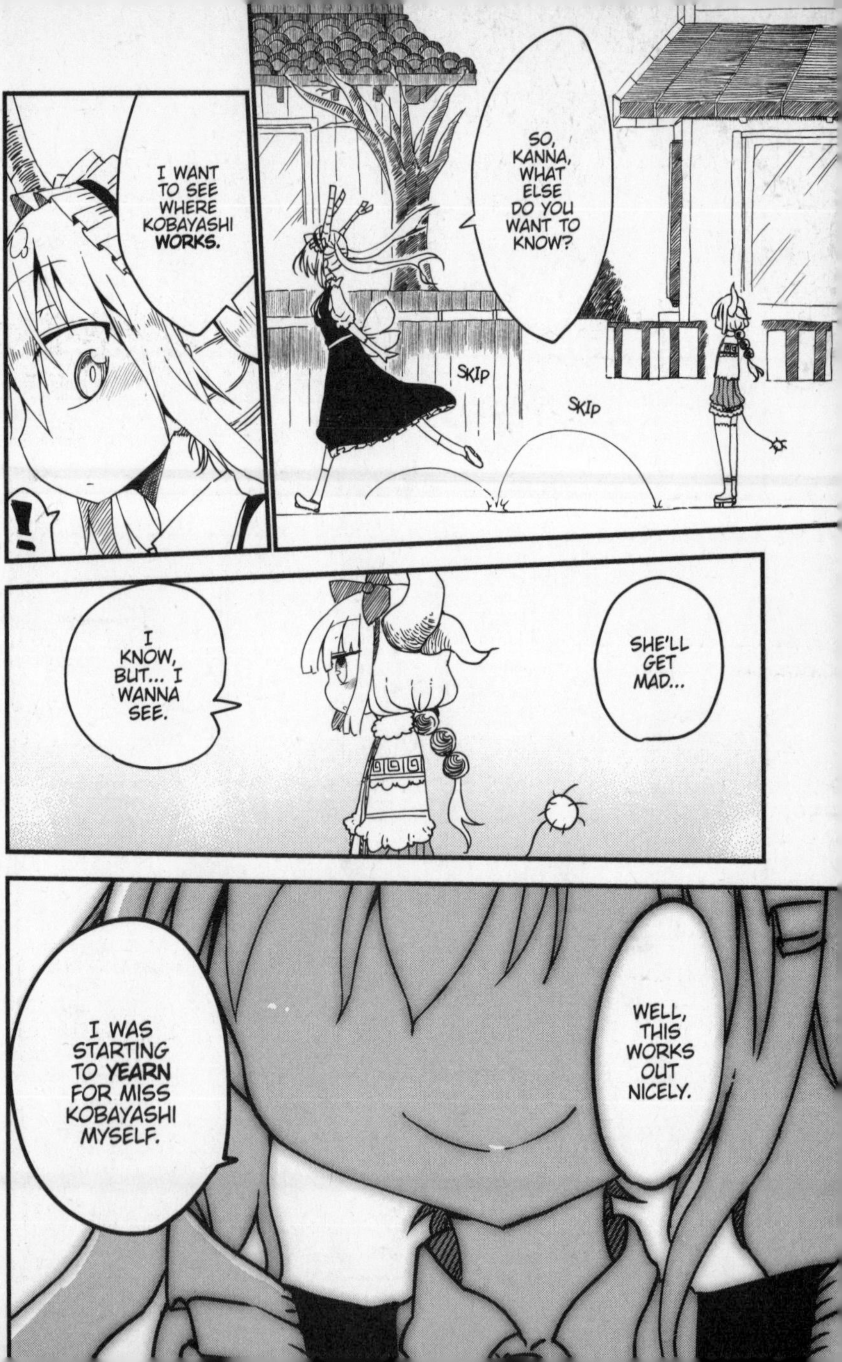
SO, KANNA, WHAT ELSE DO YOU WANT TO KNOW?
SKIP
SKIP
I WANT TO SEE WHERE KOBAYASHI WORKS.
!
SHE'LL GET MAD...
I KNOW, BUT... I WANNA SEE.
WELL, THIS WORKS OUT NICELY.
I WAS STARTING TO YEARN FOR MISS KOBAYASHI MYSELF.

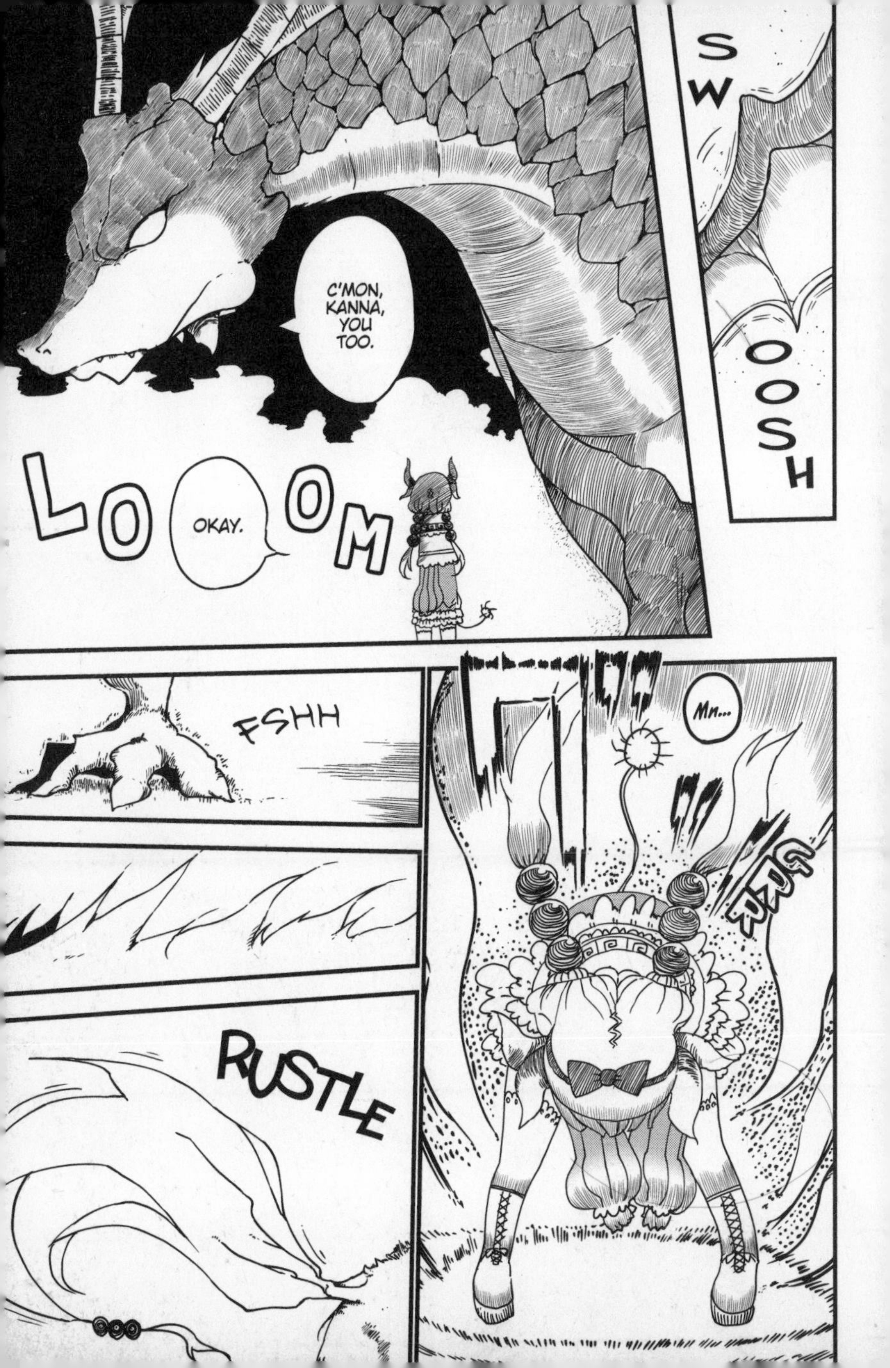
SWOOSH
C'MON, KANNA, YOU TOO.
LOOOM
OKAY.
Mn...
FSHH
RUSTLE

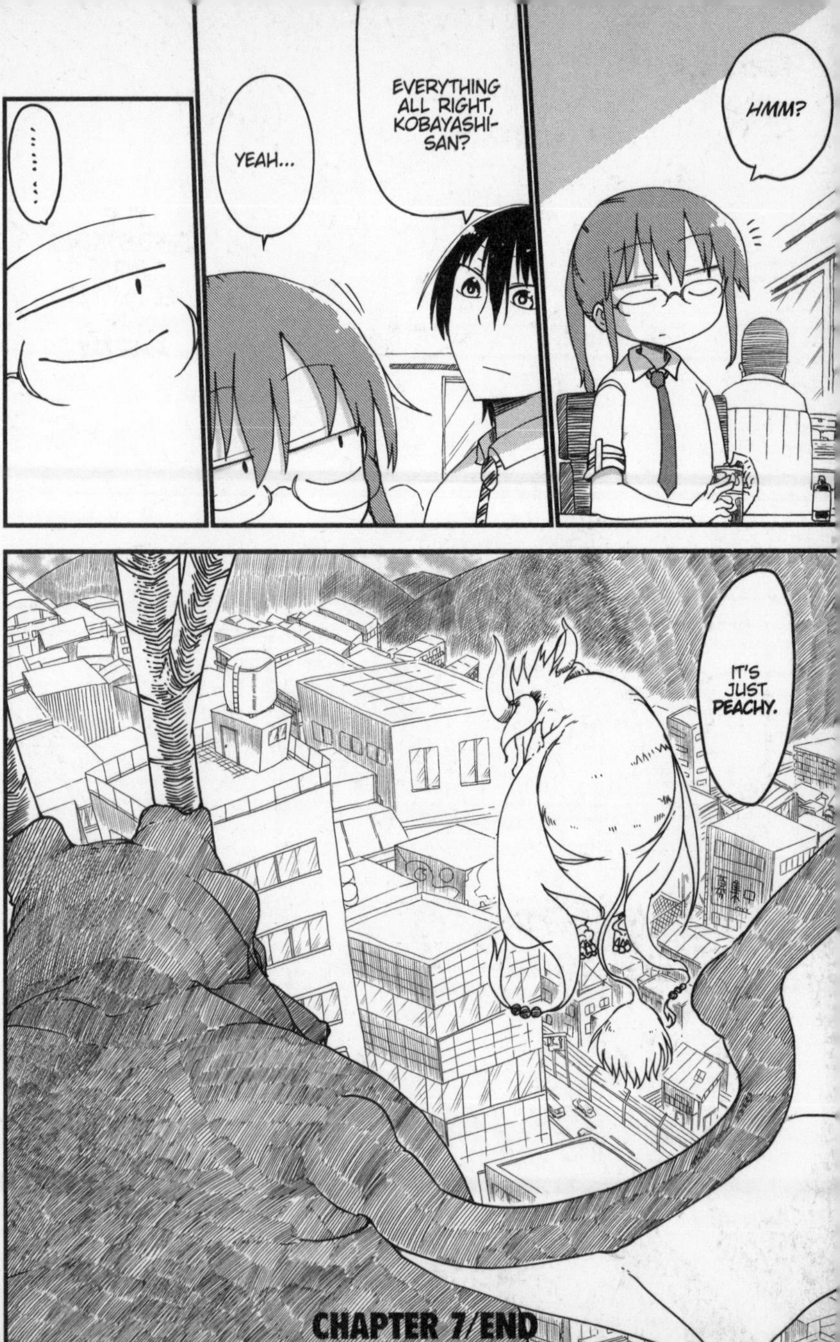
HMM?
EVERYTHING ALL RIGHT, KOBAYASHI-SAN?
YEAH...
......
IT'S JUST PEACHY.
CHAPTER 7/END

# Chapter 8

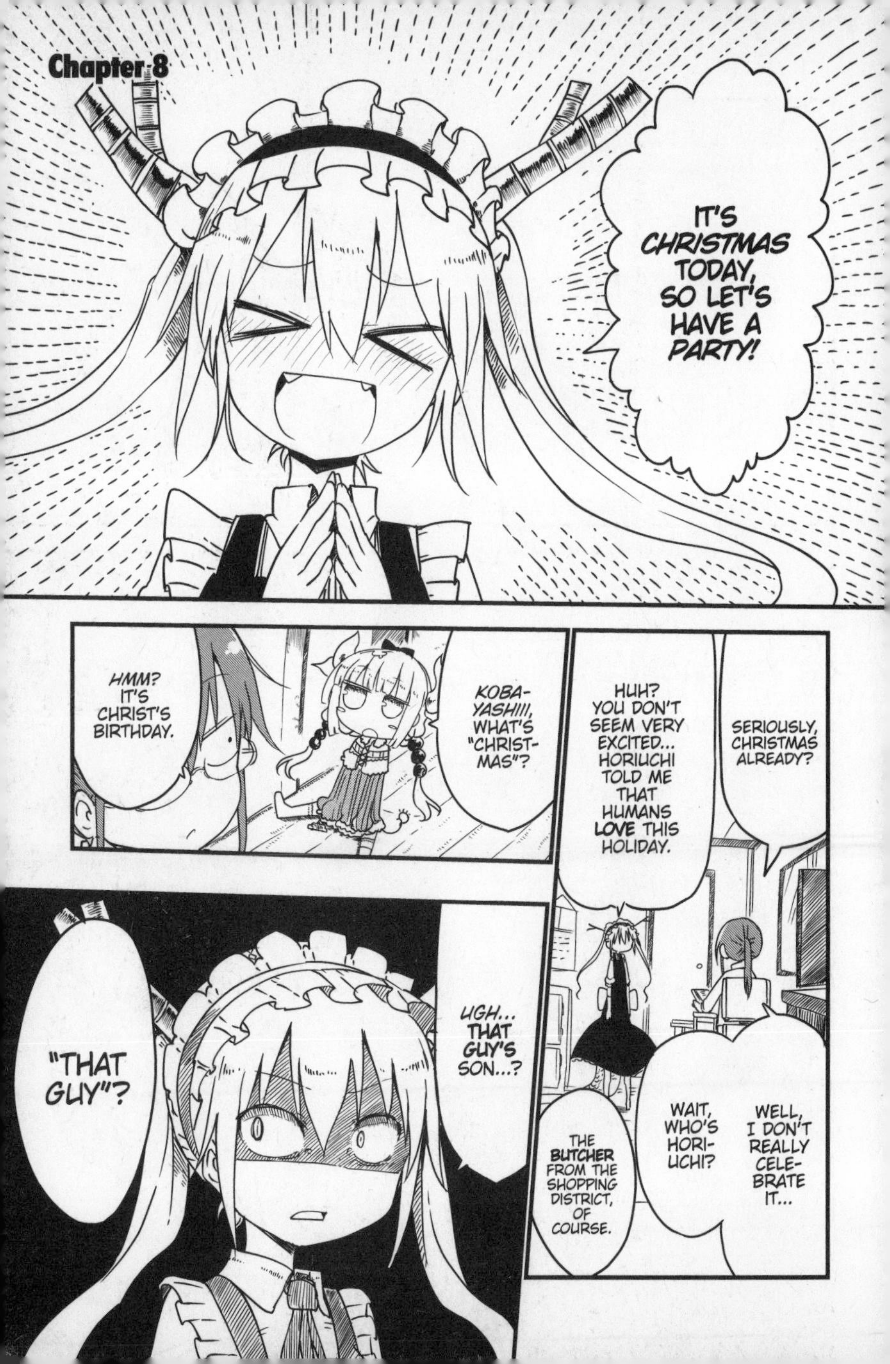
IT'S CHRISTMAS TODAY, SO LET'S HAVE A PARTY!
SERIOUSLY, CHRISTMAS ALREADY?
HUH? YOU DON'T SEEM VERY EXCITED... HORIUCHI TOLD ME THAT HUMANS LOVE THIS HOLIDAY.
WELL, I DON'T REALLY CELE-BRATE IT...
WAIT, WHO'S HORI-UCHI?
THE BUTCHER FROM THE SHOPPING DISTRICT, OF COURSE.
KOBA-YASHIII, WHAT'S "CHRIST-MAS"?
HMM? IT'S CHRIST'S BIRTHDAY.
UGH... THAT GUY'S SON...?
"THAT GUY"?

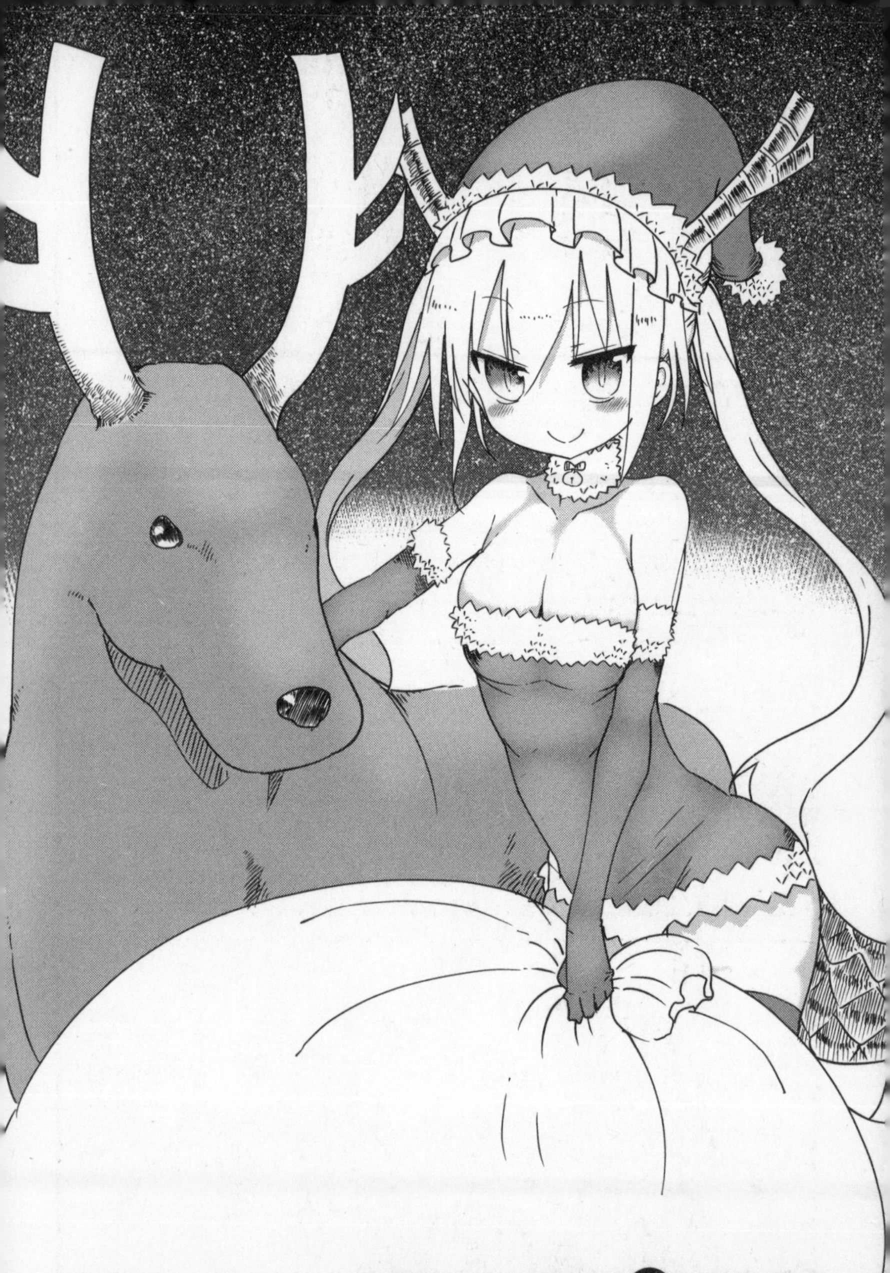

# CHAPTER 8 : TOHRU & CHRISTMAS

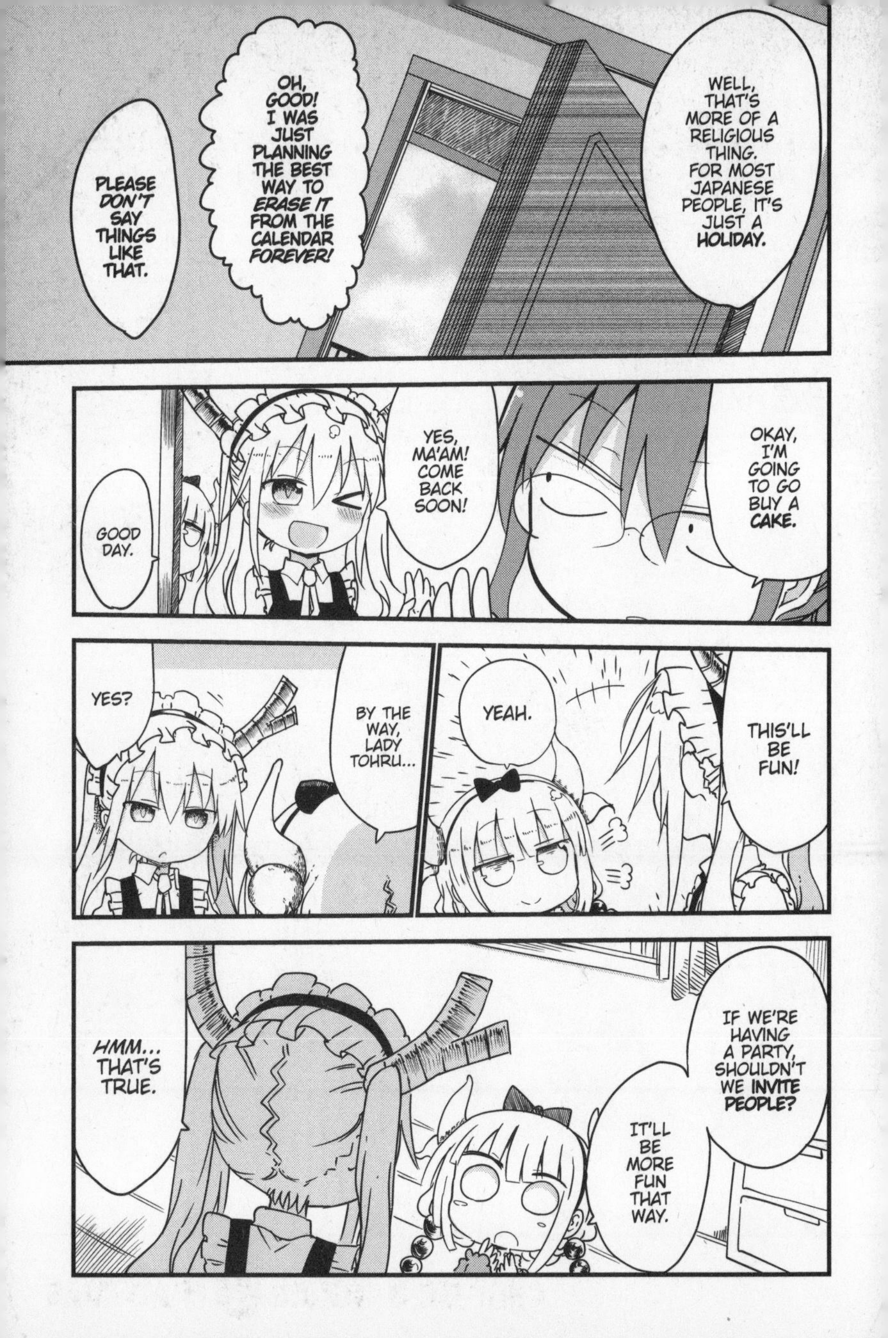
WELL, THAT'S MORE OF A RELIGIOUS THING. FOR MOST JAPANESE PEOPLE, IT'S JUST A HOLIDAY.
OH, GOOD! I WAS JUST PLANNING THE BEST WAY TO ERASE IT FROM THE CALENDAR FOREVER!
PLEASE DON'T SAY THINGS LIKE THAT.
OKAY, I'M GOING TO GO BUY A CAKE.
YES, MA'AM! COME BACK SOON!
GOOD DAY.
THIS'LL BE FUN!
YEAH.
BY THE WAY, LADY TOHRU...
YES?
IF WE'RE HAVING A PARTY, SHOULDN'T WE INVITE PEOPLE?
IT'LL BE MORE FUN THAT WAY.
HMM... THAT'S TRUE.

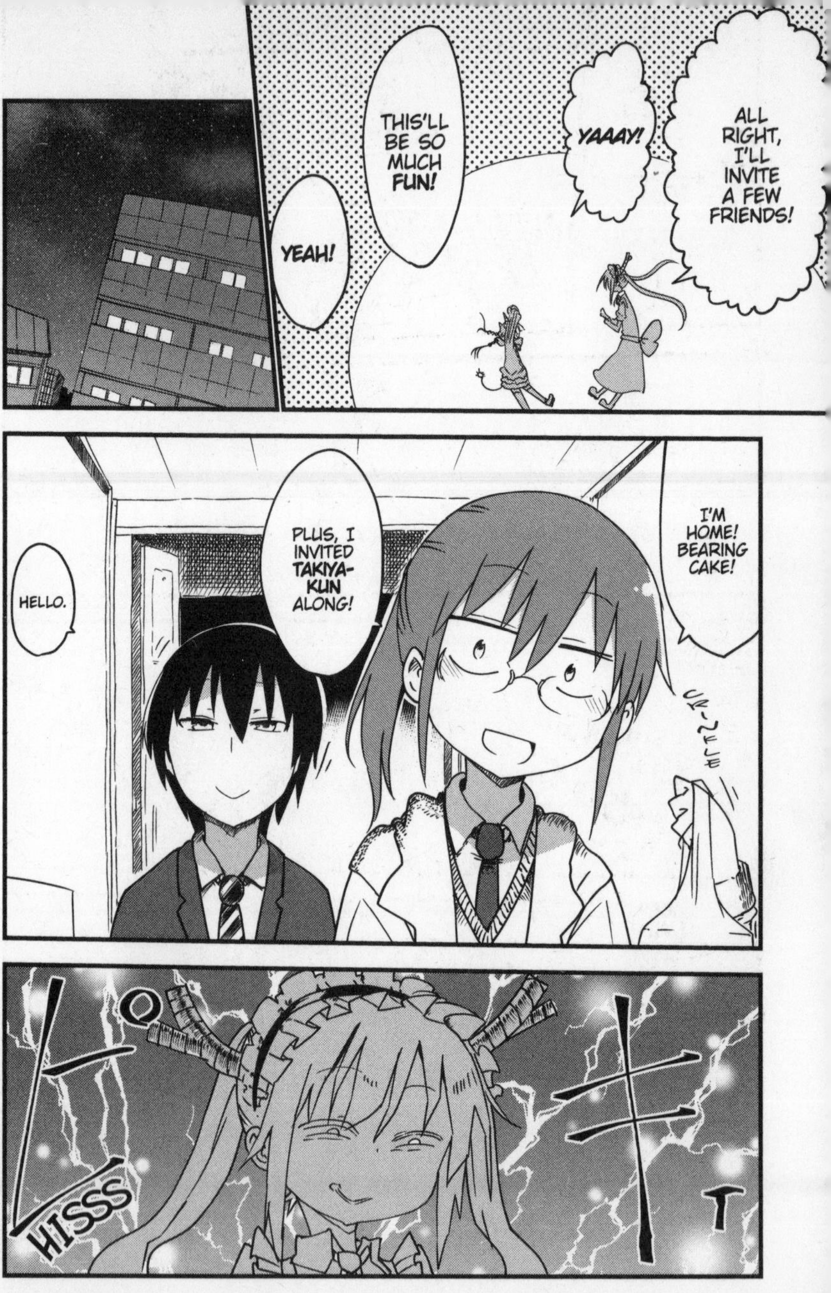
ALL RIGHT, I'LL INVITE A FEW FRIENDS!
YAAAY!
THIS'LL BE SO MUCH FUN!
YEAH!
I'M HOME! BEARING CAKE!
PLUS, I INVITED TAKIYA-KUN ALONG!
HELLO.
HISSS

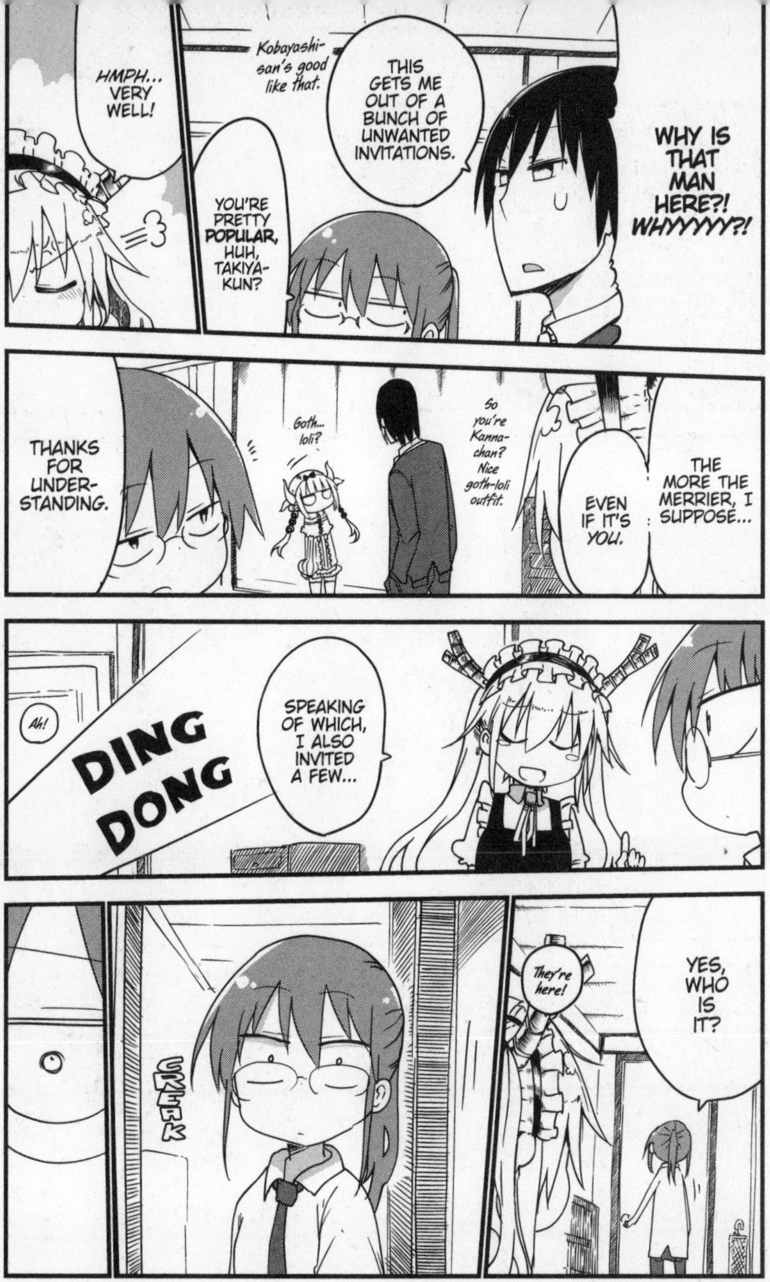
WHY IS THAT MAN HERE?! WHYYYYY?!
THIS GETS ME OUT OF A BUNCH OF UNWANTED INVITATIONS.
Kobayashi-san's good like that.
YOU'RE PRETTY POPULAR, HUH, TAKIYA-KUN?
HMPH... VERY WELL!
THE MORE THE MERRIER, I SUPPOSE...
EVEN IF IT'S YOU.
So you're Kanna-chan? Nice goth-loli outfit.
Goth... loli?
THANKS FOR UNDER-STANDING.
SPEAKING OF WHICH, I ALSO INVITED A FEW...
DING DONG
Ah!
YES, WHO IS IT?
They're here!
CREAK

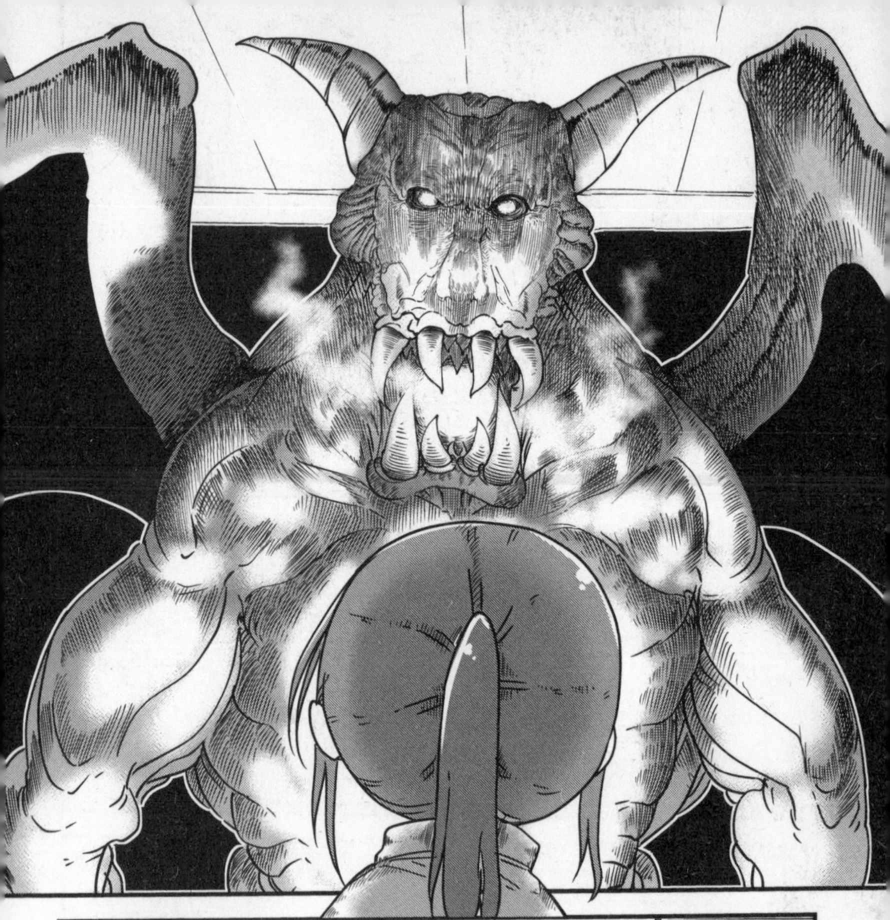
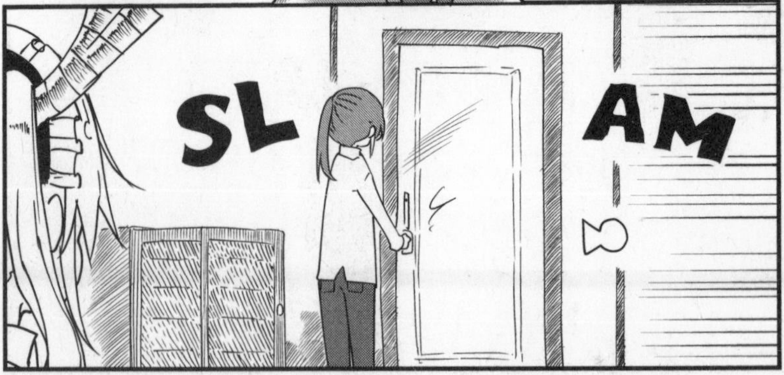
SL AM

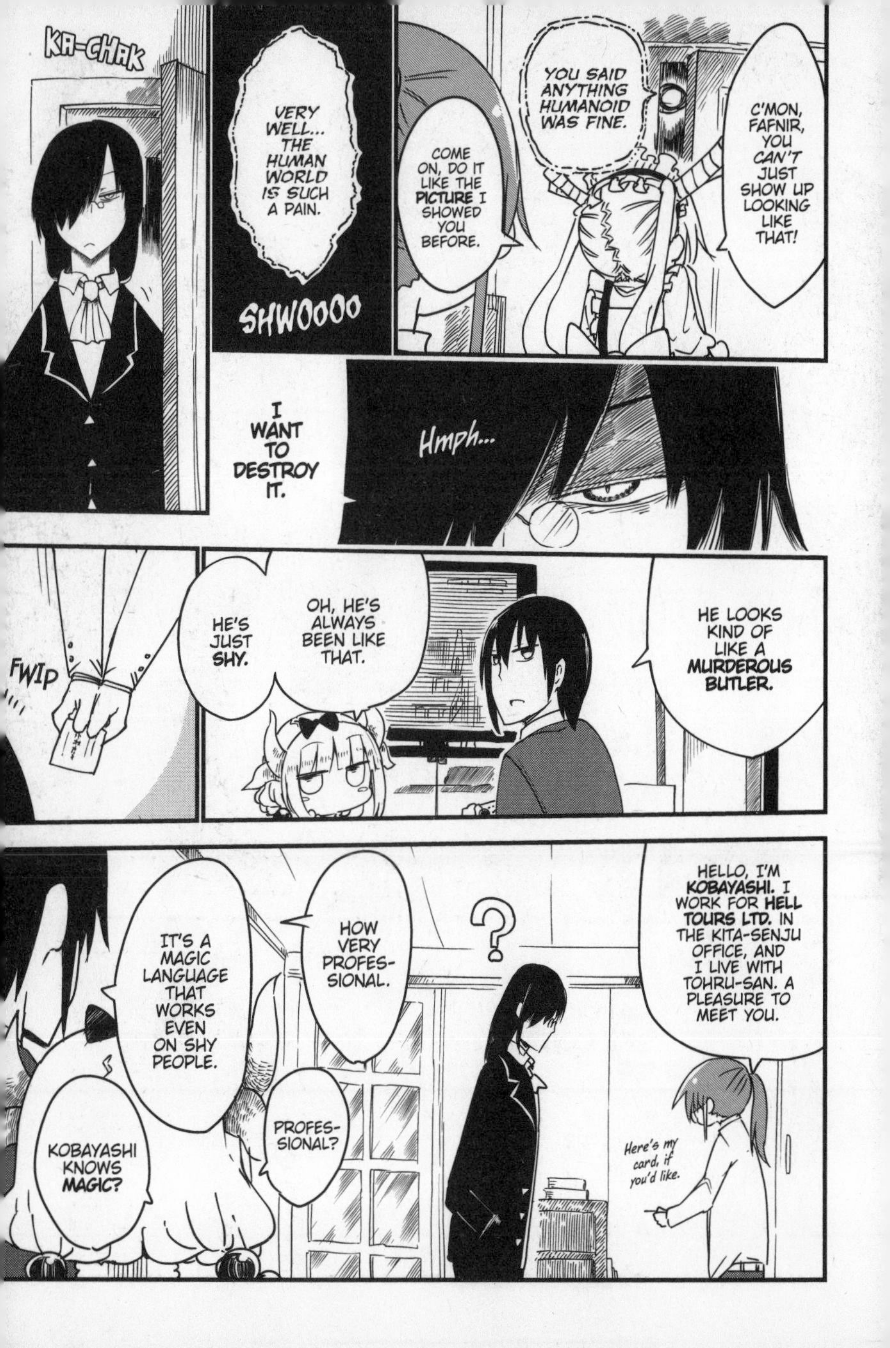
C'MON, FAFNIR, YOU CAN'T JUST SHOW UP LOOKING LIKE THAT!
YOU SAID ANYTHING HUMANOID WAS FINE.
COME ON, DO IT LIKE THE PICTURE I SHOWED YOU BEFORE.
VERY WELL... THE HUMAN WORLD IS SUCH A PAIN.
SHWOOOO
Hmph...
I WANT TO DESTROY IT.
KA-CHAK
HE LOOKS KIND OF LIKE A MURDEROUS BUTLER.
OH, HE'S ALWAYS BEEN LIKE THAT.
HE'S JUST SHY.
FWIP
HELLO, I'M KOBAYASHI. I WORK FOR HELL TOURS LTD. IN THE KITA-SENJU OFFICE, AND I LIVE WITH TOHRU-SAN. A PLEASURE TO MEET YOU.
Here's my card, if you'd like.
?
HOW VERY PROFES-SIONAL.
PROFES-SIONAL?
IT'S A MAGIC LANGUAGE THAT WORKS EVEN ON SHY PEOPLE.
KOBAYASHI KNOWS MAGIC?

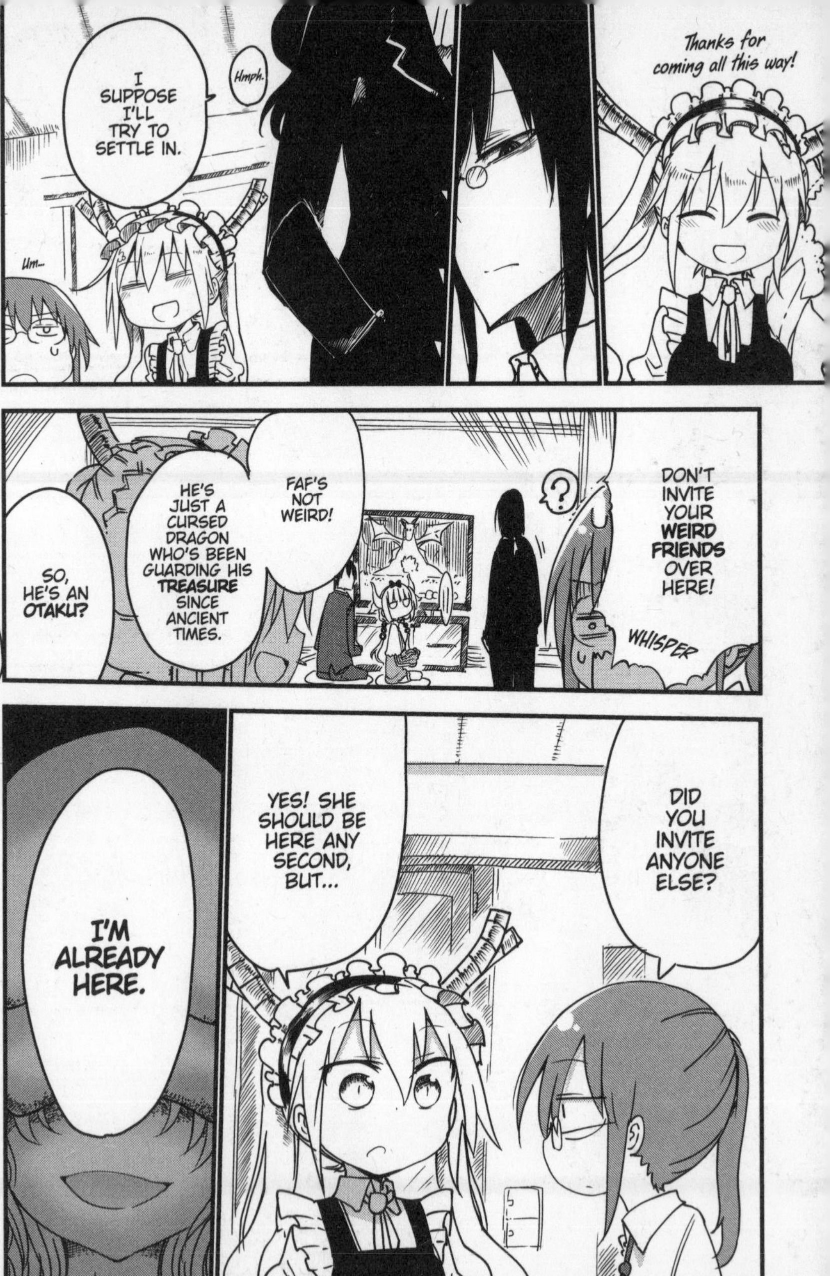
Thanks for coming all this way!
Hmph.
I SUPPOSE I'LL TRY TO SETTLE IN.
Um...
DON'T INVITE YOUR WEIRD FRIENDS OVER HERE!
?
WHISPER
FAF'S NOT WEIRD!
HE'S JUST A CURSED DRAGON WHO'S BEEN GUARDING HIS TREASURE SINCE ANCIENT TIMES.
SO, HE'S AN OTAKU?
Pretty much.
DID YOU INVITE ANYONE ELSE?
YES! SHE SHOULD BE HERE ANY SECOND, BUT...
I'M ALREADY HERE.

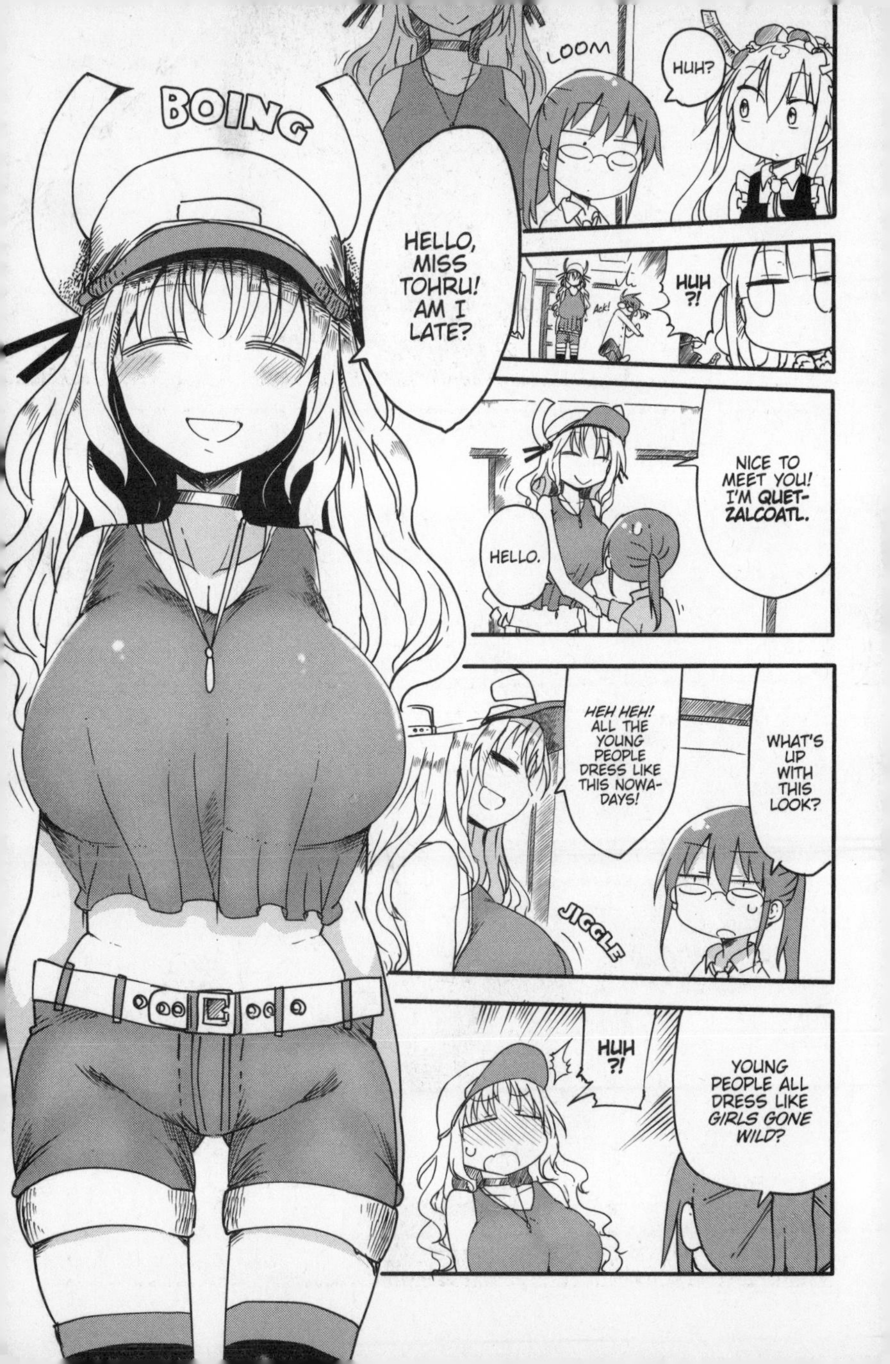
HUH?
LOOM
HUH ?!
Ack!
NICE TO MEET YOU! I'M QUETZALCOATL.
HELLO.
WHAT'S UP WITH THIS LOOK?
HEH HEH! ALL THE YOUNG PEOPLE DRESS LIKE THIS NOWADAYS!
JIGGLE
YOUNG PEOPLE ALL DRESS LIKE *GIRLS GONE WILD?*
HUH ?!
BOING
HELLO, MISS TOHRU! AM I LATE?

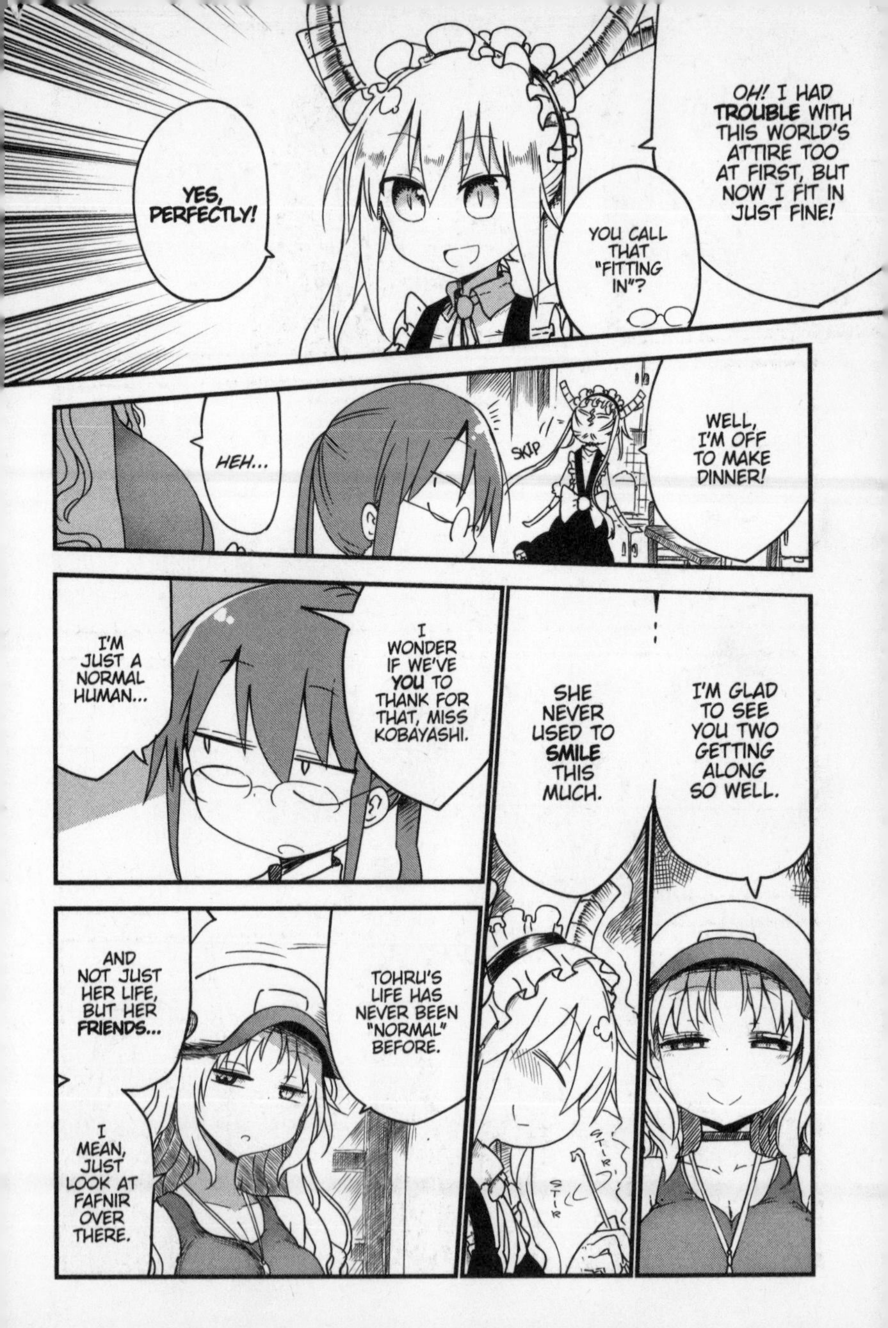

OH! I HAD TROUBLE WITH THIS WORLD'S ATTIRE TOO AT FIRST, BUT NOW I FIT IN JUST FINE!
YOU CALL THAT "FITTING IN"?
YES, PERFECTLY!
WELL, I'M OFF TO MAKE DINNER!
SKIP
HEH...
!
I'M GLAD TO SEE YOU TWO GETTING ALONG SO WELL.
SHE NEVER USED TO SMILE THIS MUCH.
I WONDER IF WE'VE YOU TO THANK FOR THAT, MISS KOBAYASHI.
I'M JUST A NORMAL HUMAN...
STIR
STIR
TOHRU'S LIFE HAS NEVER BEEN "NORMAL" BEFORE.
AND NOT JUST HER LIFE, BUT HER FRIENDS...
I MEAN, JUST LOOK AT FAFNIR OVER THERE.

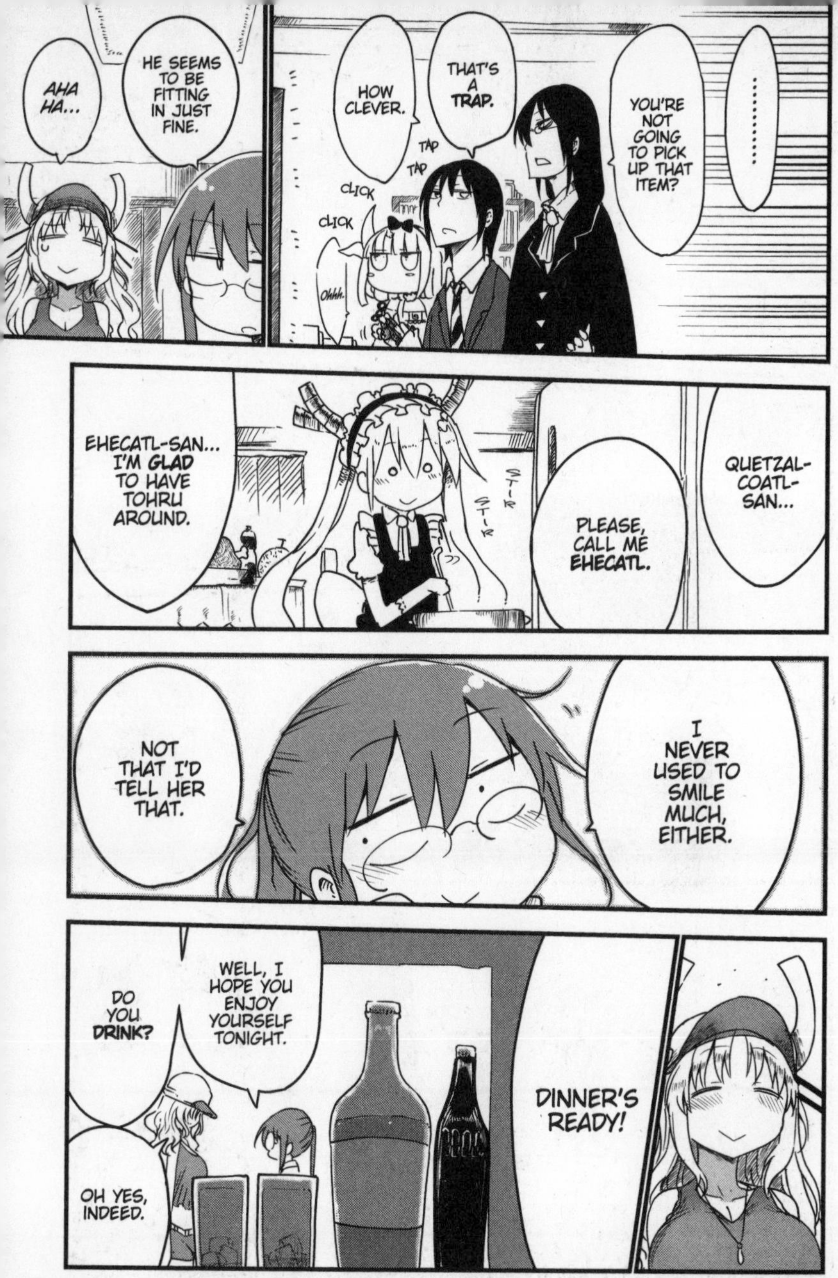
......
YOU'RE NOT GOING TO PICK UP THAT ITEM?
THAT'S A TRAP.
TAP TAP
HOW CLEVER.
CLICK CLICK
Ohhh.
HE SEEMS TO BE FITTING IN JUST FINE.
AHA HA...
QUETZALCOATL-SAN...
PLEASE, CALL ME EHECATL.
STIR STIR
EHECATL-SAN... I'M GLAD TO HAVE TOHRU AROUND.
I NEVER USED TO SMILE MUCH, EITHER.
NOT THAT I'D TELL HER THAT.
DINNER'S READY!
WELL, I HOPE YOU ENJOY YOURSELF TONIGHT.
DO YOU DRINK?
OH YES, INDEED.

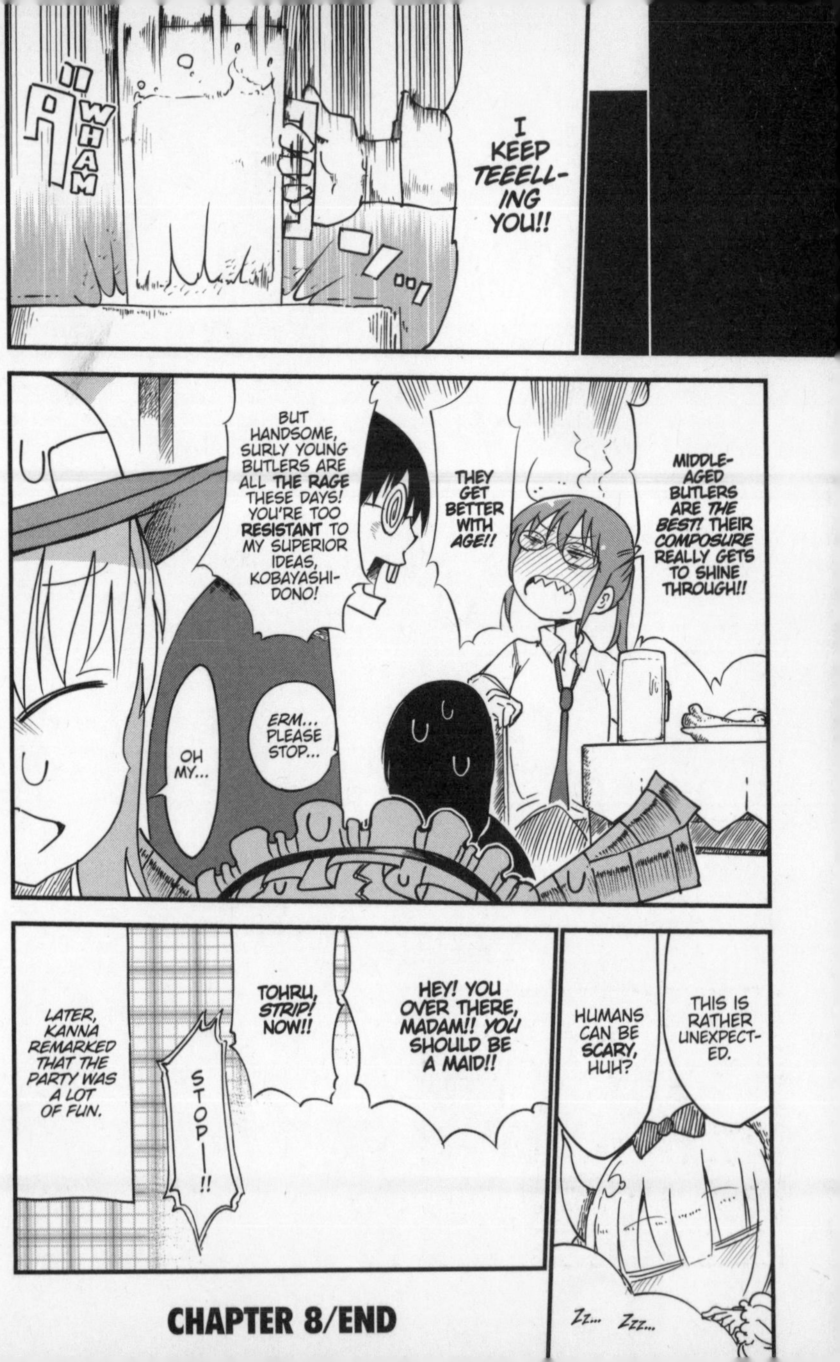
I KEEP TEEELLING YOU!!
WHAM
MIDDLE-AGED BUTLERS ARE THE BEST! THEIR COMPOSURE REALLY GETS TO SHINE THROUGH!!
THEY GET BETTER WITH AGE!!
BUT HANDSOME, SURLY YOUNG BUTLERS ARE ALL THE RAGE THESE DAYS! YOU'RE TOO RESISTANT TO MY SUPERIOR IDEAS, KOBAYASHI-DONO!
ERM... PLEASE STOP...
OH MY...
THIS IS RATHER UNEXPECTED.
HUMANS CAN BE SCARY, HUH?
Zz... Zzz...
HEY! YOU OVER THERE, MADAM!! YOU SHOULD BE A MAID!!
TOHRU, STRIP! NOW!!
STOP—!!
LATER, KANNA REMARKED THAT THE PARTY WAS A LOT OF FUN.

**CHAPTER 8/END**

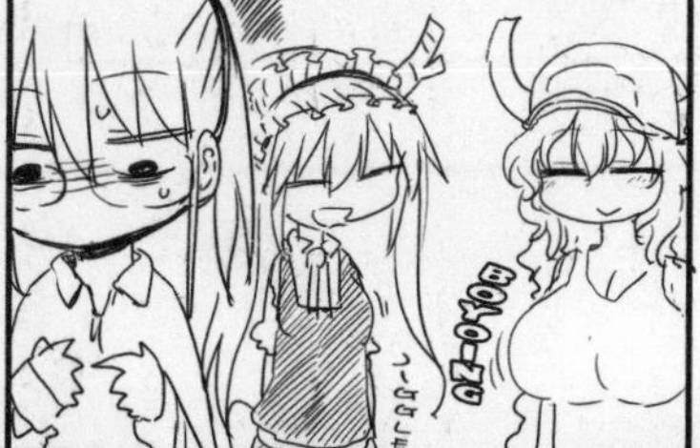
BOYO-ING!!

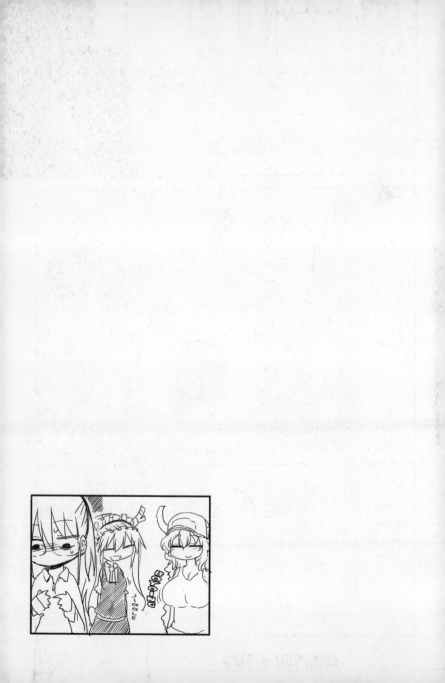

Miss Kobayashi's
Dragon Maid

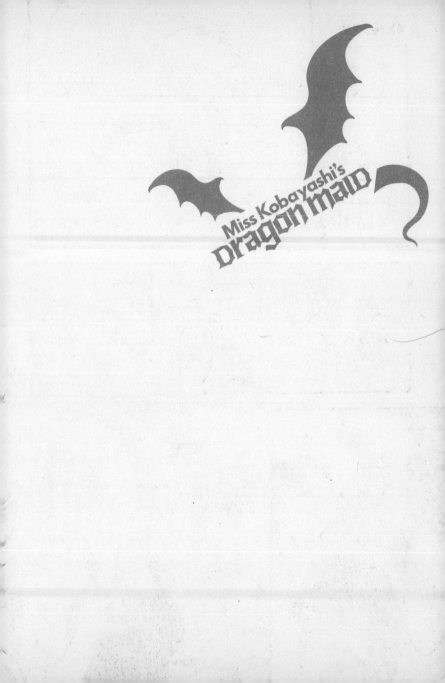

# Chapter 9

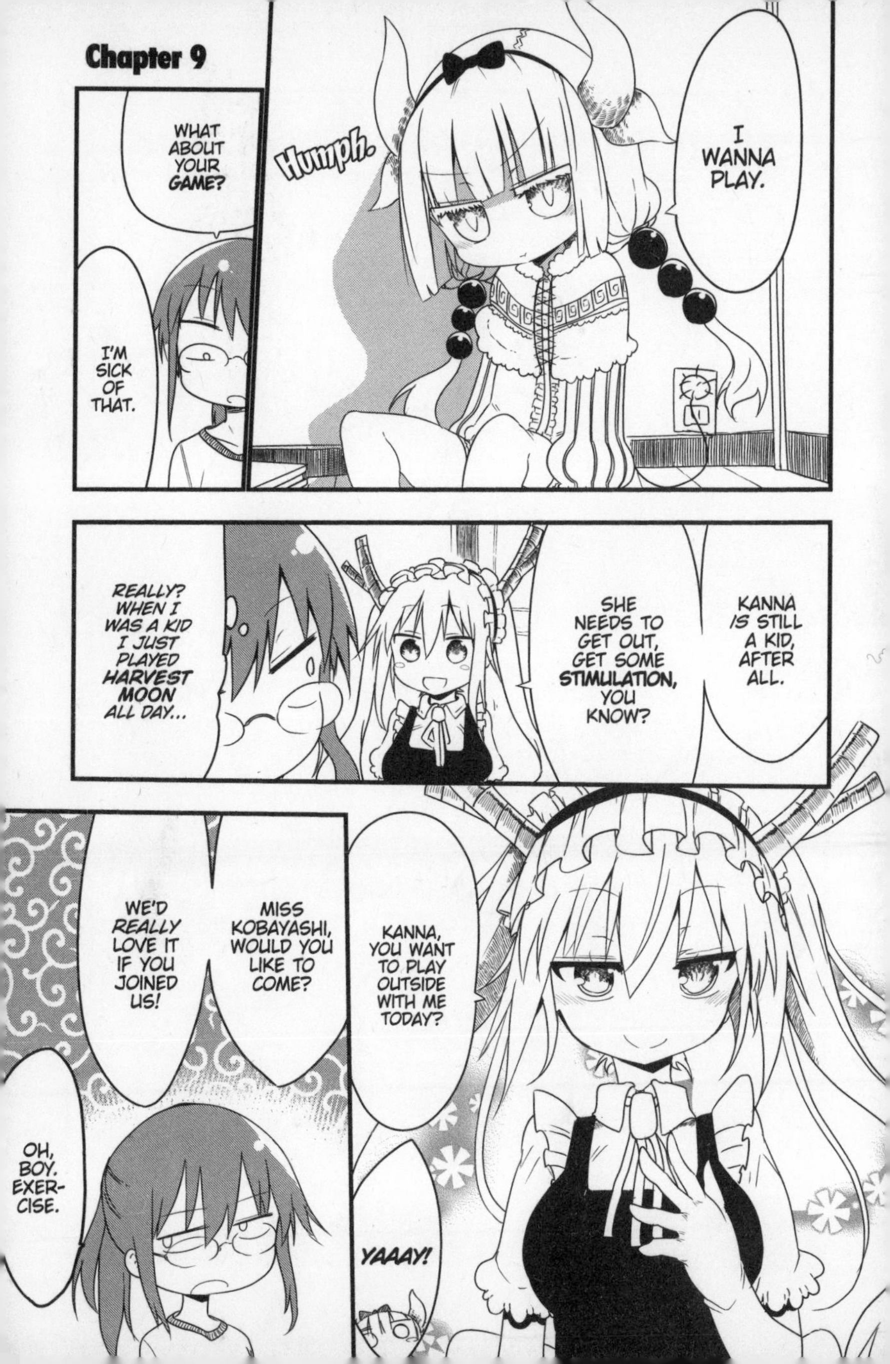
I WANNA PLAY.
Humph.
WHAT ABOUT YOUR GAME?
I'M SICK OF THAT.
KANNA IS STILL A KID, AFTER ALL.
SHE NEEDS TO GET OUT, GET SOME STIMULATION, YOU KNOW?
REALLY? WHEN I WAS A KID I JUST PLAYED HARVEST MOON ALL DAY...
KANNA, YOU WANT TO PLAY OUTSIDE WITH ME TODAY?
YAAAY!
MISS KOBAYASHI, WOULD YOU LIKE TO COME?
WE'D REALLY LOVE IT IF YOU JOINED US!
OH, BOY. EXERCISE.

# CHAPTER 9: TOHRU & THE DANGEROUS GAME

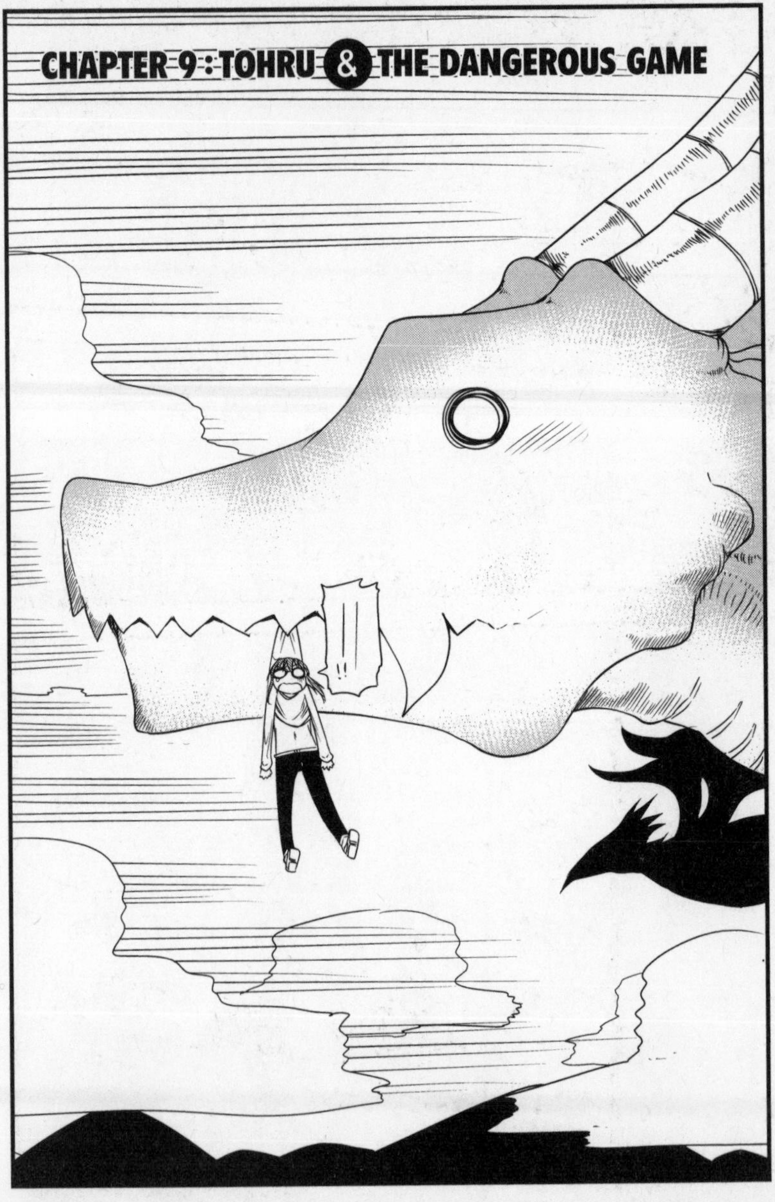
!!

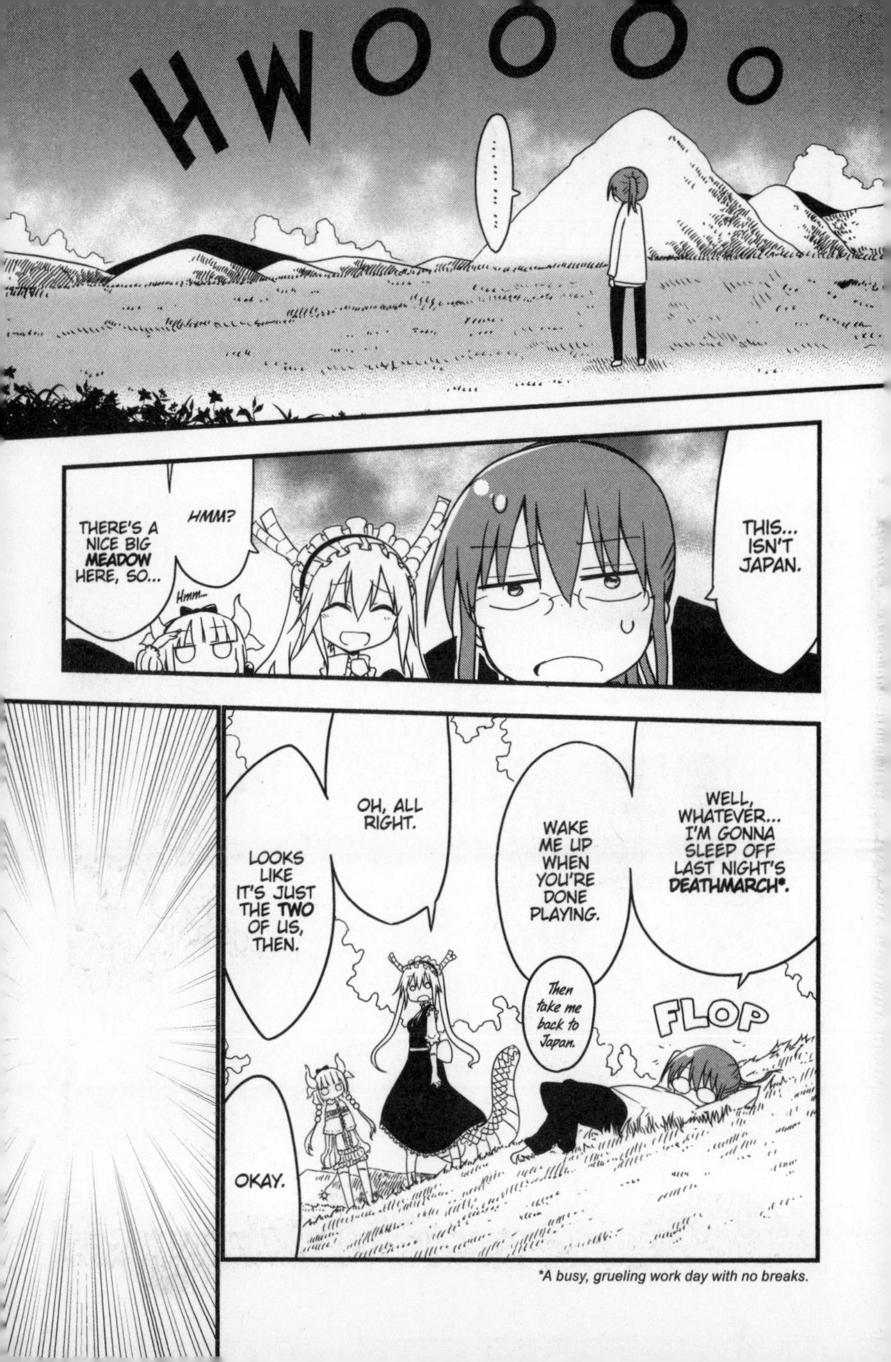
HWOOOO
……
THIS... ISN'T JAPAN.
HMM?
THERE'S A NICE BIG MEADOW HERE, SO...
Hmm...
WELL, WHATEVER... I'M GONNA SLEEP OFF LAST NIGHT'S DEATHMARCH*.
WAKE ME UP WHEN YOU'RE DONE PLAYING.
Then take me back to Japan.
FLOP
OH, ALL RIGHT.
LOOKS LIKE IT'S JUST THE TWO OF US, THEN.
OKAY.

*A busy, grueling work day with no breaks.

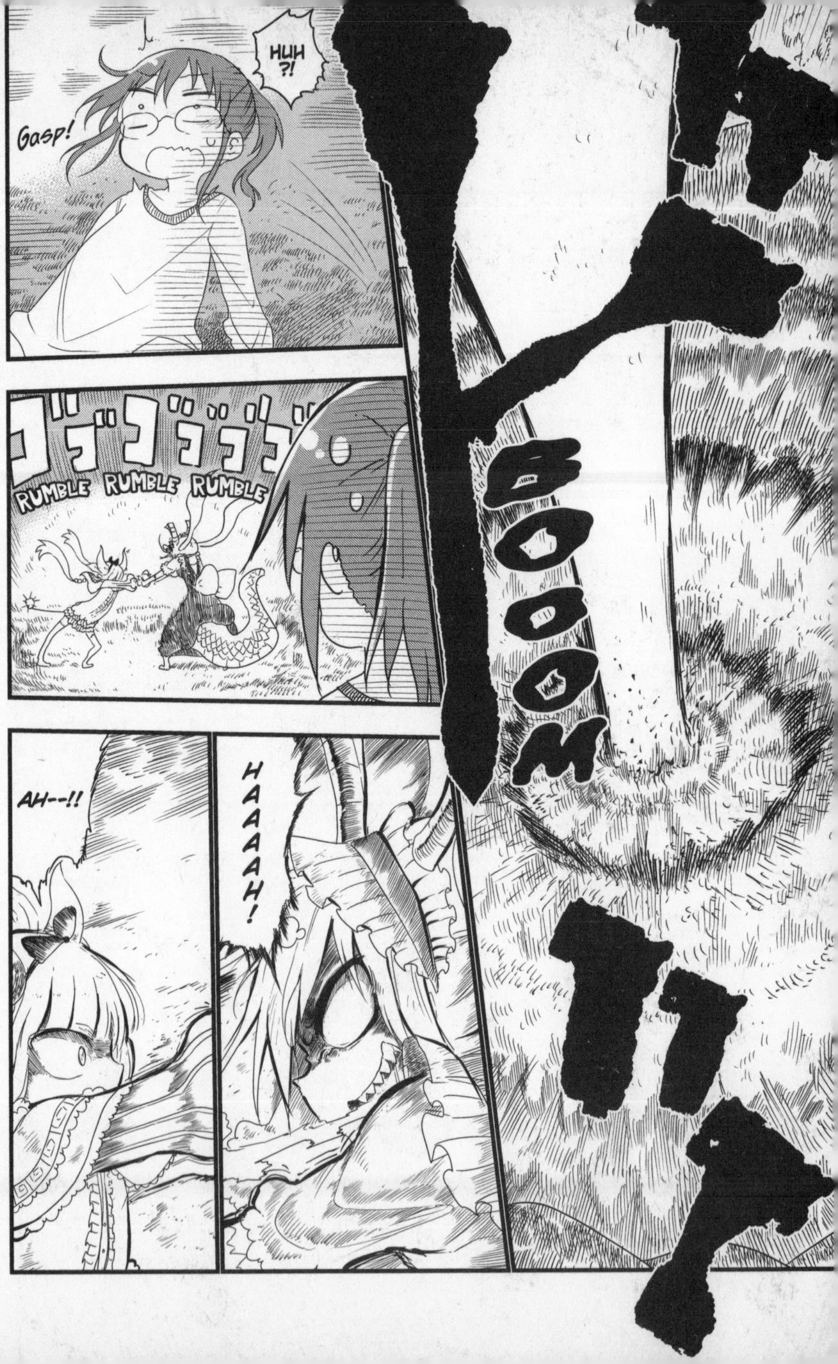
BOOOOM
HUH ?!
Gasp!
RUMBLE RUMBLE RUMBLE
HAAAAAH!
AH--!!

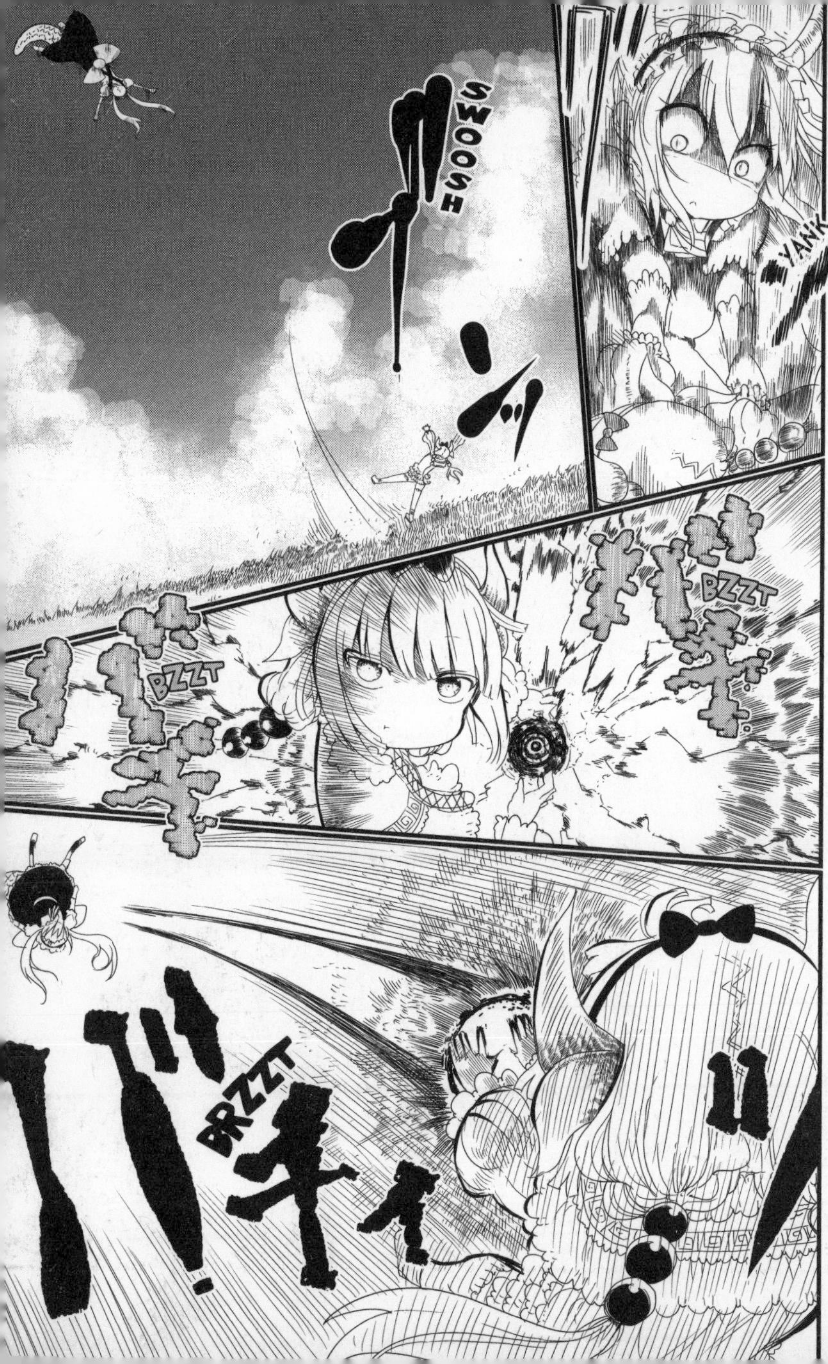
YANK
SWOOSH
BZZT
BZZT
BRZZT

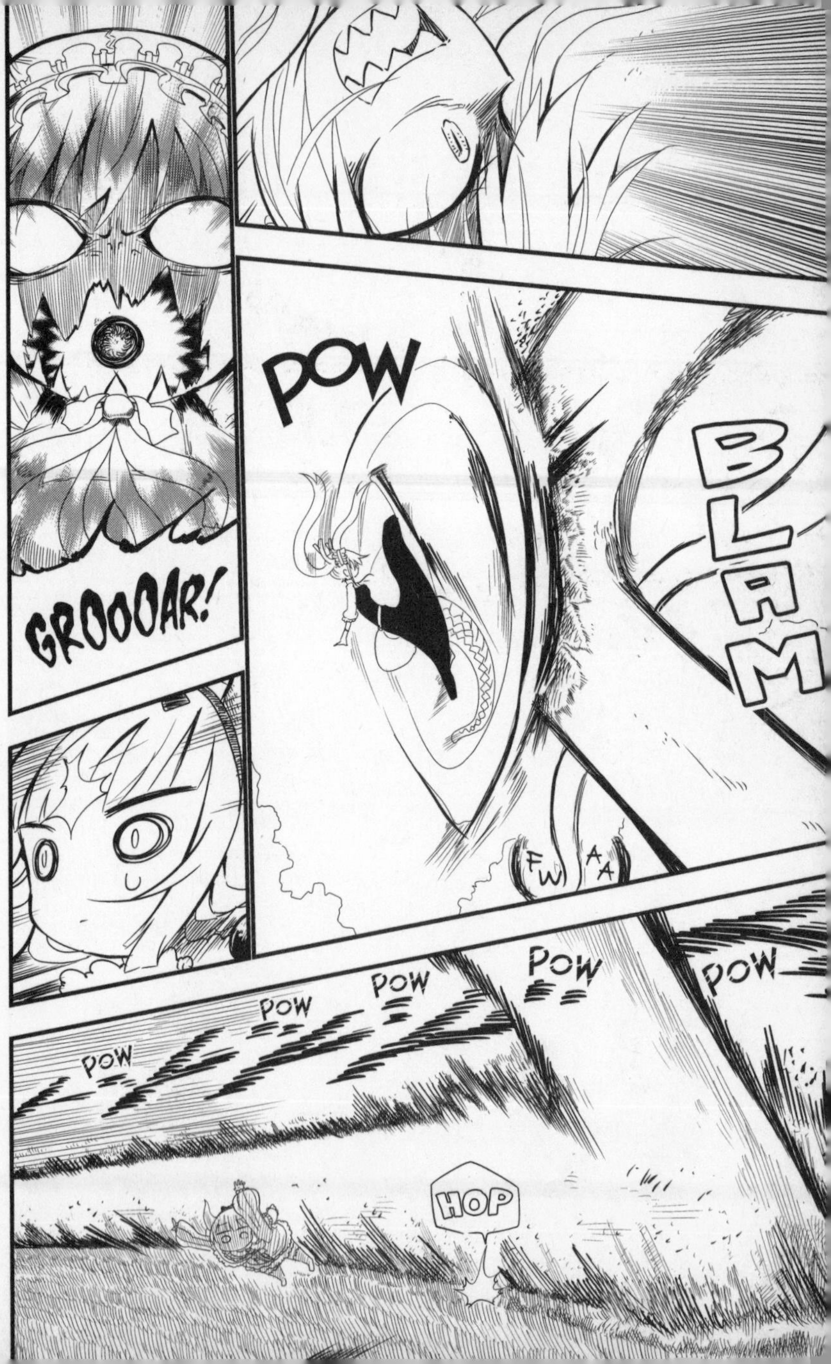

BLAM
POW
FWAA
GROOOAR!
POW
POW
POW
POW
POW
HOP

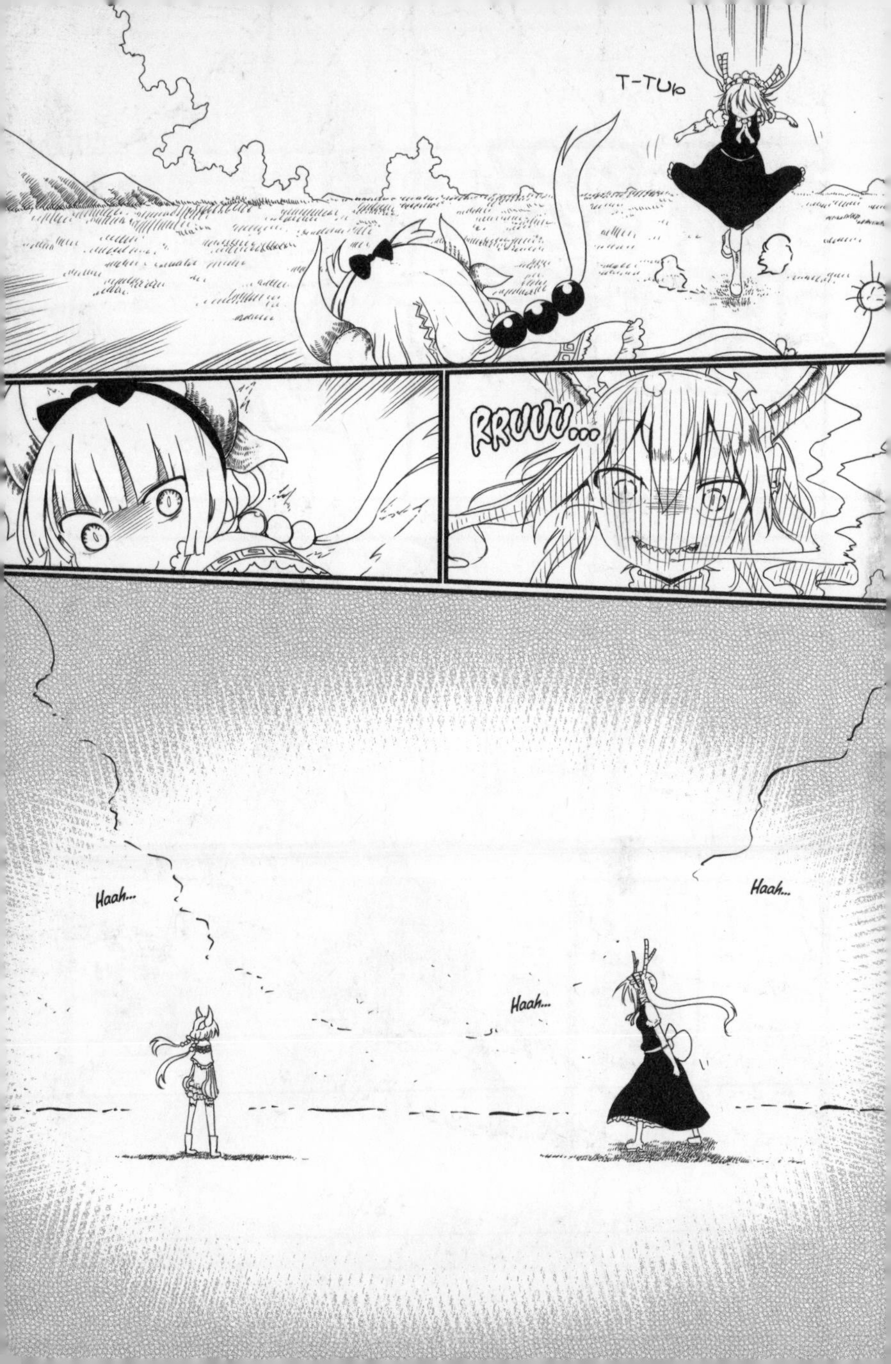
T-TUp
RRUUU...
Haah...
Haah...
Haah...

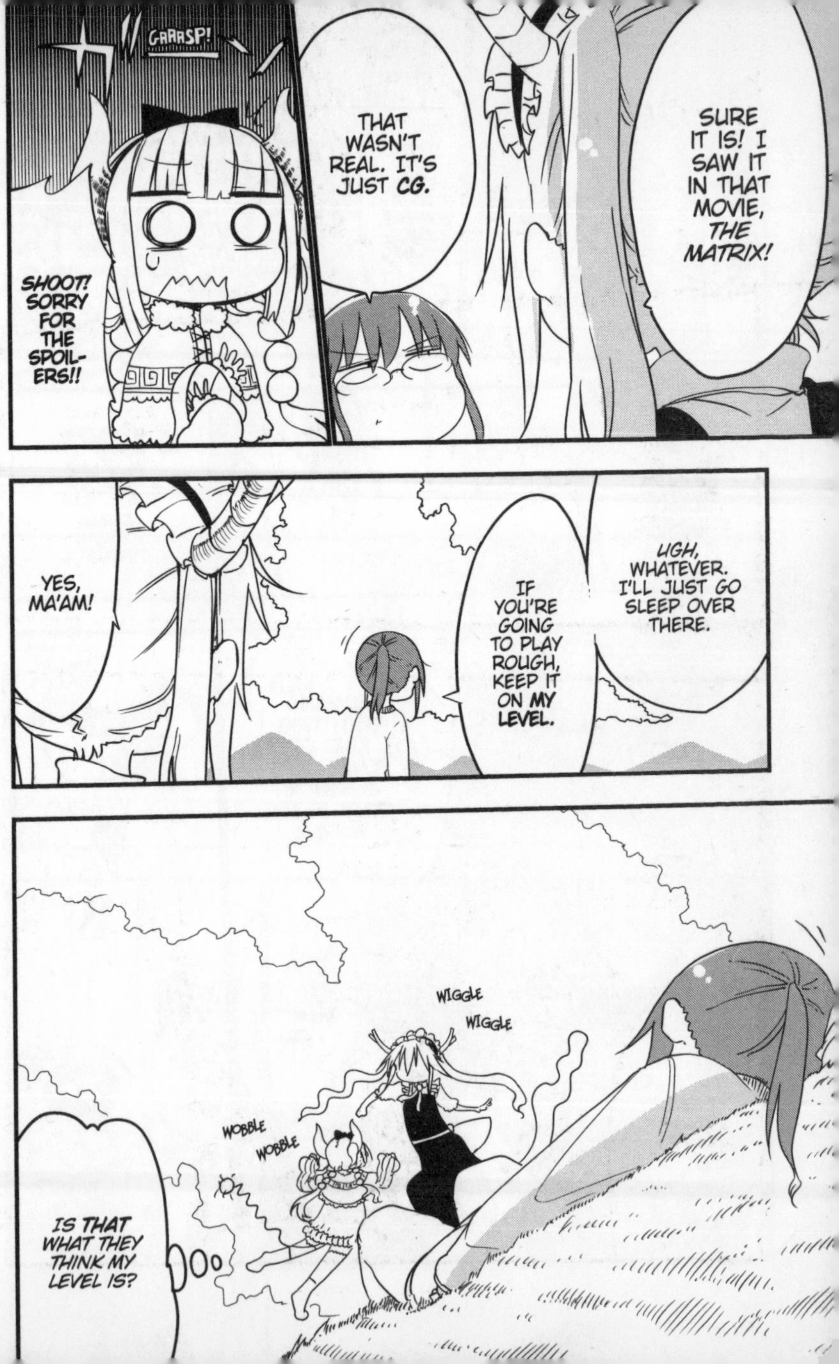
SURE IT IS! I SAW IT IN THAT MOVIE, THE MATRIX!
THAT WASN'T REAL. IT'S JUST CG.
GAAASP!
SHOOT! SORRY FOR THE SPOIL-ERS!!
UGH, WHATEVER. I'LL JUST GO SLEEP OVER THERE.
IF YOU'RE GOING TO PLAY ROUGH, KEEP IT ON MY LEVEL.
YES, MA'AM!
WIGGLE
WIGGLE
WOBBLE
WOBBLE
IS THAT WHAT THEY THINK MY LEVEL IS?

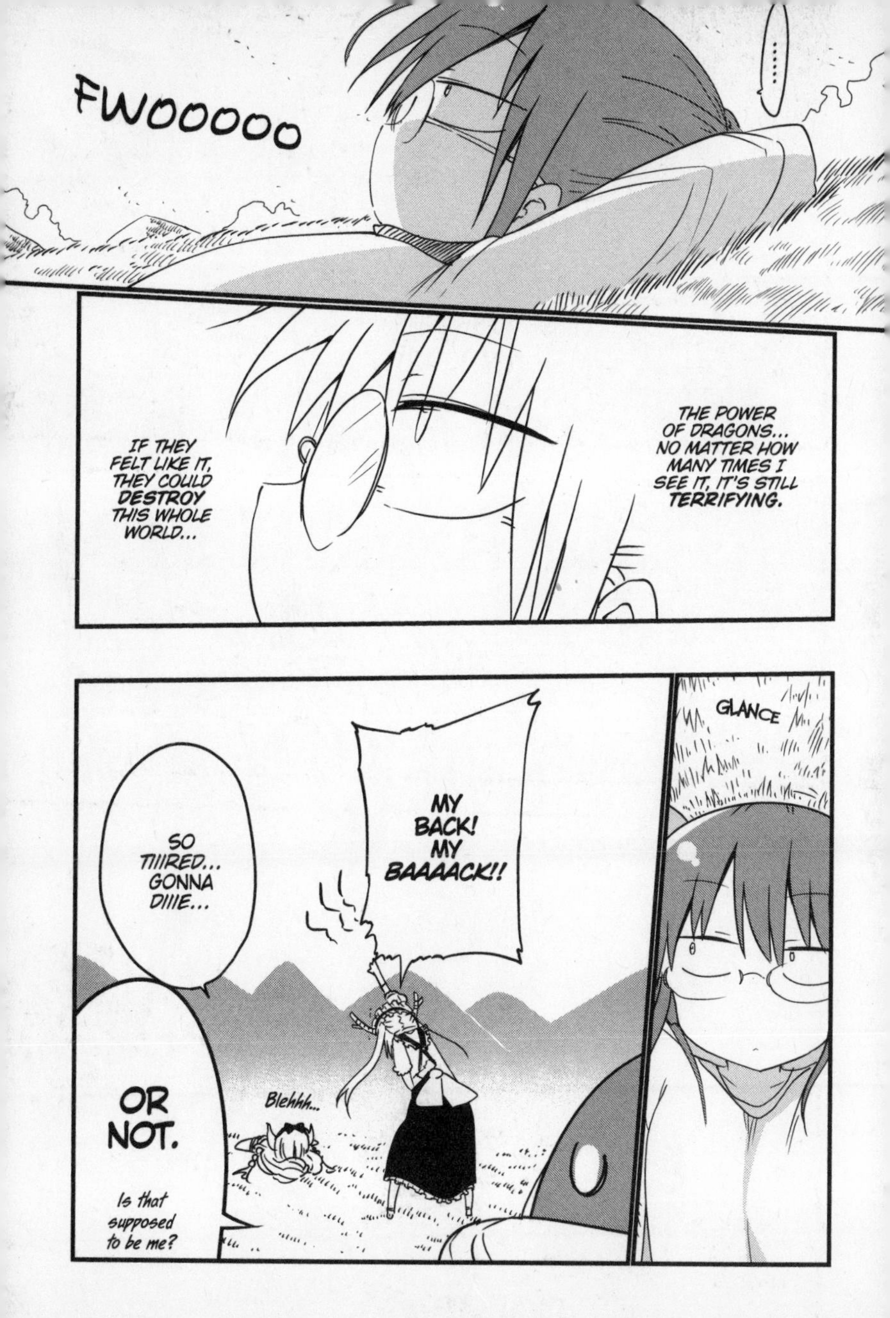
......
FWOOOOO
THE POWER OF DRAGONS... NO MATTER HOW MANY TIMES I SEE IT, IT'S STILL TERRIFYING.
IF THEY FELT LIKE IT, THEY COULD DESTROY THIS WHOLE WORLD...
GLANCE
MY BACK! MY BAAAACK!!
SO TIIIRED... GONNA DIIIE...
OR NOT.
Blehhh...
Is that supposed to be me?

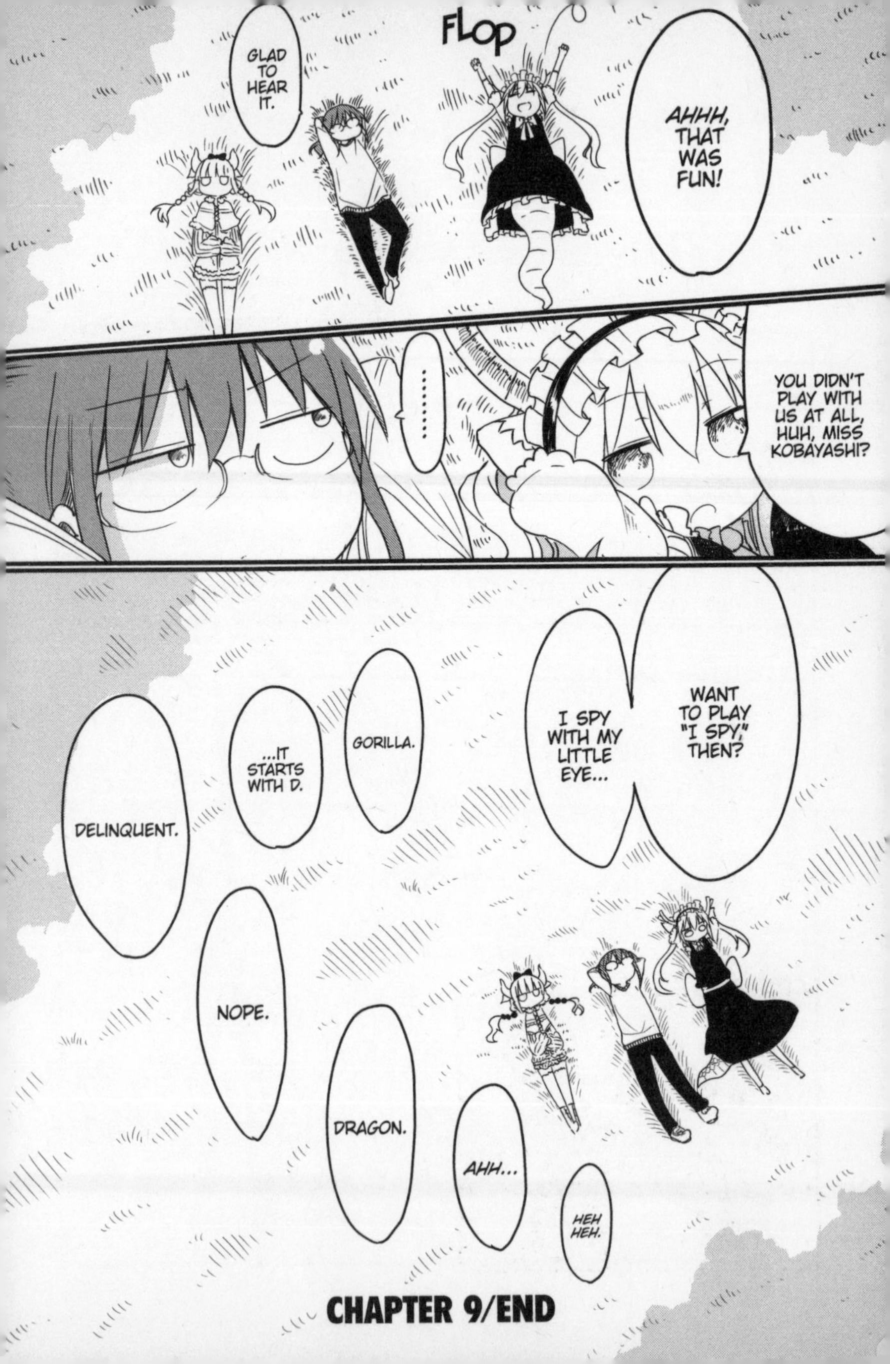
FLOP
AHHH, THAT WAS FUN!
GLAD TO HEAR IT.
YOU DIDN'T PLAY WITH US AT ALL, HUH, MISS KOBAYASHI?
......
WANT TO PLAY "I SPY," THEN?
I SPY WITH MY LITTLE EYE...
GORILLA.
...IT STARTS WITH D.
DELINQUENT.
NOPE.
DRAGON.
AHH...
HEH HEH.
CHAPTER 9/END

They really got into it for a while.
WIGGLE
......
WOBBLE

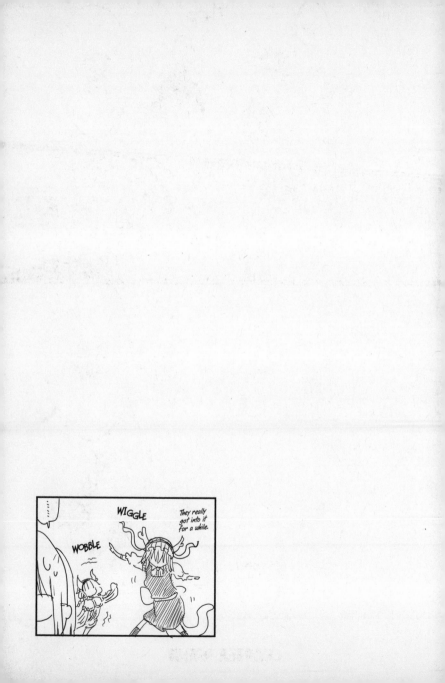

Miss Kobayashi's
Dragon Maid

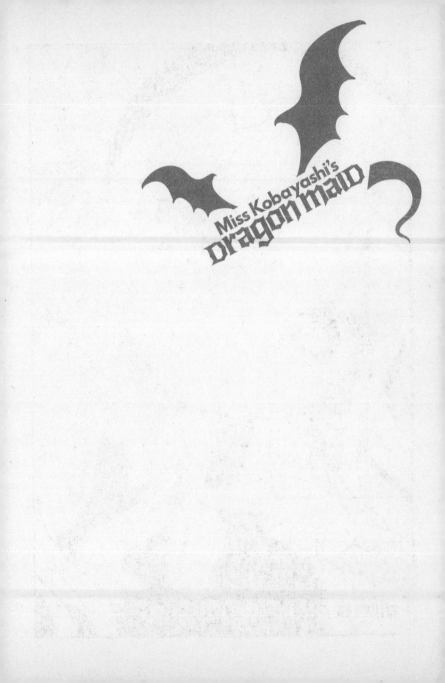

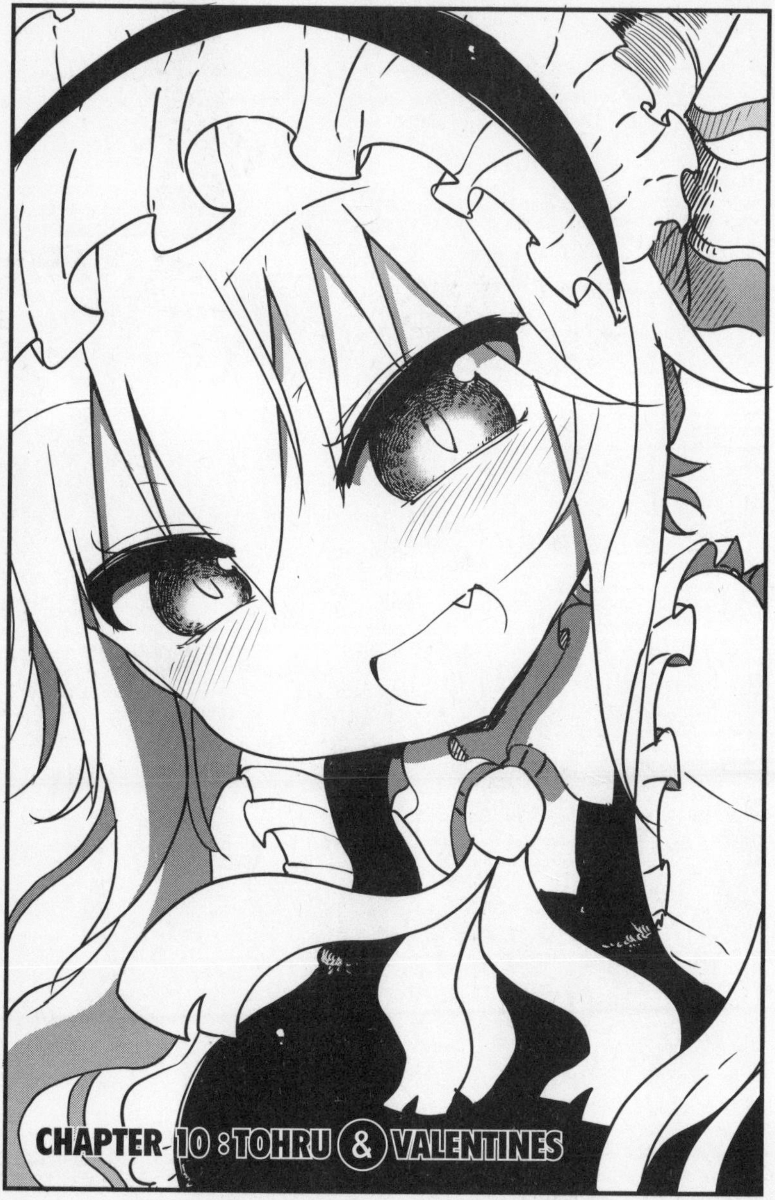
CHAPTER 10 : TOHRU & VALENTINES

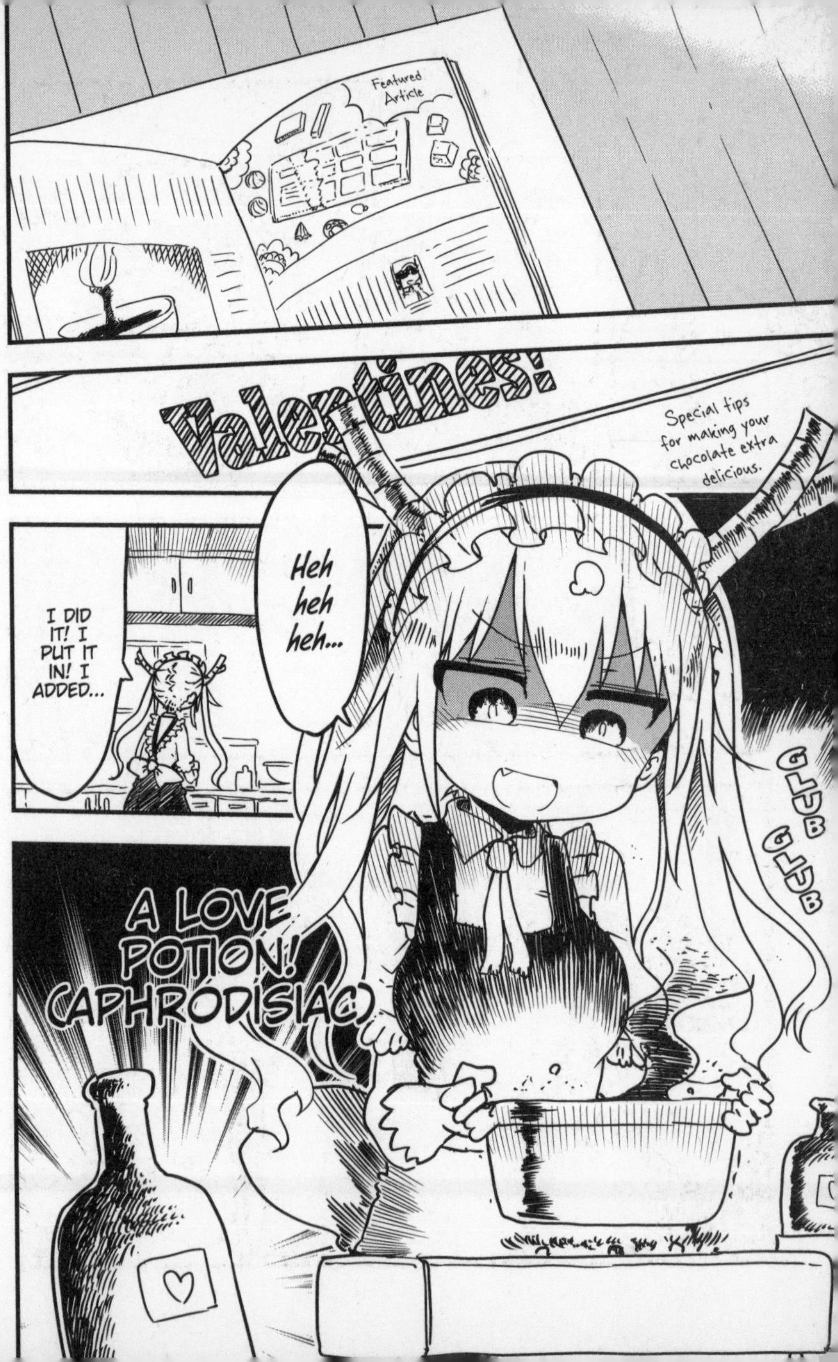
Featured Article
Valentines!
Special tips for making your chocolate extra delicious.
Heh heh heh...
GLUB GLUB
I DID IT! I PUT IT IN! I ADDED...
A LOVE POTION! (APHRODISIAC)

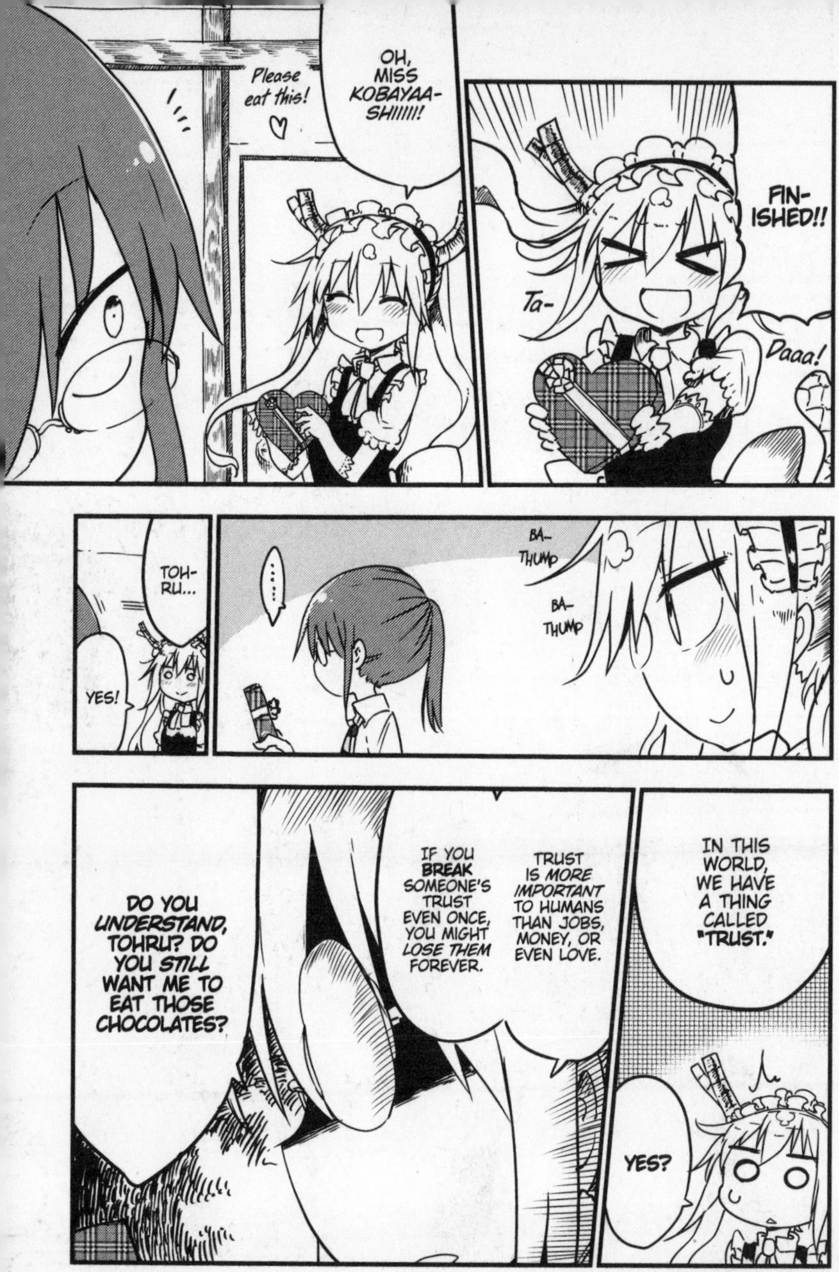
FIN-ISHED!!
Ta-
Daaa!
OH, MISS KOBAYAA-SHIIIIII!
Please eat this! ♡
BA-THUMP
BA-THUMP
...
TOHRU...
YES!
IN THIS WORLD, WE HAVE A THING CALLED "TRUST."
YES?
TRUST IS MORE IMPORTANT TO HUMANS THAN JOBS, MONEY, OR EVEN LOVE.
IF YOU BREAK SOMEONE'S TRUST EVEN ONCE, YOU MIGHT LOSE THEM FOREVER.
DO YOU UNDERSTAND, TOHRU? DO YOU STILL WANT ME TO EAT THOSE CHOCOLATES?

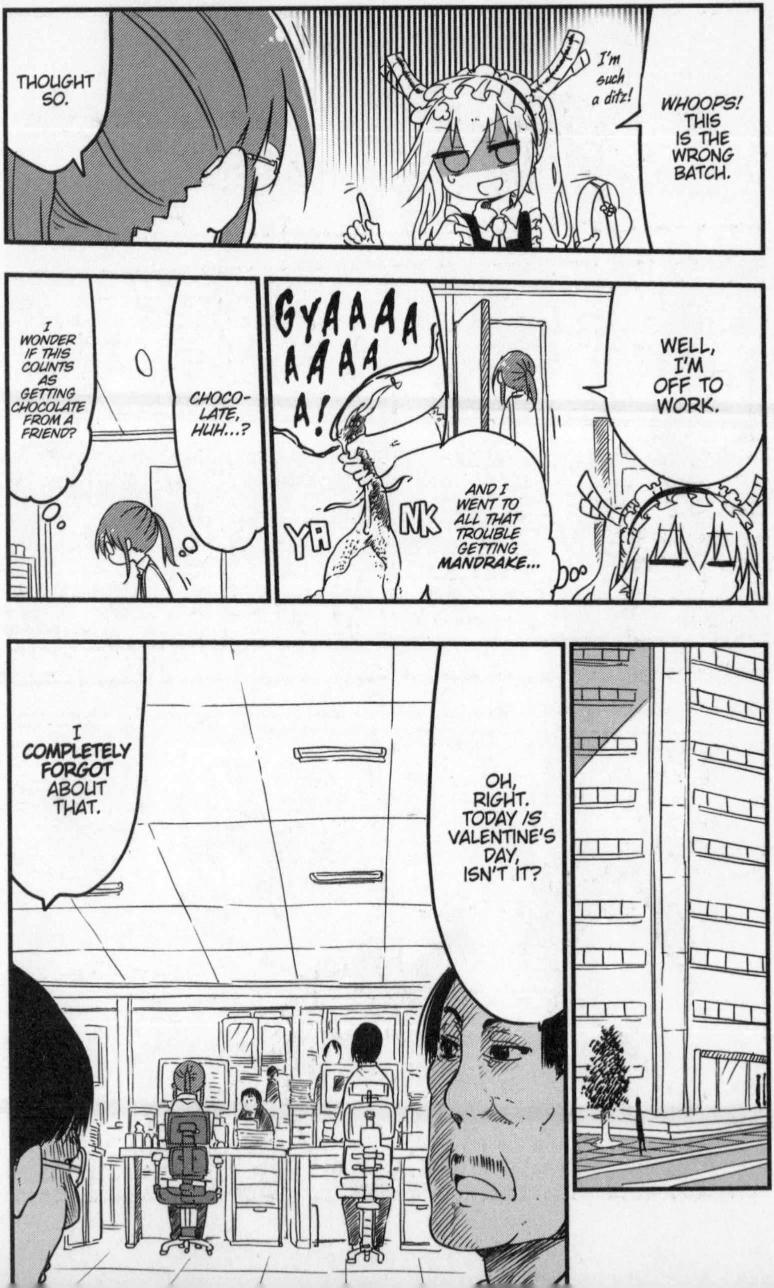
WHOOPS! THIS IS THE WRONG BATCH.
I'm such a ditz!
THOUGHT SO.
WELL, I'M OFF TO WORK.
AND I WENT TO ALL THAT TROUBLE GETTING MANDRAKE...
GYAAAAAAAAAA!
YANK
CHOCO-LATE, HUH...?
I WONDER IF THIS COUNTS AS GETTING CHOCOLATE FROM A FRIEND?
OH, RIGHT. TODAY IS VALENTINE'S DAY, ISN'T IT?
I COMPLETELY FORGOT ABOUT THAT.

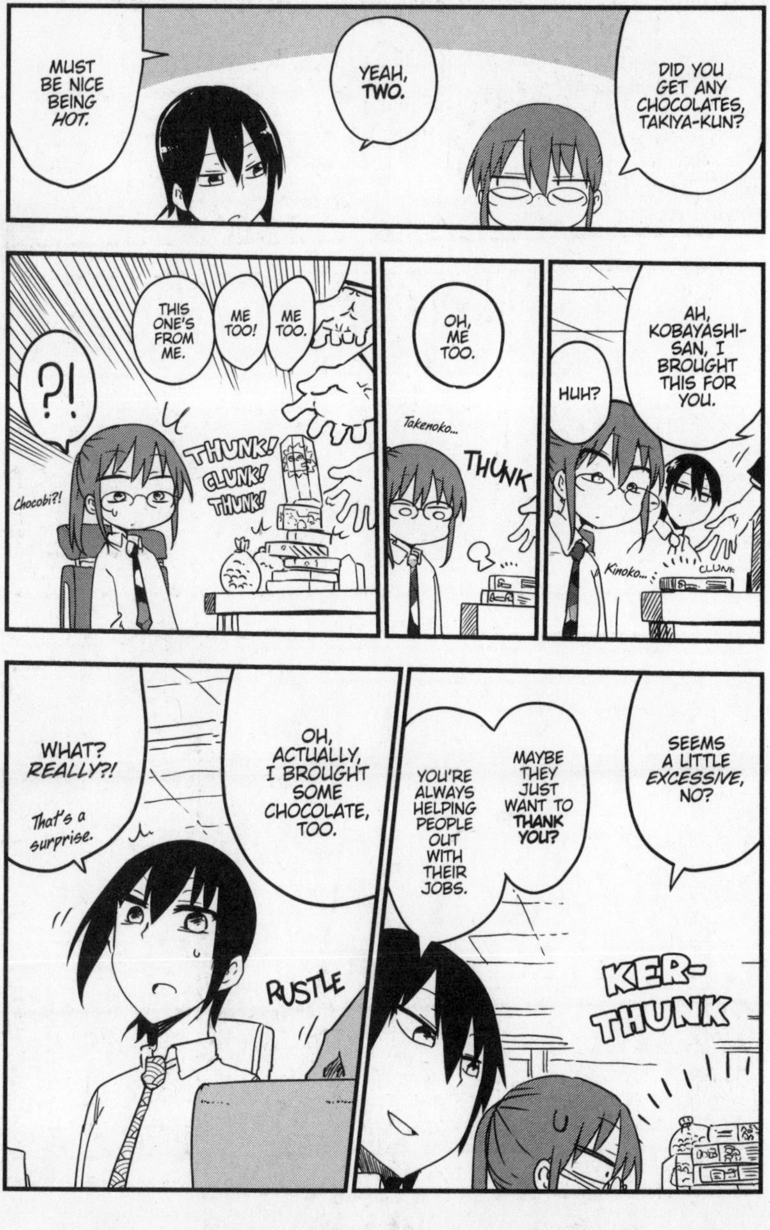
DID YOU GET ANY CHOCOLATES, TAKIYA-KUN?
YEAH, TWO.
MUST BE NICE BEING HOT.
AH, KOBAYASHI-SAN, I BROUGHT THIS FOR YOU.
HUH?
Kinoko...
CLUNK
OH, ME TOO.
Takenoko...
THUNK
ME TOO.
ME TOO!
THIS ONE'S FROM ME.
THUNK! CLUNK! THUNK!
?!
Chocobi?!
SEEMS A LITTLE EXCESSIVE, NO?
MAYBE THEY JUST WANT TO THANK YOU?
YOU'RE ALWAYS HELPING PEOPLE OUT WITH THEIR JOBS.
KER-THUNK
OH, ACTUALLY, I BROUGHT SOME CHOCOLATE, TOO.
WHAT? REALLY?!
That's a surprise.
RUSTLE

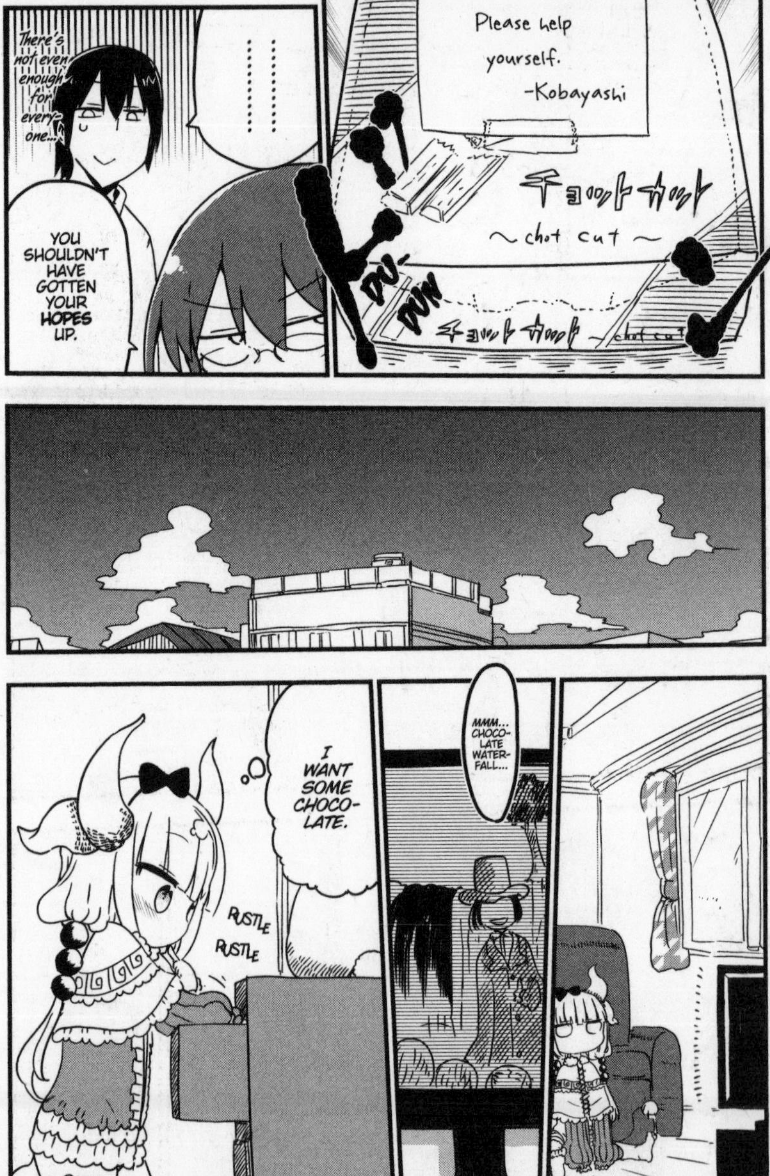
Please help yourself. -Kobayashi
チョットカット
~chot cut~
DU-DUN
チョットカット
chot cut
......
There's not even enough for every-one...
YOU SHOULDN'T HAVE GOTTEN YOUR HOPES UP.
....
MMM... CHOCO-LATE WATER-FALL...
I WANT SOME CHOCO-LATE.
RUSTLE
RUSTLE

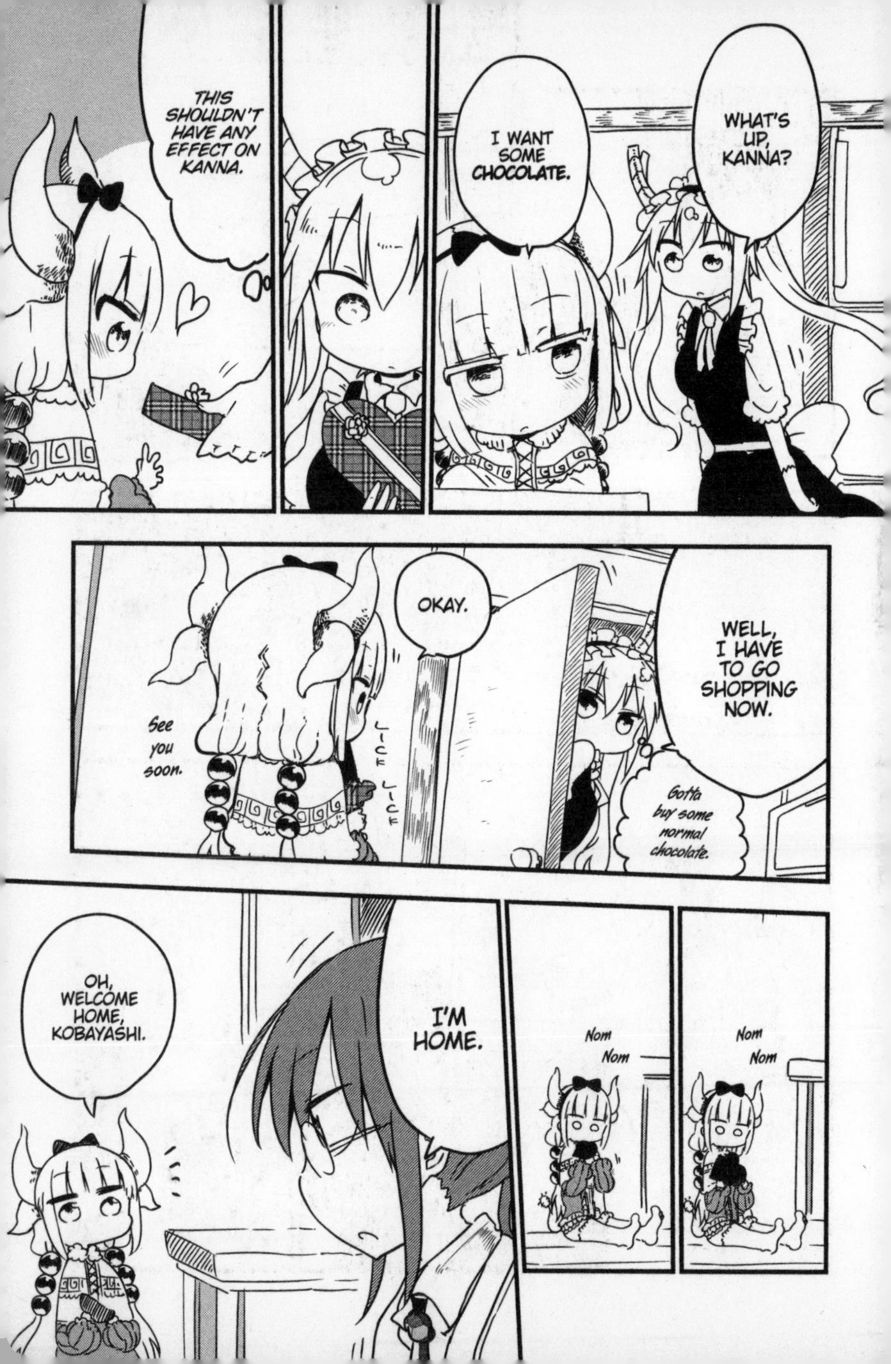
WHAT'S UP, KANNA?
I WANT SOME CHOCOLATE.
THIS SHOULDN'T HAVE ANY EFFECT ON KANNA.
WELL, I HAVE TO GO SHOPPING NOW.
Gotta buy some normal chocolate.
OKAY.
LICK LICK
See you soon.
Nom Nom
Nom Nom
I'M HOME.
OH, WELCOME HOME, KOBAYASHI.

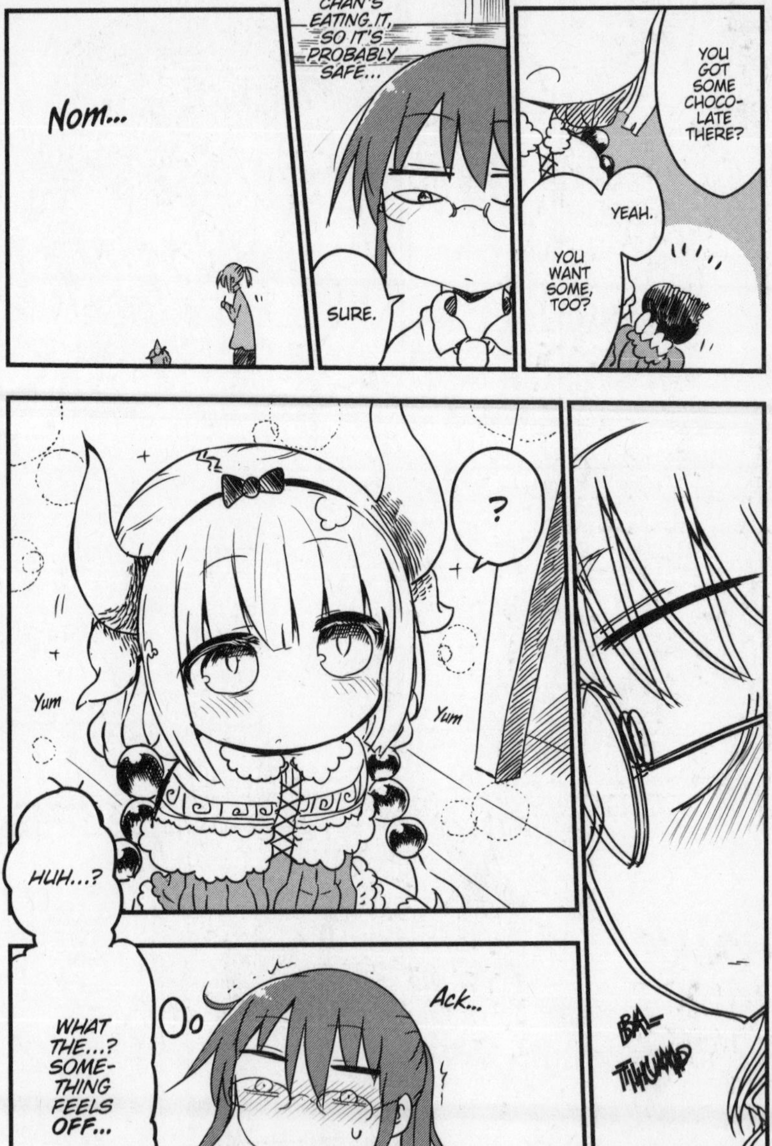
YOU GOT SOME CHOCOLATE THERE?
YEAH.
YOU WANT SOME, TOO?
KANNA-CHAN'S EATING IT, SO IT'S PROBABLY SAFE...
SURE.
Nom...
BA-THUMP
?
Yum
Yum
HUH...?
Ack...
WHAT THE...? SOMETHING FEELS OFF...

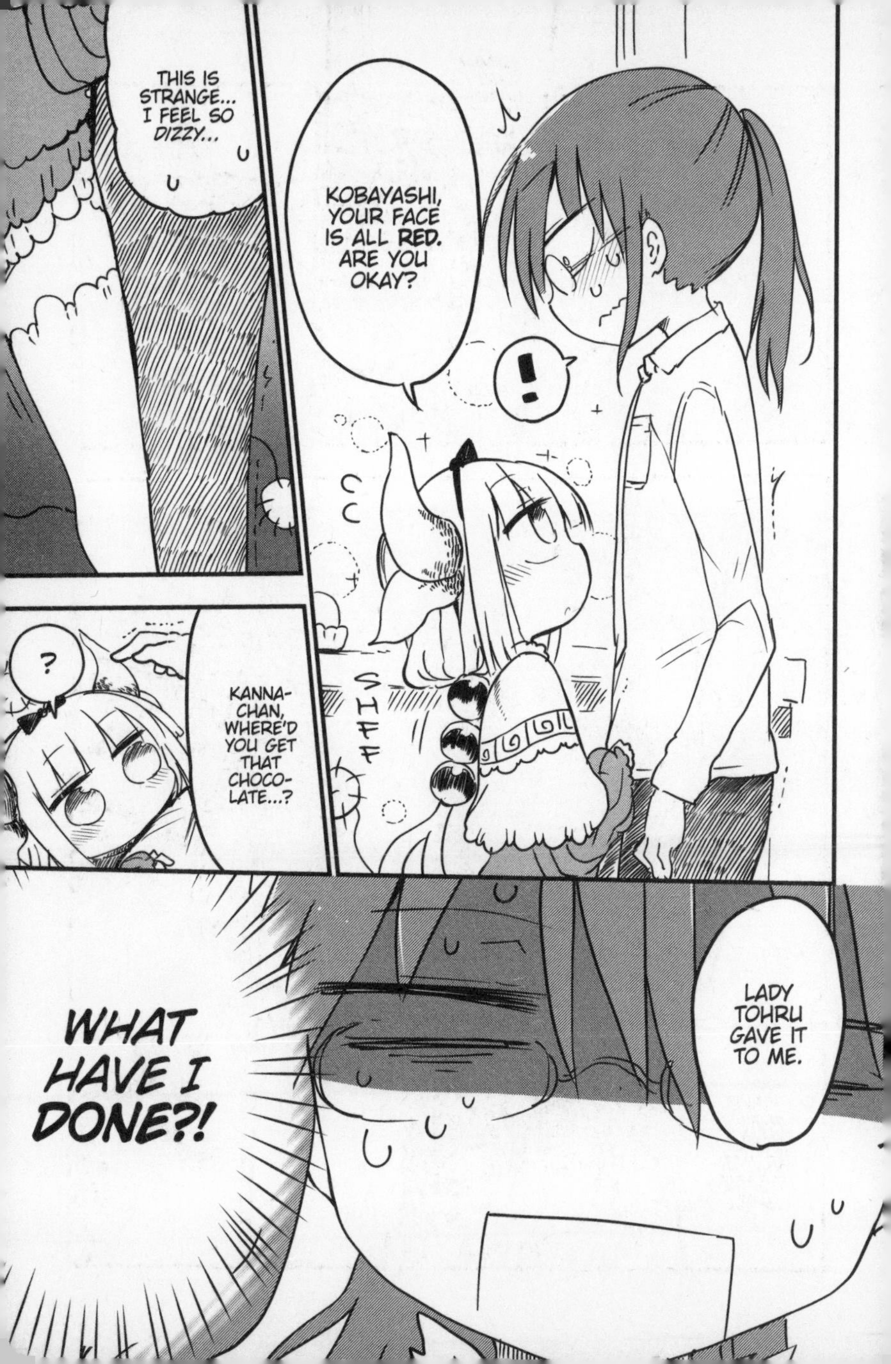
KOBAYASHI, YOUR FACE IS ALL RED. ARE YOU OKAY?
!
SHFF
THIS IS STRANGE... I FEEL SO *DIZZY*...
KANNA-CHAN, WHERE'D YOU GET THAT CHOCO-LATE...?
?
LADY TOHRU GAVE IT TO ME.
WHAT HAVE I DONE?!

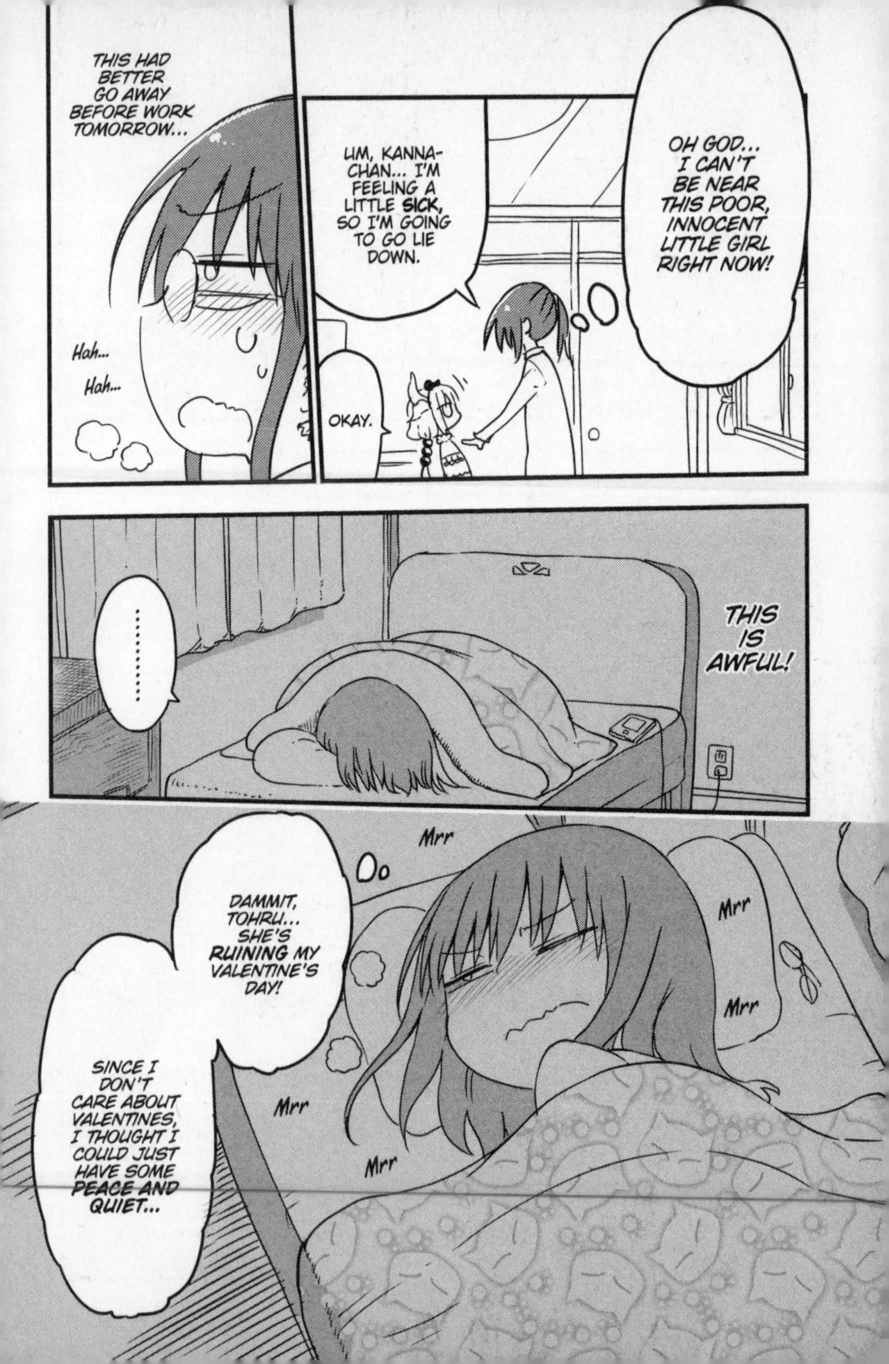
OH GOD... I CAN'T BE NEAR THIS POOR, INNOCENT LITTLE GIRL RIGHT NOW!
UM, KANNA-CHAN... I'M FEELING A LITTLE SICK, SO I'M GOING TO GO LIE DOWN.
OKAY.
THIS HAD BETTER GO AWAY BEFORE WORK TOMORROW...
Hah...
Hah...
THIS IS AWFUL!
.........
Mrr
Oo
Mrr
Mrr
DAMMIT, TOHRU... SHE'S RUINING MY VALENTINE'S DAY!
SINCE I DON'T CARE ABOUT VALENTINES, I THOUGHT I COULD JUST HAVE SOME PEACE AND QUIET...
Mrr
Mrr

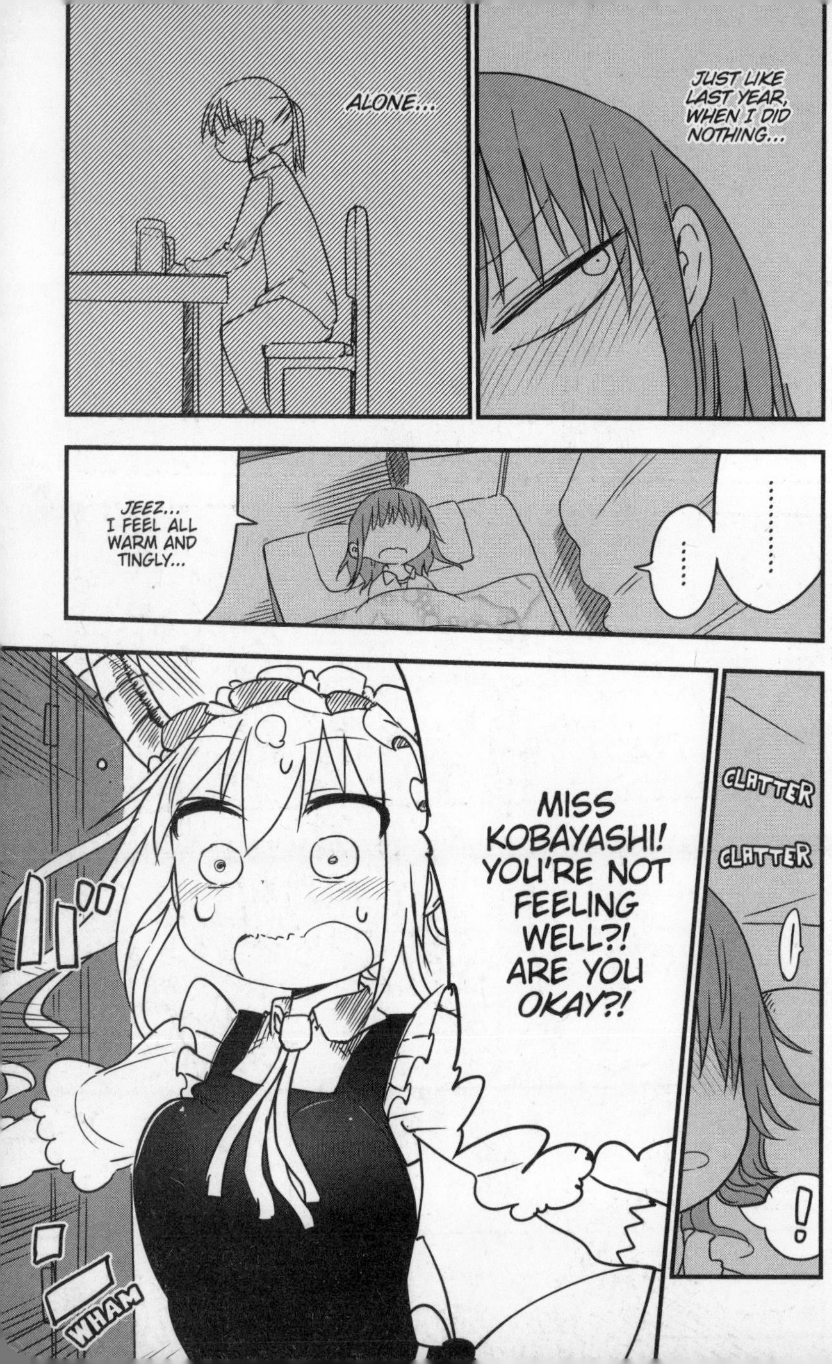
JUST LIKE LAST YEAR, WHEN I DID NOTHING...
ALONE...
......
......
JEEZ... I FEEL ALL WARM AND TINGLY...
CLATTER
CLATTER
!
!
MISS KOBAYASHI! YOU'RE NOT FEELING WELL?! ARE YOU OKAY?!
WHAM

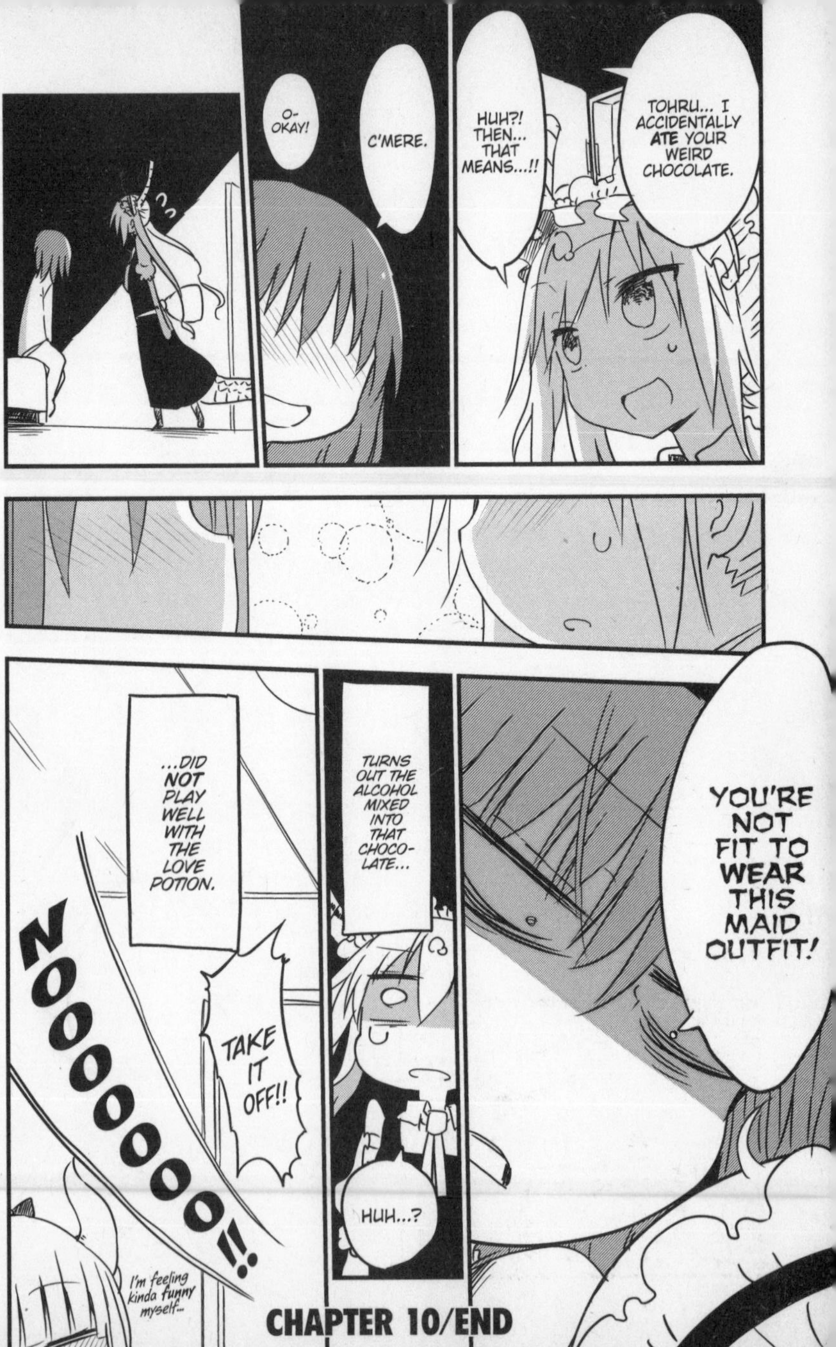
TOHRU... I ACCIDENTALLY ATE YOUR WEIRD CHOCOLATE.
HUH?! THEN... THAT MEANS...!!
C'MERE.
O-OKAY!
YOU'RE NOT FIT TO WEAR THIS MAID OUTFIT!
TURNS OUT THE ALCOHOL MIXED INTO THAT CHOCO-LATE...
HUH...?
...DID NOT PLAY WELL WITH THE LOVE POTION.
TAKE IT OFF!!
NOOOOOOO!!
I'm feeling kinda funny myself...

CHAPTER 10/END

Huh?
Ugh...

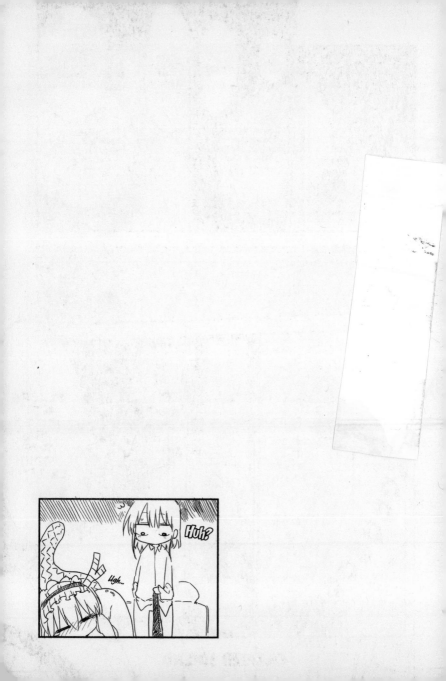

# AFTERWORD

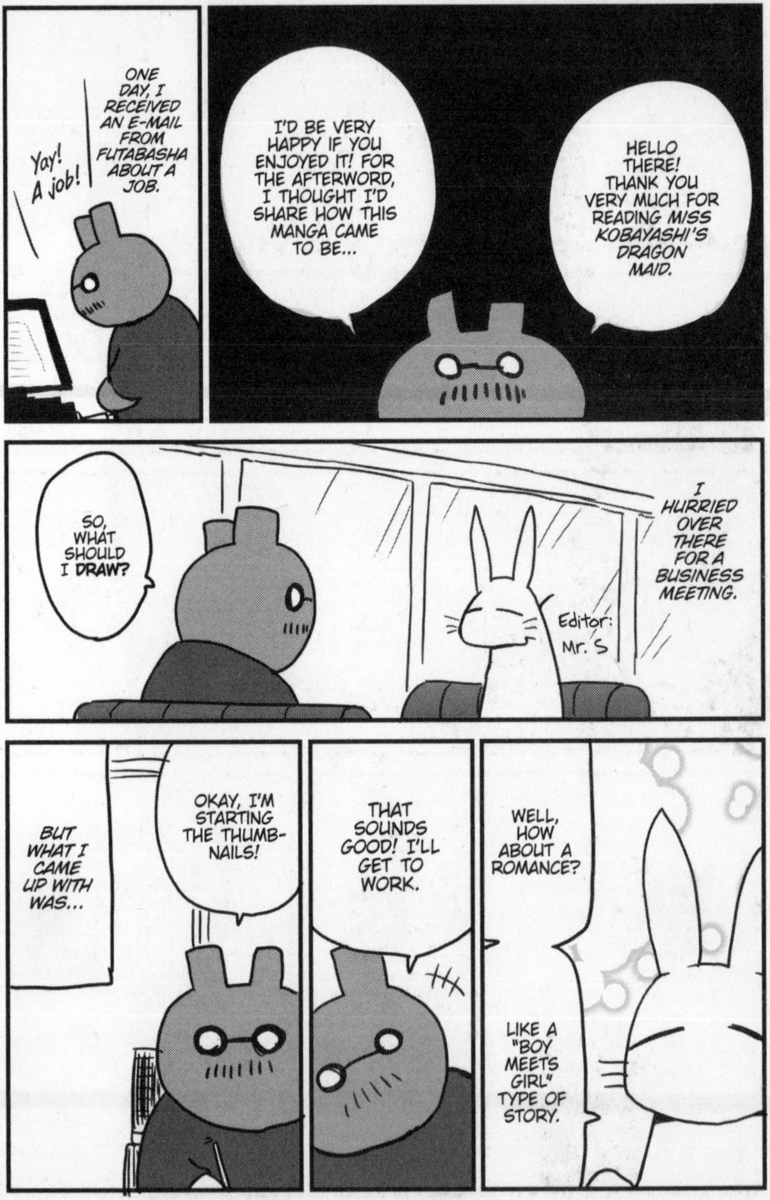
HELLO THERE! THANK YOU VERY MUCH FOR READING MISS KOBAYASHI'S DRAGON MAID.
I'D BE VERY HAPPY IF YOU ENJOYED IT! FOR THE AFTERWORD, I THOUGHT I'D SHARE HOW THIS MANGA CAME TO BE...
ONE DAY, I RECEIVED AN E-MAIL FROM FUTABASHA ABOUT A JOB.
Yay! A job!
I HURRIED OVER THERE FOR A BUSINESS MEETING.
Editor: Mr. S
SO, WHAT SHOULD I DRAW?
WELL, HOW ABOUT A ROMANCE?
LIKE A "BOY MEETS GIRL" TYPE OF STORY.
THAT SOUNDS GOOD! I'LL GET TO WORK.
OKAY, I'M STARTING THE THUMB-NAILS!
BUT WHAT I CAME UP WITH WAS...

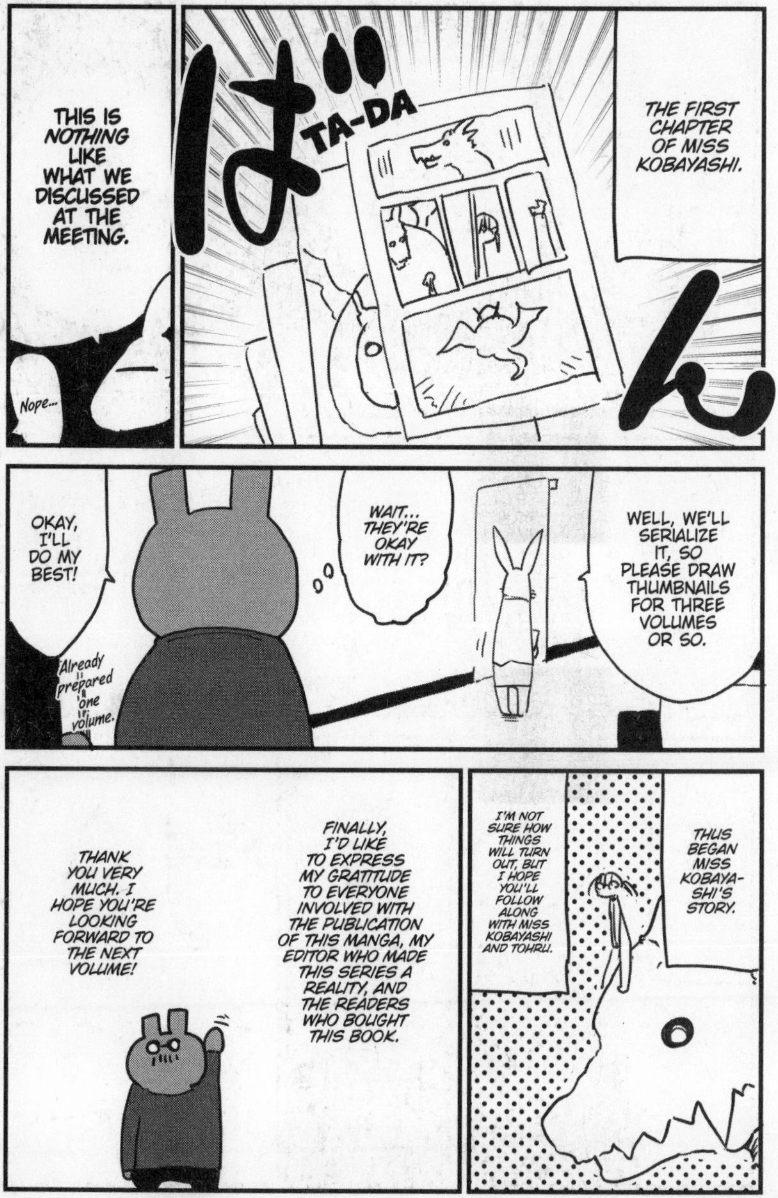
THE FIRST CHAPTER OF MISS KOBAYASHI.
ばん
TA-DA
THIS IS NOTHING LIKE WHAT WE DISCUSSED AT THE MEETING.
Nope...
WELL, WE'LL SERIALIZE IT, SO PLEASE DRAW THUMBNAILS FOR THREE VOLUMES OR SO.
WAIT... THEY'RE OKAY WITH IT?
OKAY, I'LL DO MY BEST!
Already prepared one volume.
THUS BEGAN MISS KOBAYASHI'S STORY.
I'M NOT SURE HOW THINGS WILL TURN OUT, BUT I HOPE YOU'LL FOLLOW ALONG WITH MISS KOBAYASHI AND TOHRU.
FINALLY, I'D LIKE TO EXPRESS MY GRATITUDE TO EVERYONE INVOLVED WITH THE PUBLICATION OF THIS MANGA, MY EDITOR WHO MADE THIS SERIES A REALITY, AND THE READERS WHO BOUGHT THIS BOOK.
THANK YOU VERY MUCH. I HOPE YOU'RE LOOKING FORWARD TO THE NEXT VOLUME!

Miss Kobayashi's
Dragon Maid

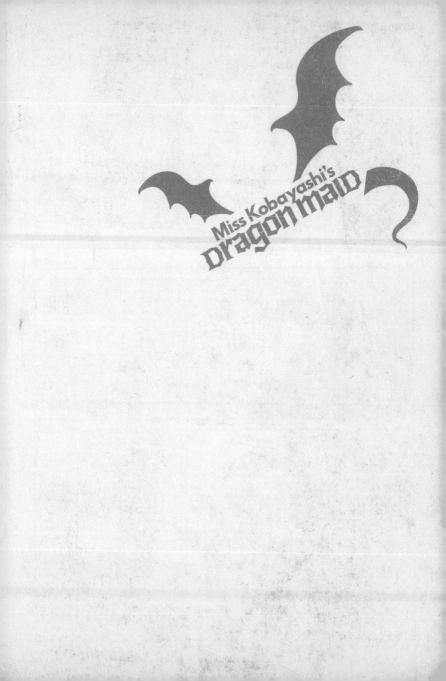

# SEVEN SEAS ENTERTAINMENT PRESENTS

# Miss Kobayashi's Dragon Maid VOL. 1

## story and art by coolkyousinnjya

TRANSLATION
**Jenny McKeon**

ADAPTATION
**Shanti Whitesides**

LETTERING
**Jennifer Skarupa**

LOGO DESIGN
**KC Fabellon**

COVER DESIGN
**Nicky Lim**

PRODUCTION MANAGER
**Lissa Pattillo**

EDITOR-IN-CHIEF
**Adam Arnold**

PUBLISHER
**Jason DeAngelis**

MISS KOBAYASHI'S DRAGON MAID VOL. 1
© coolkyousinnjya 2013
All rights reserved.
First published in Japan in 2013 by Futabasha Publishers Ltd., Tokyo.
English version published by Seven Seas Entertainment, LLC.
Under license from Futabasha Publishers Ltd.

Seven Seas books may be purchased in bulk for promotional, educational, or business use. Please contact your local bookseller or the Macmillan Corporate and Premium Sales Department at 1-800-221-7945, extension 5442, or by e-mail at MacmillanSpecialMarkets@macmillan.com.

Seven Seas and the Seven Seas logo are trademarks of Seven Seas Entertainment, LLC. All rights reserved.

ISBN: 978-1-626923-48-5

Printed in Canada

First Printing: October 2016

10 9 8 7 6 5 4 3 2 1

## FOLLOW US ONLINE: *www.gomanga.com*

# READING DIRECTIONS

This book reads from *right to left*, Japanese style. If this is your first time reading manga, you start reading from the top right panel on each page and take it from there. If you get lost, just follow the numbered diagram here. It may seem backwards at first, but you'll get the hang of it! Have fun!!

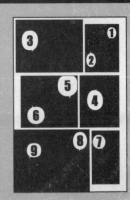